Think Ab
Multiage C

Think About...
Multiage Classrooms

An Anthology of Original Essays

Edited by

Robin Fogarty

TRAINING AND PUBLISHING, INC.

Arlington Heights, Illinois

Think About . . . Multiage Classrooms: An Anthology of Original Essays
Second Printing

Published by IRI/SkyLight Training and Publishing, Inc.
2626 S. Clearbrook Drive
Arlington Heights, Illinois 60005
Phone 800-348-4474, 847-290-6600
FAX 847-290-6609
info@iriskylight.com
http://www.iriskylight.com

Creative Director: Robin Fogarty
Managing Editor: Julia E. Noblitt
Editor: Monica Phillips
Proofreader: Sabine Vorkoeper
Formatter: Heidi Ray
Type Compositor: Donna Ramirez
Illustration and Cover Design: David Stockman
Book Design: Bruce Leckie
Production Supervisor: Bob Crump

© 1995 IRI/SkyLight Training and Publishing, Inc.
All rights reserved.

Printed in the United States of America.
ISBN 1-57517-003-5

Library of Congress Catalog Card Number: 95-79280

667B-8-96-V
Item Number 1345

For Robert Anderson and John Goodlad,
pioneers of the nongraded classroom

Contents

Foreword ix
Introduction xi

SECTION I
Images

INTRODUCTION 3

THE LITTLE RED SCHOOLHOUSE
Robin Fogarty 5

WHAT WE DO AT CONCRETE ELEMENTARY
Mardi B. Jones and Don Jeanroy 19

SECTION II
Information

INTRODUCTION 37

THE WAXING AND WANING OF NONGRADEDNESS
Barbara Nelson Pavan 39

RESEARCH IN NONGRADED ELEMENTARY SCHOOLS: SIMPLE IS BEAUTIFUL
Roberto Gutiérrez and Robert E. Slavin 49

REINVENTING SCHOOL: TEACHERS' PERSPECTIVES ON
MULTIAGE CLASSROOMS
David Marshak 87

SECTION III
Implementation

INTRODUCTION 111

NONGRADED EDUCATION: A REPORT FROM ASPEN, COLORADO
Marilyn Hughes 113

INSTRUCTIONAL STRATEGIES IN A MULTIAGE PRIMARY CLASSROOM
Kathy Magee 141

TECHNOLOGY FOR TEACHING AND LEARNING
Frank Betts 163

SECTION IV
Insights

INTRODUCTION 189

CRITICAL INSIGHTS FROM THE CLASSROOM
Kay J. Williams 191

JOURNEY OF CHANGE: THE NONGRADED SCHOOL
Jacquie Anderson 207

Authors 235

Index 239

Foreword

In the following pages the reader will find a most valuable collection of essays dealing with one of the most interesting dimensions of educational transformation. Robin Fogarty once again has demonstrated a keen awareness of the important thinking that is currently going on about how best to organize classrooms and schools, and she makes available a rich array of materials from which readers can easily draw. As in her previous edited volume, *The Multiage Classroom: A Collection* (IRI/SkyLight Training and Publishing, 1993), she has selected with skill and care a broad and inclusive range of arguments and experiences. This volume comprises the best of the references to which teachers, administrators, and school patrons can now turn for information and guidance.

As the editor has wisely observed, multiage grouping is an age-old idea, and it is not possible to discuss it apart from the complex setting within which it occurs and also without embracing or acknowledging other labels or terms that are rife in the literature. What is not always realized, however, is that nearly all of the age-old multiage practices (such as in the little red schoolhouse, as noted in the introduction) were not really deliberate, which is to say consciously preferred over the age-segregated options that have dominated the past century or so of schooling. This anthology offers abundant evidence combined with educational and social advantages to children. Little wonder that the reader must ultimately conclude that multiaging has in fact become a predominant theme in the current literature as well as an increasingly predominant practice.

I have found this to be a stimulating read and I predict that all those who start reading it will have a hard time putting it down. I congratulate IRI/SkyLight Training and Publishing for its strong contributions, through this and other materials, to the fruitful discussion that will surely be stimulated.

ROBERT H. ANDERSON

Introduction

> It is impossible for ideas to compete in the marketplace if no forum for their presentation is provided or available.
>
> —Thomas Mann

Picture the little red schoolhouse and the diversity of ages, abilities, and interests that coexist under one roof. Imagine the young ones practicing their numbers, the intermediates reciting their rhetoric, and the seniors writing their lessons from literature and history. Think about the competitive spirit that is a natural outgrowth of sibling rivalry and the empathic tolerance that balances the conflict inherent in the family settings of the multiage classroom in the one-room schoolhouse. Listen to the rhythm of the classroom as the teacher orchestrates multiple talents and teaching in this microcosm of the society of the day.

What is the legacy of the little red schoolhouse? Are there lessons that are relevant today? How might the children of the '90s benefit from this historically honored institution for the K–12 classroom? Is the one-room schoolhouse a real and relevant model for educational reform in this decade?

Using the one-room schoolhouse as a metaphor for multiage groupings, the purpose of this anthology is to provide the forum for presentation that Thomas Mann refers to. This anthology gathers under one cover a substantive review of original essays that explore the concepts, characteristics, and controversies that surround this age-old idea.

The voices in the field represent theoreticians, statisticians, and practitioners alike, as the picture of the multiage groupings takes focus for the viewer. Section I, entitled "Images," begins with two essays that help the reader envision multiage school settings. Three different classrooms are highlighted in the opening piece with "slice of life" looks into primary, intermediate, and senior-level multiage clusters. The second essay presents snapshots of an entire school as a bigger picture of the multiage structure.

The second section, "Information," leads the reader into a literature review of multiage groupings. Historical trackings, a synopsis of the research, and the benefits and limitations of multiage classrooms are the essence of this informative section.

Armed with the vision and the facts about multiage classrooms, Section III discusses the issues of implementation. This section is aimed at the practical concerns of actually organizing, using, and evaluating multiage classrooms. The three essays provide valuable guidelines for the practitioner. One report lays out the planning process. Another essay focuses on instructional strategies. And a third piece weaves technology into the fabric of the multiage classroom in the little red schoolhouse of today.

Coming full circle, the book ends with two essays that chronicle the critical issues surrounding the intricacies of successful multiage classrooms. The final section, "Insights," thus provides a reflective moment to internalize the many implications and subtleties that accompany multiage groupings of students.

All in all, this group of essays is designed to provide a bird's-eye view of a critical issue emerging from educational reform: multiage classrooms. Read about multiage groupings and see what you think.

SECTION I

Images

*Art
is the difference
between seeing
and just
identifying.*

—Jean Mary Norman

SECTION I
Images

Connoisseurs in any field acquire their expertise through schooling, life experience, and finally, total immersion in their field of study. To become a connoisseur of the multiage classroom requires similar rigor. To become fully cognizant of the many intricacies and complex workings of the multiage classroom, to understand the subtleties at work, connoisseurs must, at some point, immerse themselves in the classroom experience.

Robin Fogarty's essay, "The Little Red Schoolhouse," does exactly that. Readers are led immediately into the heart of school—the classroom. In each of three cases, the connoisseur flavors multidimensional components of the nongraded classrooms. The first tasting occurs in a primary setting, in which very young children explore, discover, and uncover the mysteries of their world. Philosophically based on the work of the well-known New Zealander, Sylvia Ashton Warner, this multiage classroom provides a rich, full-bodied experience as youngsters in that primary cluster evidence the true nature of children reaching out into their environment with unbridled curiosity and creativity.

A second flavor is presented in the intermediate years as the reader steps into the multiage classroom known as "Kinc.," an abbreviation for Kids Incorporated. In this scenario, the reader joins the students in an outdoor educational setting—a Civil War cemetery. The flavors are rich as these eight- to twelve-year-old youngsters use their skills in art, history, literature, and math to explore and learn in this fertile learning environment. Finally, a senior cluster of fifteen- to eighteen-year-olds focuses on age-old philosophical dilemmas such as truth and justice, individuals and equality, courage and survival.

A companion essay, "What We Do at Concrete Elementary," opens the doors of the classroom and takes the reader into the hallways of the school for a more comprehensive tasting. In this larger setting, Mardi Jones and Don Jeanroy orchestrate an immersion experience in which the reader samples the balancing of myriad elements in action. Jones and Jeanroy explore a collaborative model of team teaching, staff development issues, the active learning strategy of cooperative learning, and the overriding concerns confronted in parent conferences and student assessment. But, does it work? Probably the most enhancing part of this essay is the author's response to this very concern.

The Little Red Schoolhouse

Robin Fogarty

A painted rainbow, a historic cemetery, and cowards turned heroes are the stuff these schools are made of. Envision the vignettes and experience three alternative programs that ignite and integrate learning for all students. Understand how creative educators are "breaking down the barriers" with nongraded, multiage, continuous progress and developmentally appropriate, untracked models of holistic, interdisciplinary, learner-centered classrooms, reminiscent of the romanticized little red schoolhouse of days gone by.

Vignette One: Somebodies Who Make the Rainbow Real: Organic Learning in the Primary Cluster

Orange construction paper strips fully stocked in a coffee can; a large black marker; a round reading table with several little chairs; shoebox "fish" games about the room; and a line formed around the teacher. Words are rehearsed and called out to classmates as they approach the front of the line: Butterfly, the Refrigerator, Raggedy Ann and Andy, Piano, Garden, Girl, Prickly, Whale, and Dumbo.

Although this article was written for *Think About . . . Multiage Classrooms,* it also appears in *Best Practices for the Learner-Centered Classroom* (IRI/Skylight Training and Publishing, 1995.)

These words are what Sylvia Ashton-Warner (1963) calls the organic words that comprise the "key vocabulary" of each child learner. Using a whole language approach to reading in the primary classroom, this New Zealander models a fully integrated learning environment that can be anchored by just one word, as illustrated in the following poems:

Deep Inside of Me
I start with just one word
One special word
Way down deep inside of me.
A word I love
A word I fear
One I can see and touch and hear.
I start with just one word
One special word
Way down deep
Inside of me.

Can do! Can do!
Now, I tell just what
That one word can do.
Popcorn pops,
Jackrabbit hops,
Grass grew.
Birdie flew.
Bluebird sings,
But, bee stings.
Now, I can tell just what
That one word can do.

Add a Few
Hmm, now that I have two
Why not
Add a few.
I tell its color
And shape
And size.
I create a picture of words
For your eyes.
Hmm, now that I have two
Why not add a few.

A Story to Tell

By gosh, by golly, by gee
I've got a whole story
Way down deep
Inside of me
A story of love, or one about fear,
One I can see
And touch and hear
By gosh, by golly, by gee
I've got a whole story
Deep down inside of me.

Peacock has lots of feathers. Peacock is in the zoo. People like to see the peacock. Peacock opens its feathers and they are SO PRETTY!

Indeed, Indeed, Indeed

I've got all the words I need.
Words that name and
Words that can do
And words to describe
Yes, all those words
That are way down deep
In my inside
Indeed! Indeed! Indeed!
I have all the words I need.

The magician does magic on stage. He did make rabbits come out from his hat. Then he did a bow.

Inside of Me

Believe it or not
All those words that I've got
Can be set free from way down deep
Inside of me
They can be thought about
Or better yet, said right out
And if I write them down
I'll have a story to say and see
A real story, to really read
From way down deep inside of me.

On t.v. I saw a chimpanzee learning to talk sign language.

He learned and he had to think because it was complicated.

That's why it took so long.

His name is CHARLY CHIMPANZEE!

Imagine the busy hustle in the classroom as the children nominate their own personal word for the day, a key word in their inner world that helps unlock the mystery of the reading process for each of them and opens the door to myriad related activities that integrate the arts and the academics into meaningful, holistic tasks.

Emily slowly traces the word *butterfly* with her finger after the teacher has written it on the orange strip. "The easel," she responds to the teacher-initiated question of how she wants to study her word today. "I'm gonna paint my butterfly in beautiful, bright colors," and off she goes to stand on the drippy, sticky butcher paper under the easel in the paint corner.

Erin chooses to "water write" her word on the blackboard, while Matt forms his word out of sea shells on the red mat. Effie uses the dusty pastels to print the word *girl*, and Eric traces the word *Dumbo* in the wet sand.

Following the chatter of the word study time, the children settle down with their handmade orange stapled booklets, which match their word orange cards, and begin their sentence writing:

"Butterfly is beautiful!"	(Emily)
"Piano is magic."	(Erin)
"Garden can grow."	(Matt)
"Girl is pretty."	(Effie)
"Dumbo can fly."	(Eric)

Some ask the teacher to help them write their sentences, others quiz each other for words they need to fill the page. When the sentences begin to string together and form stories, the children receive sticky dots for punctuating their ideas. The teacher helps the children add headings and titles, and their writing develops. Then, once the sentences are written and crayoned pictures adorn the day's pages, the buzz begins again as partners share their stories with each other.

This scenario repeats each morning until the month ends and the orange word booklets are taken home to parents. The parents know that the goal is for the child to read the sentence booklet to anyone who will listen, including goldfish, grandparents, and the neighbor next door. For every reading, a signature is collected on the inside cover for a Monday morning tally.

Over time, as the year progresses, these youngsters have nine sentence booklets and color coordinated cards for each month of school and a shoebox overflowing with their specially requested words. With the focus on authentic assessment (Burke 1992), these artifacts provide ongoing evidence of the students' development. In fact, the final assessment tool is a tenth booklet that holds a page from each of the previous ones. The children have quite a time deciding exactly which pages to select for their finished portfolio.

Although the activities in this primary classroom resemble those of many early childhood programs, there are several key elements to silhouette: this is an nongraded class with four-, five-, and six-year-olds included; the curriculum is fully integrated (Fogarty 1991) through a language arts focus, with music, art, math, science, and social studies creeping into the daily activities through the word boxes and sentence books; and the program provides a platform for genuine investigations and class projects. In addition, the parents are an integral part of the action and the assessment process.

Interestingly, the integration of curriculum permeates every aspect of this classroom as the students learn from each other. For they not only learn their own words, but they're privy to other children's dynamic vocabulary as they interact with these shoebox treasures. They alphabetize, categorize, and prioritize the words as they internalize the learning through reading, writing, listening, and speaking.

> The rainbow is one example of the serendipitous effects of the shoebox curriculum. After Alan paints his "rainbow," lots of children want his word too. In fact, "rainbow" becomes so contagious, a special event is planned and the entire class paints a rainbow so big and so beautiful that they decide to display it over the length of the windowed wall. There is magic as the sunlight filters through the many colors of paint.

Integrated learning and multiage grouping champion this classroom (see fig. 1). Breaking down the barriers is natural with these "somebodies who make the rainbow real."

Vignette Two: Kids Incorporated and the Cemetery Study: A Multiage Alternative for the Intermediate Cluster

> Kinc., the logo for Kids Incorporated, hangs precariously over the doorway that opens into a double classroom with a large folding wall. The shelves that line the windowed wall are packed and stacked with brightly

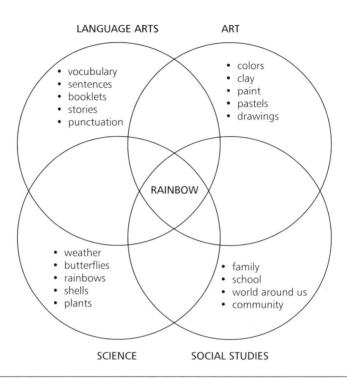

Figure 1. Emergent Theme: Primary Whole Language Classroom

colored plastic dishpans stuffed with books and papers—some neatly, others randomly, but all punctuated with various writing instruments.

The students are of various sizes, ages, and abilities, and display various levels of industry. About the room are clusters of students: three girls look at a Beverly Cleary book; two boys are talking about after-school sports; several youngsters, boys and girls, are puzzling over the gerbil cage; while some of the older girls giggle at the boys in the hall.

The side board displays the Track Sheet, a listing of the day's events, but interestingly, only two items carry a time designation: 11:30 A.M.– Lunch and 2:30 P.M. –Safety Assembly. Next to the Track Sheet, two girls check their names off of the Homework Due List.

Two teachers talk near the center of the room. Their desks are located in a back-to-back island surrounded by tables of students and learning centers. Near the sink is the science table, completely covered with artifacts that run the gamut from gerbils in training and broken rock specimens, to a jungle of plants and a disorganized assortment of magnets, tools, slides, and the treasured microscope.

Opposite the popular science laboratory is the never-ending activity of what appears to be a simulation of musical chairs. As one child relinquishes a headset, three others scramble for the vacated chair.

Art drips from the walls and hangs from a wire network that crisscrosses the room in a random scrabble design.

Frayed file folders labeled Math Skill Packets are indexed alphabetically in a blue milk crate. A parent-helper checks off assignments at the skill center as a sandy-haired student hands them to her.

This pandemonium quickly diminishes as the 9:00 A.M. bell rings and the younger teacher starts the morning housekeeping chores by taking attendance. With no time to spare, the seasoned teacher holds up the sign Novel Groups and the migration of students begins.

Kids Incorporated is an alternative school *within* a school. It comprises two teachers; fifty-four children, aged eight to twelve; siblings; and parent volunteers. The vision of the two teachers is to create a school setting that embodies the natural elements of the family that nurture authentic learning.

To foster cooperation and a sense of collegiality and team spirit across the various age levels, an extensive outdoor education week is intentionally built into the fall schedule of events. Using the summer and the month of September and part of October to raise money, the teachers plan a mid-October trip to a camp.

Parents have been polled for talent and willingness to participate in small-group sessions scheduled throughout the week. In a backbreaking schedule of events that runs from 7:00 A.M. until 9:00 P.M. are many learning opportunities. Among the featured classes are: (1) Robinson Crusoe, a shelter-building, overnight excursion; (2) The Cemetery Study, a Civil War history lesson that incorporates art and literature; (3) Noodle Mania, a cooking class to prepare noodles and soup for lunch; (4) Bear Hunt, a hiking class where plaster casts of animal tracks are made; and (5) Old McDonald's Farm, a morning of genuine farm chores at the ranch.

Choices are made by students as they fill their schedule from the menu of fifty-plus class offerings. Ghost stories, told around the campfire by a dad who participates in community theater, exemplify a whole-group activity and the diversity of parental involvement.

Integrating curricula is a natural outgrowth of the learning experiences designed for Kinc. To illustrate how significant learning such as cooperation and critical thinking is threaded (Fogarty 1991) through each camp activity, the Cemetery Study Unit is a good example (see fig. 2).

Working in small archeological dig–type groups, students choose from a list of tasks in their cemetery packet. The suggested activities include:
1. Create five art etchings or rubbings including borders, symbols, lettering, and numerals.
2. Find two epitaphs that appear on the tombstones and write two more.

Figure 2. Threading Life Skills: Multiage (Gr. 3–6) Classroom

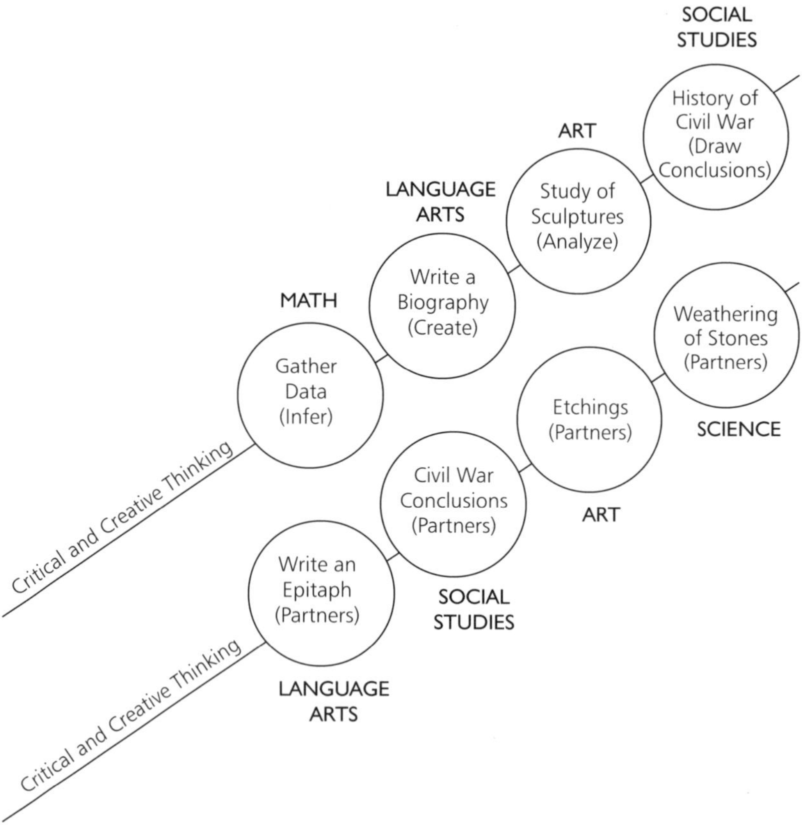

- SOCIAL STUDIES — History of Civil War (Draw Conclusions)
- ART — Study of Sculptures (Analyze)
- LANGUAGE ARTS — Write a Biography (Create)
- MATH — Gather Data (Infer)
- SCIENCE — Weathering of Stones (Partners)
- ART — Etchings (Partners)
- SOCIAL STUDIES — Civil War Conclusions (Partners)
- LANGUAGE ARTS — Write an Epitaph (Partners)

Critical and Creative Thinking

3. Answer historical questions by viewing various tombstones and gathering pertinent data.
4. Draw a map of the cemetery or a particular part of the cemetery.
5. Gather mathematical information and generate statistical data for generalizations about the Civil War.
6. Investigate the weathering of the tombstones and the conditions of the earth in the cemetery and draw some conclusions.

Learning experiences orchestrated over the week set the stage for activities and interactions for the rest of the year. More importantly, unbreakable bonds are made among the students—young and old, new and familiar. The team building begins with the force of a hurricane. Back at school, the winds always seem gentle by comparison.

Vignette Three: How Courage Is Like the Rain: A Philosophy Study for the Senior Cluster

Courage? What does it mean? What comes to mind? Hero. Sudden. Unexpected. Save a child. Train track rescue. *Profiles in Courage.* Inner self. Recognition. War hero. Medals. Purple Heart. Strength. Cowardice. *Catch-22.* Moral courage. *The Wizard of Oz.* Stand up! Stand out! Famous. High dive. Risk. Bungee jump. Untested. Undetected. Under pressure. Surprise, like a summer shower. Rain.

The brainstorm flows through its natural cycle: a burst of ideas, a lull, reignited associations, silliness, novelty, and a final wind down. The teacher pounces on that final word, *rain*, and asks, "How is courage like the rain?"

Heads together, pens poised, the small groups discuss possible comparisons as one team starts to write on the large poster paper: "Courage is like the rain because both . . . hmmm, both can happen suddenly; they can come upon you unexpectedly; and . . . .Wait, I've got it . . . they often result in a change for you. If you get caught in the rain and get wet, you change your clothes. If you act in a courageous way it may change how you feel about yourself."

So goes the latest scenario in the senior cluster. Staffed with a teacher team that consists of a guest artist, a visiting attorney, a guidance counselor, and a literature teacher, this philosophy study targets students from the senior cluster levels—incoming freshmen through graduating seniors.

Designed around the age-old discipline of philosophy, students are exposed to an interdisciplinary approach to subject matter. They experience content through the dilemma, paradox, and ambiguity inherent in the universally compelling philosophical issues: truth, justice, equality, authority, wisdom, courage, life, death, and love.

Interwoven in the puzzle are opportunities to explore the issues in myriad domains. For example, in an experiment with authority, students read about historically renowned authority figures, Hitler, Stalin, and McCarthy, and compare them with the authority figures in their own lives. In turn, literature becomes a springboard for historical simulations, real-life role plays, journaling, and depictions of authority through the visual and performing arts.

> "Courage is like the rain . . . isn't that a fresh idea? Let's explore some of the ideas a bit further. For example, what do you mean when you say courage is unexpected? Give us a real illustration."
>
> "Well, when you step on the high dive and you look down, you're really afraid of the fall. Yet, you prepare, just as you've done in practice many times before; you proceed through your ritual of standing at the invisible spot, stepping through the approach, focusing yourself mentally, and performing the precision dive with skill and grace. That's courage, if you ask me."
>
> "I agree. That's certainly a grand display of physical courage. What else?"
>
> "To stand up for what you believe, in front of your friends, when you know you're in the minority. I think that shows courage."
>
> "Tell us more about that."
>
> "Maybe you like classical music because you've had to learn it and play it in orchestra, but your friends want to listen to hard rock or rap. Even though it's a simple example, we can really pressure each other to the point that it does take some courage to stick to your own ideas."
>
> "That's so true, isn't it? How about one more example of courage?"
>
> "Cowards can be courageous. My grandpa says that a lot of guys in the war ended up as decorated heroes, but they weren't all that heroic in the beginning. Once their plane was shot down or they found themselves in prison camp, their courage got them through."
>
> "Yeah! It's like when someone rescues a kid from a fire or rushes into the street and throws a child free from the path of a car—the courage just happens suddenly, unexpectedly. And someone who seems more like a coward in other situations proves himself a hero with courage."

The integration to the various subjects is evident in this scenario. The fertile themes of courage, trust, and love are transformed into an investigative question and then easily "webbed" out to the various disciplines for appropriate instructional activities and aligned with key goals (Fogarty 1991).

Figure 3 suggests other subject matter content in a rich web of interdisciplinary activities. This investigation centers around the question: How common is courage? Sparked by that query, investigations in the various disciplines are ignited with activities and accompanying outcomes. Multiple forms of literature are available for student selection. One team studies Hemingway, another compares and contrasts a film to a book, and still another group reads and comments on *Catch-22*. All are focused on the question, "How common is courage?"

Figure 3. Selected Theme: Senior Cluster

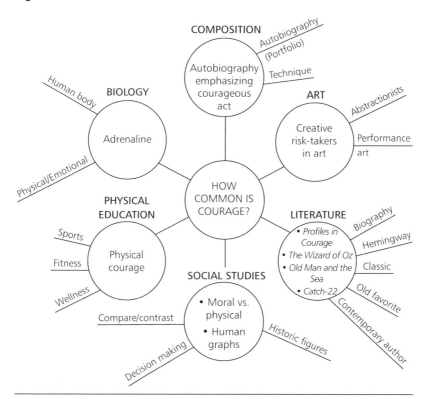

Figure 4. Call for Presentations

Please prepare an answer to the essential question: "How Common Is Courage?" You may use one or any combination of the following expressive forms:

☐ Art   ☐ Music   ☐ Drama
☐ Writing   ☐ Speaking   ☐ Other

You may work by yourself or in collaboration with one or two others.

Presentations begin next week. You will have 25 minutes to present and 5 minutes for feedback. Please sign up for a time.

To culminate the study of courage, a handout calling for presentations is distributed (see fig. 4). Presentations are as varied as the presenters. Creativity flourishes and debate is lively as students grapple with an unknown. After all, who really knows how common courage is?

A painted rainbow, a historic cemetery, and cowards turned heroes are the stuff these schools are made of.

References

Anderson, R. H. 1993. The return of the nongraded classroom. *Principal* (January): 9–12.

Anderson, R. H., and B. N. Pavan. 1993. *Nongradedness: Helping it to happen.* Lancaster, Pa.: Technomic Publishing.

Ashton-Warner, S. 1963. *Teacher.* New York: Simon & Schuster.

Bellanca, J., and R. Fogarty. 1991. *Blueprints for thinking in the cooperative classroom.* Palatine, Ill.: IRI/Skylight Training and Publishing.

Burke, K., ed. 1992. *Authentic assessment: A collection.* Palatine, Ill.: IRI/Skylight Training and Publishing.

———. 1994. *The mindful school: How to assess authentic learning.* Palatine, Ill.: IRI/Skylight Training and Publishing.

Costa, A. L. 1991. *The school as a home for the mind: A collection of articles.* Palatine, Ill.: IRI/Skylight Training and Publishing.

Costa, A., J. Bellanca, and R. Fogarty, eds. 1992. *If minds matter: A foreword to the future, Vol. I.* Palatine, Ill.: IRI/Skylight Training and Publishing.

———. 1992. *If minds matter: A foreword to the future, Vol. II.* Palatine, Ill.: IRI/Skylight Training and Publishing.

Fogarty, R. 1990. *Keep them thinking: A handbook of model lessons, Level II.* Palatine, Ill.: IRI/Skylight Training and Publishing.

———. 1991. *The mindful school: How to integrate the curricula.* Palatine, Ill.: IRI/Skylight Training and Publishing.

Fogarty, R., and J. Bellanca. 1987. *Patterns for thinking: Patterns for transfer.* Palatine, Ill.: IRI/Skylight Training and Publishing.

Fogarty, R., D. Perkins, and J. Barell. 1992. *The mindful school: How to teach for transfer.* Palatine, Ill.: IRI/Skylight Training and Publishing.

Goodlad, J. I., and R. H. Anderson. 1987. *The nongraded elementary school* (rev. ed.). New York: Teachers College, Columbia University.

Jacobs, H. H, ed. 1989. *Interdisciplinary curriculum: Design and implementation.* Alexandria, Va.: Association for Supervision and Curriculum Development.

Pavan, B. N. 1973. Good news: Research on the nongraded elementary school. *Elementary School Journal* (March): 233–42.

Richmond, G. H. 1973. *The micro-society school: A real world in miniature.* New York: Harper & Row.

What We Do at Concrete Elementary

Mardi B. Jones and Don Jeanroy

At 7:55 on a sunny Monday morning, hefty yellow school buses lumber to the curb, huff to a halt, and unload their young passengers. For the next ten minutes, organized chaos reigns.

Brightly clad children, hugging notebooks and backpacks, scamper in a hundred different directions. This scene repeats itself daily in schoolyards across the country, but at Concrete Elementary School, high in the Cascade Mountains of northern Washington state, 450 children are scurrying to a different kind of classroom.

Students work at levels that match their abilities.

Here, "family groups" replace the traditional graded classroom. Instead of plodding through a rigid, chronological program, students work at levels that match their abilities. They progress through a curriculum that keeps pace with their capabilities as they learn together over a span of age and grade levels.

By grouping children this way, it is possible for teachers to use strategies that will be more responsive to the individual needs of the children. Meanwhile, ongoing authentic assessments replace the annual practice of promotion and retention.

The basic goal of Concrete Elementary School's Continuous Progress Program is to nurture the diversity and growth of children's knowledge by removing artificial barriers. This allows the children to proceed at their own pace. Students learn, not by lecture and rote, but through their own active involvement and participation in the educational process. In short, they learn by doing in a nongraded environment, and they love it.

The concept is bold. For the faculty at Concrete Elementary, it meant taking a chance and revamping the entire educational structure that had been in place for so long. But on the cusp of a new century, and with a dramatically different world only a heartbeat away, they believed change was necessary. Their motto is simple: "Educating for the twenty-first century is not a list of new ideas or a set of guidelines or the transmission of information. It is a way of thinking."

"We'll never go back to teaching within the framework of a graded classroom."

Now in its second full year of operation, the program is successful on a number of levels, from the students' excitement to the teachers' enthusiasm and commitment. "We'll never go back to teaching within the framework of a graded classroom," is a phrase that is repeated often at Concrete Elementary. "We'll never go back to the old way of teaching."

Background

For decades there has been a call for more flexibility in the grouping and progression of children in their early years of schooling. This call has come with the recognition that (1) each child is unique, with individual needs, abilities, and interests; and (2) children develop and learn at different rates and in different ways.

Dr. Don Jeanroy, principal at Concrete Elementary, wrestled with the problems of reaching all students and developing a way to meet their needs while at the same time allowing them to advance at their own rate. In 1989, the school submitted a grant to the Office of Superintendent of Public Instruction in Olympia, Washington. State officials approved the grant and funding was made available through the Schools for the 21st Century program. Jeanroy and the faculty began to put a well-thought-out plan into action.

Jeanroy explains their Continuous Progress Program and how it came about:

> At Concrete Elementary, we realized we had a responsibility to recognize the individuality of each child and to do everything necessary to cater to it. We began to explore the various possibilities for achieving the level of instruction we desired, while keeping an eye on the individual learning needs of each student.
>
> Our first task was to define our problems and our goals. We were faced with two basic issues. One was the unpleasant task of retaining children. That is, making them retake a year if they were not ready to move on. In the old vernacular, "flunking" them. In our opinion, this odious practice was detrimental to the student, as well as stressful to the child's teacher and family. Clearly, something had to change.
>
> Second, we were challenged by the "gifted" children—that 5 percent who finished early and yearned for more than their grade level was prepared to give them. Their needs were a priority too.
>
> These students represented both ends of the education scale. We also knew that students in the middle ranges learn at different rates. We felt a strong need to provide for those learners as well.
>
> During the year before we established our current program, we formed committees of teachers and parents to research and visit other schools that had multiage classroom programs. Our most successful observations took place in British Columbia. The provincial government had mandated nongraded classroom programs at the primary levels throughout the province.
>
> However, with each program we visited we could not find that "perfect" match to satisfy our needs. We did gain enough information to develop a greater understanding of the nongraded format and we were able to design our own "continuous progress" program from these visitations.

For three months at the end of the school year, Jeanroy met weekly with the twelve teachers who were going to implement the new Multiage Class (MAC) program in grades one through five. They planned, discussed, and decided how they were going to function within a multiage format.

"This process required a great deal of trust building, cooperation, and sharing on everyone's part," Jeanroy explains. "We recognized that we were going to take a great professional 'risk,' and that it was critically important for us to be as well prepared as possible."

As principal, Jeanroy was directly involved in the selection of the teachers for the MAC program and had a great deal of confidence in their ability. His major role, then, was to guide and encourage their growth, and to support them in their efforts to try something new.

Faced with these challenges, the faculty started to redefine their educational program and tailor all they had learned to fit Concrete Elementary.

"We started with the multiage classroom concept and called it our Continuous Progress Program," says Jeanroy. "This program defined our goals and gave us a framework to proceed from. Within this framework we developed a variety of tools that helped us achieve our educational objectives."

> *Multiage grouping allows the flexibility to place children according to need, ability, or interest.*

The three basic tools are multiage classrooms, team teaching, and cooperative learning. These are reinforced by instructional aids such as whole language/thematic units, cross-aged tutoring, multiple intelligence learning styles, and the immersion process in Chapter 1 and remedial math programs. There are also special programs for student motivation, including the successful Self Manager and Conflict Manager programs, principal's awards, and schoolwide parties and assemblies.

What Is a Multiage Classroom?

At Concrete Elementary, the teachers feel that multiage grouping allows the flexibility to place children according to need, ability, or interest—not just by age or grade level alone. This all but eliminates the problems associated with a yearly transition from one grade to another. It also increases opportunities for cooperation, particularly with older students helping younger ones.

A natural outcome of multiage classrooms is role modeling for children. Students can learn from other children around them, and young children are stimulated intellectually by older children. Vertical arrangements provide each class with students who set examples. This increases the social maturity of the younger ones. The children have a broader social experience, with opportunities to lead and to follow, to collaborate, and to make stable peer relationships.

Another plus is that older children develop self-reliance and responsibility. This is excellent preparation for secondary school. Greater opportunities for cross-age tutoring exist as age-grade lines for instruction are eliminated.

Children work at their own maximum pace, helping each other by intention or invitation. The program is not geared to the work of a single year but can be adjusted over a two- or three-year period. A child of low scholastic ability is able to take longer to progress through the lower school without repetition of a whole year's work. The structure of the class is more stable, with the top-level children moving out at the end of any year and the others remaining.

We have found that the fear that children will lose contact with their own age group is unfounded. Children mix freely outside the classroom, take part in age-group activities for the whole school, and are able to combine with their age-peers for special sessions if necessary.

Ideally, most children will have more than one year with the same teacher; a teacher who will have the opportunity to know them and their parents very well. School/home cooperation is strengthened when teachers and parents are comfortable with each other.

Team Teaching: A Cornerstone of Our MAC Program

Team teaching at Concrete Elementary provides for variety and flexibility. Teams are assigned to work with each multiage block, and these teams may work with students for up to three years. This provides continuity and a sense of family for students and teachers alike.

Teachers are free to use their own creative styles and still remain within the overall framework of the program. Some teachers work both separately and together. Some work together with some separation, while others work 100 percent together.

Marilyn Lane, a bright, energetic, primary-level teacher, has been teaching for eight years at Concrete Elementary. She was one of the presenters of the Continuous Progress Program concept to the State Education Agency in 1989, and she has worked closely with the program as it has developed to its present structure.

Lane works with Hallie Elms, a five-year veteran at Concrete. Their classes, Family Groups A and B, are the equivalent of a first and second grade combination in continuous progress.

"We call them Family Groups because families care for each other," explains Lane. "In a multiage setting, students learn to care for one another in the classroom. Hopefully, that carries over onto the playground, on the bus, and in the lunchroom. This is another reason we do cross-age tutoring. If you know a child's name and have worked with that child on a one-on-one basis, you tend to be kinder to them in situations outside the classroom."

> "In a multiage setting, students learn to care for one another in the classroom."

Lane and Elms have two separate classrooms, connected by a six-foot opening in the wall. "We are physically separate, but together," Lane explains.

"We may not have doors open all the time, and we don't run back and forth—but the work is similar," continues Elms. "The kids are comfortable with our system. We all share."

Elms adds that their classes work together about 30 percent of the week. "Kids are working with kids. We work together with math, music, and performance time. We do our field trips together, too."

Lane and Elms enjoy their partnership. Lane explains, "The best part of team teaching is that we generate more ideas on the themes we are teaching. We are theme based in our whole language approach. By team teaching we can share ideas and materials."

Elms adds with a laugh, "This also cuts down on the time and energy in preparing the class, too!"

Lane and Elms agree that "team teaching allows for your teaching partner to fill in the blank spots—your area of weakness. It helps the students by allowing us to offer a variety of information on a given subject. Two heads are better than one."

These teachers also agree that team teaching makes it comfortable to share original ideas. "Team teaching allows you to have someone to bounce your ideas off of," adds Elms. "Team teaching has a built-in support system."

Lane and Elms offer words of advice. "If you are planning to team teach, move into it slowly. The first year, pick two or three themes you have material for and you feel comfortable with. Then blend the material and work together."

Lane cautions, "You must be very careful that you and your team teacher have similar teaching styles. Find someone to work with who has similar expectations."

Jaci Gallagher and Meridith Loomis have been team teaching Family Groups D and E for two years. Theirs is a three-year, age/grade classroom spread, incorporating third-, fourth-, and fifth-year students. Both teachers support the concept and feel there are many advantages to team teaching.

"Team teaching has a built-in support system."

"You can take advantage of your team teacher's strengths," explains Loomis. "Jaci's is math. Mine is language arts. Our students get the best of both worlds."

"Team planning is also an advantage," adds Gallagher. "If one person gets stuck, the other can help."

"I feel, as team teachers, we are more open to asking for suggestions," Gallagher continues. "Another advantage is that we are together so much, we know what each other is doing."

"We can bounce ideas off each other," Loomis continues, "and Jaci knows me well enough to know what I like and what I am capable of—so she answers with that in mind."

Both teachers add this advice: "It is a big advantage to share teaching philosophies. If you are considering team teaching with another person, go into their room and watch them. Get a feel for how they teach, and be very sure it fits your style of teaching."

Down the hall is another oversized classroom. Fifty mobiles, depicting the individual states of the Union, swing from the ceiling and an "America the Beautiful" banner covers the far wall. The room is a hive of activity, but controlled and with a purpose. Students work in small groups, some reading, some tapping on a computer.

"We work 100 percent together," explains teacher Deborah Money. Along with her partner, Barbara Hawkings, Money teaches more than fifty students in one large classroom. They call their family group the Mohawks.

"We both instruct. While one teacher is teaching the class, the other one circulates throughout the room to help students and reinforce the subject matter," explains Money. "This type of setting is the only way to go as far as instructing and encouraging at the same time. We love it!"

The Mohawks' room is divided into two areas: lecture hall and activity hall. They cover certain topics each day, then the students break up to cluster in small groups and work on projects.

"All of our work revolves around our thematic units," continues Money. "This month we are studying the 'Nifty, Fifty United States.' This theme is carried throughout all our learning units such as math, social studies, and language arts."

Points are earned as projects are finished, and the students know they can bring their work to either teacher for verification of completion. "The students have two teachers to call their own," says Money.

"Barbara and I talk with each other in front of the students about topics and teaching styles. We think it is important for the students to see two adults working together as a team. It is important that they see the process of cooperation."

The daily instructional curriculum is integrated so that the usual blocks of reading, math, spelling, etc., mesh together. The teaching process "blends" many academic areas. For example, reading, math, and science can be taught together as the students research a cooking project or do a shopping project with the use of a local newspaper. This same concept can be extended as the students study the environment, take a look at prehistoric times, or develop a model of the stock market.

Teachers are primarily responsible for choosing and implementing the curriculum. Often it does not reflect the direction contained in the textbooks "adopted" for the classroom. Basal readers and other textbooks are used, but as a supplement to the curriculum focus decided on by the teacher.

In most cases, instruction centers around research-based topics and, as a result, the library is the primary resource tool in the school. Also, the parents and the community act as excellent resources for the students as they "dig up" information on their topic.

Staff Development

All the teachers at Concrete Elementary were given many hours of training before the Continuous Progress Program began. For example, they had twenty-four hours of initial cooperative learning training plus a follow-up with the trainer. The trainer went into each classroom for a minimum of three hours to work with teachers on the implementation of cooperative learning activities. They also had eighteen hours of inservice training on the use of theme-related units in teaching reading, math, writing, social studies, and science.

> The parents and the community act as excellent resources for the students.

In addition, the faculty honed their skills in staff communication, decision making, conflict resolution, goal setting, and in recognizing and applauding success at two weekend retreats. They also attended a three-weekend seminar on the implementation of seven different learning styles in the teaching/learning process. Multiple intelligences, as this process is called, explores learning centers and teaching strategies. Many of the teachers have adopted this instructional method and are using it successfully in the classroom.

Another ongoing inservice experience deals with portfolio and personal assessment techniques. Teachers are developing skills in different authentic assessment procedures as well as developing progress report cards and conference schedules. Other ongoing inservice programs use an interrelated curriculum to identify basic student outcomes and track the students' progress.

Cooperative Learning

The cross-age tutoring process is a natural outgrowth of the MAC program. Within each family group, there is a wonderful opportunity for the children at each level to assist children of another age level.

Initially older children assist the younger children, but as the year progresses it is not uncommon for the younger children to work at the same level with the older children or to assist the older ones. Throughout this entire process, it is very important for the concepts of cooperative learning to be fully implemented within each family group.

At the same time, intermediate level children frequently work with children at the primary level. This is done at a time that is convenient for the teachers. The faculty considered formalizing the process by developing an "adopt-a-kid" approach, but later decided to keep it less structured and make it a process whereby the older child earns the right to work in a primary classroom with any child who needs help.

An extra bonus occurs when student social skills improve as well.

Cooperative learning is a natural in family groups and an extra bonus occurs when student social skills improve as well. Meridith Loomis and Jaci Gallagher explain: "It's good the students see Jaci and me cooperating. They see how to work with others in the real world. We also use each other as an example of working together toward a common goal. They see us as a real-life application of cooperation."

These teachers feel the system works best if the classes are split in terms of age for short periods of time during the day. "The kids have a sense of identity," explains Loomis. "They can say, 'This is my classroom and Mrs. Loomis is my teacher.' Our students know they have a personal space within the multiage classroom framework. This gives them individual ownership within the whole."

By definition, cooperative learning is working within a group, where each individual has clearly defined roles and all are working toward common goals. "For example, we built sugar-cube pyramids last week," Jaci Gallagher explains. "The students were split into multiaged groups of four. The goal of each group was to complete a sugar-cube pyramid. The students' first task was to assign themselves roles within the group structure. There was a foreman (the builder), a recorder to write down the building process, an encourager to keep the group going with positive reinforcement, and a checker to see if the computations were correct. Each person had a role in building the pyramid."

"We are not just working in a group," continues Loomis. "To be successful, cooperative learning must have roles and goals. Of course our goal is to have them do this on their own. They are learning a life skill.

And it works. Now they come up with their own goals and roles while working independently on a project. We don't have to tell them. It's great to see this happen!"

The teachers see clear advantages to cooperative learning as it is applied in the multiage classroom setting. "They are definitely learning from each other," says Loomis. "The younger students draw on the older kids' experiences. When our students see their classmates excel, it gives them incentive to try new things. What better way to learn?"

> The younger students draw on the older kids' experiences.

Loomis and Gallagher teach the child as an individual. "We read in cross arrangements," Gallagher explains. "Fifth-year students read with third-year students. The kids aren't strapped with the stigma of 'reading in a lower reading group.'"

"When all ages are in a group, kids aren't singled out as 'top' or 'bottom' students," Loomis continues. "This is a big advantage. Blending skills for the good of all."

Parent Conferences and Student Assessment

In the past, parent-teacher conferences were regimented into twenty-minute sessions conducted over a three- or four-day period at the end of the first trimester. These were very cumbersome to schedule, and by the end of the first day, the teachers were emotionally drained.

To change the process, teachers were encouraged to schedule parent conferences on their own. The conferences begin in late October and run through mid-December. Each conference is limited to a maximum of forty-five minutes and other specialist teachers are encouraged to participate in the conferences.

On the average, most teachers schedule two or three conferences per week to occur during their planning time or after school. They also do the "easier" conferences first and wait until after the trimester is over in December to do the more difficult ones.

To compensate the teachers for the added hours required by this format, they have the option of using the regular districtwide parent conference time at their own discretion, provided they remain in the school building. This could include preparing curriculum, conferring with other teachers, or tending to other related tasks.

During the parent-teacher conference, the teachers share a narrative report card with the parents. This is a drastic change from the standard "letter grade" report card used in the past.

The basic format of the narrative report card is stored on a computer disk compatible with APPLE IIe or GS programs. During the course of the trimester, the teachers can "call up" the narrative report card for any given child and record any achievements or concerns related to the child. Each classroom has a computer available for the teacher's use in doing report cards and other computer-related tasks.

The narrative report card indicates the progress a student has made in language arts, math, science/social studies, handwriting, and social development. Within each category, the teacher will describe the classroom program or curriculum currently being taught. This includes a brief description of the goals of the program, the activities and projects being worked on, and the homework expectations. Then the teacher will summarize where a given child is functioning within the program.

> "The letter grade report card never told us anything about what was going on in the school."

A typical narrative report card could range from two to five pages in length. It can be developed by the teacher over the length of the entire grading period and, when finished, can serve as a "profile" of the child's current achievement level.

The teachers were initially concerned that the parents would not understand the narrative report card format and still wanted the traditional "grade point average" summary, even at the earliest primary grade levels. However, the typical response was, "Now we have a better understanding of the total program our children are experiencing. The letter grade report card never told us anything about what was going on in the school. It only gave us an indication as to where our child was functioning. This new narrative report card is much more personal."

Concrete Elementary's Chapter 1 and math (LAP) programs had, in the past, operated on the traditional pull-out basis, with the children leaving their regular classrooms each day for twenty-five to thirty minutes to participate in the Chapter 1/LAP programs. However, they discovered that less than 10 percent of the children ever "tested out" of these programs.

They have redesigned the program, and now children with the most severe problems are assigned to Chapter 1 and LAP during the first sixty days of the school year. While they are with the "specialists," the children are totally immersed for the entire morning in reading and language experience. The afternoon is spent with math activities. Children with less severe problems are involved during the second and third trimesters.

When the children are returned to their regular family groups, an instructional assistant is assigned to work with them during the next trimester as a follow-up to their experience. As a result of the school's efforts in this direction, more than 44 percent of the children "tested out" of the program during the first year.

Before trying this approach, Concrete Elementary had to get the approval of the Washington State Chapter 1/LAP Office. The state was very supportive and assisted the school in making changes in order to get better results for the children.

Does It Work?

All the careful planning, preparation, and restructuring is in vain if the overall concept does not work. Though after two years of it, the faculty and staff can point to indicators that say, "Yes, the multiage, continuous progress program does work."

For example, the following improvements have been seen at Concrete Elementary because of the restructuring activities:

- Average student daily attendance has increased from 89 percent to 93 percent.

- No student was retained or held back during the first full year. All of the children are somewhere on the spectrum in working toward their educational goals. They are considered in continuous progress.

- Discipline referrals to the office were reduced by 47 percent in one year.

- Parent interest in the multiaged program increased significantly during the first two years. Sixty-eight percent of the parents wanted their child in a MAC classroom in the first year. This year, 82 percent of the parents wanted a MAC classroom for their child. As a result, two new MAC family groups had to be created.

- In the past two years, out of a faculty of twenty-eight teachers, there have been only two staff changes, and these were brought about by retirement.

None of the changes at Concrete Elementary has occurred without a cost. Everyone paid the price in a lot of hard work and many long hours. But they would never go back to where they were before. All who are involved feel they now provide a better education for the children. And the teaching staff is very highly motivated and dedicated.

As the children scamper to the bus and wave at their teachers gathering on the sidewalk to see them off, they carry with them an enthusiasm that spreads throughout the community. Their message is simple, "School is fun; we like to learn." The children are unaware of why or how the changes occurred—they just look forward to going to school each day.

Success can be measured by test scores, statistics, and achievement parameters. It can also be measured by enthusiasm and the sheer joy of learning. Concrete Elementary scores high on both counts. The faculty still has challenges and goals to work toward in the education process, but they can look back at a series of triumphs with pride.

The teachers share their students' enthusiasm for a nongraded system with the simple edict, "We will never go back to what we were doing before!"

References

Anderson, R. H., and B. N. Pavan. 1993. *Nongradedness: Helping it to happen.* Lancaster, Pa.: Technomic Press.

Elementary School Principals' Association of Washington. 1992. *Developmentally appropriate practices—Resource book for savvy principals.* Olympia, Wash.: Author.

Gaustad, J. 1992a. *Making the transition from graded to nongraded primary education.* Eugene: Oregon School Study Council, University of Oregon.

———. 1992b. *Nongraded education.* Eugene: Oregon School Study Council, University of Oregon.

Glasser, W. 1990. *The quality school.* New York: Harper & Row.

Goodlad, J. I., and R. H. Anderson. 1987. *The nongraded elementary school.* New York: Teachers' College Press, Columbia University.

Hunter, M. 1992. *How to change to a nongraded school.* Alexandria, Va.: Association for Supervision and Curriculum Development.

Malen, B., and R. T. Ogawa. 1990. *Community involvement: Parents, teachers and administrators working together.* Boston: Allyn and Bacon.

McDonald, J., ed. 1993. *Open education as a component of restructuring.* Bloomington, Ind.: Center for Evaluation, Development, and Research, Phi Delta Kappa.

Miller, B. A. 1989. *The multigrade classroom: A resource for small rural schools.* Portland, Ore.: Northwest Regional Educational Laboratory.

———. 1994. *Keeping children at the center: Implementing the multiage classroom.* Portland, Ore.: Northwest Regional Educational Laboratory.

Province of British Columbia Ministry of Education. 1989a. *The primary program—Resource document.* Victoria, B. C.: Author.

———. 1989b. *The intermediate program—Resource document.* Victoria, B. C.

Washington Roundtable. 1994. *School centered renewal.* Seattle, Wash.

Washington State Office of the Superintendent of Public Instruction. 1993. *Moving toward multiaged programs.* Olympia, Wash.

SECTION II

Information

*To treat
your facts with
imagination is one
thing, but to imagine
your facts is another.*

—John Burroughs

SECTION II

Information

To provide the facts, data, and issues that are the cornerstone for conversations regarding multiage groupings, Section II offers insightful information from leading voices in the field.

Barbara Pavan opens the section with a historical perspective that traces the waxing and waning of nongradedness from the '60s to the present. In this comprehensive essay, the author discusses the various elements that weave multiage, nongraded groupings into the fabric of education. She begins with a detailed look at what happened in the '60s and '70s with open classroom concepts, schools without walls, the humanitarian approach to students through values clarification, and individualized progress programs, and illustrates how the whole movement was suddenly and decisively aborted. With the launch of Sputnik, the fundamental, back-to-basics, traditional way became the focus. Moving into the '80s, Pavan looks at the philosophy behind the Coalition of Essential Schools, directed by Ted Sizer, which brought about a revival of the nongraded approach. Continuing the historical journey, Pavan highlights the present course of the '90s in which school reform targets learner-centered schooling and in doing so, places multiage groupings into the limelight again.

In the second essay of this section, Roberto Gutiérrez and Robert Slavin present extensive and comprehensive discussions of the research base for nongradedness. It is complete with rationale, a discussion of methodology, specific categories, and a summary of the research. The authors also address acceleration policies and look at how relevant the early research may be.

In the final esssay, David Marshak provides an insightful piece on how teachers perceive the social and psychological benefits of multiage classrooms. Interestingly, the author delineates the benefits—from the teachers' perspective—for the students, the teachers, and the parents. Marshak presents a brief look at the disadvantages of multiage classrooms and concludes by suggesting that the multiage model offers insight into what twenty-first century schools might become.

For readers investigating the concept of multiage classrooms, this section provides some answers. The facts are here; the evidence is clear. Informed conversations resulting from these readings are sure to yield meaningful results.

The Waxing and Waning of Nongradedness

Barbara Nelson Pavan

A nongraded school is one in which grade-level designations are not used for students or classes. Progress is reported by indicating the tasks completed and the manner of learning, not by A,B,C,D,E,F or G,S,U or similar rating systems. A team of teachers generally works with a team of students who are regrouped frequently according to student needs or interests and the particular task or activity. Most of these groups are multiage, heterogeneous groups learning together as they pursue complex problem-solving activities and projects in interdisciplinary thematic units. Students are active participants in their learning and in the collection of multiple sources of documentation to be used for assessment and evaluation. Continuous pupil progress is not movement through a predetermined sequence of curriculum levels, but an individual expansion of knowledge, skills, and understanding.

The paragraph above describes nongradedness as it was practiced at the Franklin Elementary School in Lexington, Massachusetts, from 1957 to 1983. In the earlier years, the stress was on the team teaching component as a way to better meet students' individual needs by providing more teachers and more grouping possibilities.

Interest in nongradedness was strong during the 1960s and the early 1970s. Many articles of general interest were published and a considerable body of research comparing nongraded and graded schools was generated with results favoring nongradedness (Pavan 1973b). Funding for creative and innovative projects was available from the federal government and a number of foundations, providing the needed "start-up" costs for many schools. In fact, this was a time when Americans had a more positive attitude than at present and believed that education could resolve our nation's problems.

A British import called "open" or "informal education" began to overshadow interest in nongradedness during the early 1970s. American educators flocked to Great Britain to see "open classrooms." In the best of these British classrooms, many located in Lancaster, the practices observed were closely attuned to the nongraded description given earlier. The source of their philosophy came from certain understandings of child development, such as Piaget's, and from the work of people such as John Dewey. The famous Plowden report (1967) was one such document that also described team teaching and reported visits to Harvard, the Franklin School, and other public schools and universities in the United States. After that report many British educators visited the Franklin School, and I was invited to visit and speak in Bradford, England, in 1974.

American receptivity to open education is explained by the close connection to that model and the major movements in twentieth-century American education. Squire (1972) brought together major writers in *A New Look at Progressive Education,* which detailed some of the parallels between progressive education and the British primary school model but failed to note any relationship to the American nongraded movement. The roots of nongradedness run deep in the progressive era of the 1920s and 1930s. The similarities of the underlying principles on which all three—progressive, nongraded, and open education—are based needs to be acknowledged. It would be instructive if we investigated our educational history more thoroughly.

The Waning

So why did nongradedness appear to fade away in the late '70s? As with any other complex innovation, there is no single cause; a number of factors contributed to the waning of nongradedness. Depending on the geographic location of a school, declining enrollment hit school districts in different years during the 1970s. With lower enrollments came the consolidation of schools, which resulted in the closing of other schools. If the nongraded programs were in the older schools, which were the logical choice for school closings, then the nongraded program ended. This was the fate of the Franklin School in 1983. However, other things were happening before then that made it more difficult to maintain the program.

When many teaching positions were available, teachers (and principals) could be placed in schools where there were compatible philosophies. However, declining enrollment in the 1970s often meant that teachers were assigned to a given school with teaching philosophies that were incompatible with nongradedness. Since money was no longer available for the intensive staff development needed to train new faculty, assigning teachers to a nongraded school who did not wish to teach in such a school made the continuation of such a program even more difficult. In a few cases, nongraded programs never were truly operational, due to insufficient staff training from the start.

Aspects of the '70s contributed to the waning of nongradedness.

As with all innovations, there is a need for continued and supportive leadership. Frequently, visionary leaders are sought after for other programs and so leave. If this happens before the program is institutionalized or before others have assumed complete ownership, the program generally falters. Additionally, when funding for equipment and supplies is cut too drastically, teachers become frustrated as they perceive that their efforts are not appreciated by the community or the central office.

There were also certain aspects of the '70s that contributed to the waning of nongradedness. Open education became associated with "free school," lack of structure, and the "hippie" drug culture. Parents and communities were upset. With the Vietnam War protests, the entire country was upset. So easy solutions were sought.

People believed schools should get "back to the basics" with increased testing using behavioral objectives. Schools should not be fun for students, but hard work. School boards, especially those in the Northeast during the 1974 oil embargo, were experiencing fiscal difficulties, and breadwinners, even high-level executives, were losing their jobs. The public was not in a generous mood. In a few cases, the John Birch Society was again able to get a member elected to the school board.

Officially, many school districts dropped nongraded or open education programs to quiet the public. However, teachers did not forget the joyous experience of watching children blossom in these programs. Many went underground and continued to operate in a nongraded mode within the constraints of their school systems.

As interest in nongradedness waned in the 1980s, research and publication about it also tapered off. Even though an analysis of thirty-seven research studies comparing nongraded and graded schools indicated that a student in a nongraded school was likely to have higher academic achievement, a better self-concept, and a more positive attitude toward school (Pavan 1977), many educators and the general public did not appear to be convinced. The tradition of gradedness, which most adults had experienced as children, was a hard one to overturn. It appears so much simpler to raise standards—such as scores on standardized achievement tests and reading levels in basal readers—as hurdles to "pass" in order to be promoted to the next grade level. This is done even as school boards proclaim that individuals learn at different rates and in different ways.

The tradition of gradedness was a hard one to overturn.

The Winds of Change, or Waxing

The inflammatory language in the 1983 publication *A Nation at Risk* unleashed a flood of other reports, but only a trickle of funding—much of which was soon rescinded or found insufficient to cover inflation. Many of these first reports called for more of the same ineffective practices from the past: increased testing of both students and teachers (especially if teachers were to receive increased salaries), expanded class hours, higher standards (meaning more retention and more transition classes), further curriculum regulations from state departments of education, and additional school days.

However, others were voicing the need to not merely add more or tinker with education, but to drastically restructure schools as they are now. The Carnegie report (1986) called for teachers to work together in teams, with teachers replacing some of the principal's function as instructional leader. These lead teachers were to function as the team leaders did at the Franklin School or in a Multi-Unit Individually Guided Education (IGE) program. The Holmes Group (1986) noted how this need for teacher collaboration would change how teachers are educated for the profession. Goodlad (1990) described how a pedagogy team models the collaborative learning process for preservice teachers.

> How did this nongraded revival happen?

Today, under Ted Sizer's direction, the Coalition of Essential Schools has philosophically returned curriculum decisions to the teachers at the high school level. A team of teachers works with a team of students to develop performance-based assessments using projects as a major learning vehicle. Junior highs are now becoming middle schools so that former secondary and elementary teachers may combine their subject matter and child-centered strengths to provide for children's needs. Elementary schools, especially the primary grades, are once again considering nongradedness. Incidentally, both the middle school movement and Sizer's coalition philosophically foster nongraded schools.

How did this nongraded revival happen? Americans seem to respond when situations reach crisis levels. *A Nation at Risk* (1983) declared a disaster—America would no longer be able to compete (remember Sputnik?). This has been reinforced by plant closings and layoffs that have led to unemployment in geographic areas and among people not used to losing their jobs.

There is widespread concern that schools are not working for our growing number of "at-risk" children. Retention rates are up, which has school boards on edge. The school district of Philadelphia alone has failed 23 percent of its first graders for the last several years (Superintendent's MIC, 1990–91). Such statistics caused a Promotion and Retention Task Force to recommend instituting nongradedness in the elementary schools.

Implementation has been limited to nongraded classes in about a dozen schools this past school year, while the district has been engaged in a massive school-based restructuring program initiated by a new superintendent.

Research supporting that retained students generally score lower than promoted students on standardized tests has been available to educators for nearly forty years (Goodlad 1952), but widespread understanding has only recently emerged with the publication of Shepard and Smith's *Flunking Grades: Research and Policies on Retention* (1989). School board members are realizing that retention is not only educationally ineffective, but very costly as more and more students spend additional years in school.

Some states have looked at their deficient educational systems and declared the need to improve in order to lure new business. These states have revamped their departments of education and educational systems in order to make school funding more equitable. The financial squeeze and the awareness that most of the past programs for "at-risk" or special education students have had minimal success has caused state legislatures to look at new ideas or, as in the case of Kentucky, to consider reviving nongrading, which had been practiced in a number of their schools in the past.

Collaboration between students and teachers is now considered necessary.

In one sense nongradedness seems as if it's being reactivated in a desperate attempt to improve schools. I would not take such a pessimistic view. I believe that thoughtful educators, many of whom have had some experience with nongrading or team teaching, understand that the present educational process of lecture, recite, and test is dysfunctional. We know so much more about learning and teaching than we knew just fifteen years ago. The brain does not just absorb new information, but seeks to connect it with previous and present knowledge. The role of motivation and other psychological principles is much better understood as it relates to learning. Teachers are learning a multitude of teaching strategies to apply in different contexts and for different goals. Collaboration between students and teachers is now considered necessary to increase learning. And many different cooperative learning models are now available to achieve the benefits of heterogeneous grouping.

Education frequently follows trends in business. The recent stress on participatory management known as school or site-based management (SBM) has involved teachers in decision making and goal setting within their schools. Like business, education is realizing that the talents of its employees have in most cases been underutilized, and at a great loss to the system.

This time around for nongradedness we should be aware that change is a slow and often painful process. Business and industry do not expect their employees to operate new systems without extensive education, and yet we educators frequently expect teachers to learn new skills in a one-day, one-shot inservice program. Kentucky originally provided a five-year phase-in period (later cut to three years by the state legislature) for nongraded primaries. The phase-in included planning periods, in-service education, and practical support from the state department of education. Even so, this was a hectic time, as the entire educational system was being revamped.

> "The nongraded plan is a system of organization."

In the 1963 edition of *The Nongraded Elementary School,* Goodlad wrote, "It should be clear by now that the nongraded plan is a system of organization and nothing more" (p.59). He goes on to explain that the structure enables the teacher to become more creative since both teachers and students are freed of the grade level confinements. In the 1987 edition he said, "What I would stress now, far more than I did then, would be the philosophy behind nongradedness and how this must infuse much more than merely school structure."

In the period between 1963 and 1987, Pavan (1972) synthesized a list of thirty-six principles of nongradedness from a thorough reading of the literature on nongrading. A copy was sent to forty-eight writers and practitioners in the field in order to provide feedback as to the clarity, validity, and comprehensiveness of the model. Thirty-nine people (81 percent) sent back usable, completed forms. The responses were overwhelmingly in agreement with the assumptions in the model. For all but one of the thirty-six statements, at least 70 percent of the respondents felt each principle was either crucial or important in a comprehensive definition of nongradedness. All but eight of the thirty-six statements were declared to be crucial or important by 80 percent or more of the respondents.

In the spring of 1987 these principles were sent to those same respondents to find out their thoughts on the subject fifteen years later. Responses were received from twenty-three of the original respondents. They suggested some language changes (for example, substituting "cognition" for "intelligence"), but otherwise the experts reaffirmed that most of the thirty-six principles are crucial to a comprehensive definition of nongradedness.

Once again their responses were used to revise the statements. The categories were also realigned and the items within the categories reordered for a more logical flow. Two dissertations (Guarino 1982; Hoffman 1985) that had used the original list were also consulted. The resulting revised version (1993) has been used with large groups of teachers and administrators from a dozen different states in training sessions, and these discussions have provided useful insight as to the understanding of the items by current practitioners. The present version enables educators to determine their comfort with and commitment to nongradedness.

The Principles of Nongradedness (Anderson and Pavan 1993) are divided into six clusters, each with six items: goals of schooling, organization, curriculum, instruction, materials, and assessments. The goals of schooling for nongradedness speak to individual differences, student autonomy, maximizing potential in many areas besides the cognitive, enjoying learning, and developing positive self-concepts. Grouping and placement in multiage, multiability groups are frequently changed based on tasks and needs. Curriculum differs as individuals differ, and integrated subject matter themes using inquiry methods are stressed. A variety of instructional strategies and materials are used as children expand their knowledge and skills and are assessed by teachers and students using multiple data sources.

Nongradedness appears to be waxing in the 1990s. Efforts are being made not only to implement nongradedness, but also to assess the degree of the implementation efforts. Too many research studies have provided only comparative results of nongraded and graded schools without documenting if nongradedness was an actuality. Two observational tools are available for such efforts. One is the nongraded behavioral indicators developed by Pavan (Anderson and Pavan 1993) and utilized by Guarino (1982), and by Sattler (1995) in her study of three continuous progress schools that have been in operation since 1976. The other tool and preliminary results are available in *The Implementation of Kentucky's Primary Program* (1994). In both the newly instituted Kentucky program and the program that is nearly twenty years old, implementation remains mostly dependent on individual teachers. Neither study found much evidence of team teaching, which facilitates schoolwide implementation.

Due to the renewed interest in nongradedness, Pavan (1992) updated the review of comparative studies of graded and nongraded schools. Since 1968, sixty-four research studies have been conducted, most of which attest to the benefits of nongraded schools for students in terms of higher academic achievement, better mental health, and more positive attitudes toward school. These results were even more pronounced when students stayed in nongraded programs for longer periods of time and when nongradedness was more effectively implemented. Additionally, at-risk students did more favorably in nongraded settings.

If this time-adequate staff development is provided and sufficient time is allowed for changes to be implemented, the benefits of nongradedness should bring joy to the children, their teachers, and, especially, their parents.

References

Anderson, R., and B. N. Pavan. 1993. *Nongradedness: Helping it to happen.* Lancaster, Pa.: Technomic Press.

Goodlad, J. 1952. Research and theory regarding promotion and non-promotion. *Elementary School Journal* 53: 150–55.

———. 1990. *Teachers for our nation's schools.* San Francisco: Jossey-Bass.

Goodlad, J., and R. Anderson. 1987. *The nongraded elementary school.* New York: Teachers College Press.

Guarino, A. R. 1982. An Investigation of Achievement, Self-Concept, and School Related Anxiety in Graded and Nongraded Elementary Schools. Ed.D. dissertation, Rutgers University.

Hoffman, M. S. 1985. The Ungraded Primary Organization in the Milwaukee Public Schools. Ph.D. dissertation, Margurette University.

The Holmes Groups. 1986. *Tomorrow's teachers: A report of the Holmes group.* East Lansing, Mich.: The Holmes Groups.

Kentucky State Department of Education. 1970. *New directions, new dimensions. Elementary programs in Kentucky.* Frankfort, Ky.: Office of Curriculum Development (ERIC ED 067-310).

National Commission on Excellence in Education. 1983. *A nation at risk.* Washington, D.C.: Government Printing Office.

Pavan, B. N. 1972. Moving Elementary Schools toward Nongradedness: Commitment, Assessment, and Tactics. Ed.D. dissertation, Harvard University.

———. 1973a. Nongradedness—One view. *Educational Leadership* 30: 401–03.

———. 1973b. Good news: Research on the nongraded elementary school. *Elementary School Journal* 73: 233–42.

———. 1977. The nongraded elementary school: Research on academic achievement and mental health. *Texas Tech Journal of Education* 4: 91–107.

———. 1992. The benefits of nongraded schools. *Educational Leadership* 50 (2): 22–25.

Plowden, B., et al. 1967. *Children and their primary schools: A report on the Central Advisory Council for Education.* London: Her Majesty's Stationary Office.

Sattler, J. M. Implementation of Nongradedness: A Study of Three Continuous Progress Schools. 1995. Ed.D. dissertation, Temple University.

School District of Philadelphia. 1991. *Superintendent's management information center.* 1990–91. Philadelphia: School District of Philadelphia, Office of Assessment.

Shepard, A., and M. L. Smith, eds. 1989. *Flunking grades: Research and policies on retention.* London: Palmer Press.

Squire, J., ed. 1972. *A new look at progressive education. ASCD yearbook.* Washington, D.C.: Association for Supervision and Curriculum Development.

Task Force on Teaching as a Profession. 1986. *A nation prepared: Teachers for the 21st century.* Hyattsville, Mass.: The Carnegie Forum on Education and the Economy.

University of Kentucky Institute on Educational Reform. 1994. *The implementation of Kentucky's primary program.* Lexington: University of Kentucky Institute on Educational Reform.

Research in Nongraded Elementary Schools
Simple Is Beautiful

Roberto Gutiérrez and Robert E. Slavin

> Greek mythology tells us of the cruel robber, Procrustes (the stretcher). When travelers sought his house for shelter, they were tied to an iron bedstead. If the traveler was shorter than the bed, Procrustes stretched him until he was the same length as the bed. If he was longer, his limbs were chopped off to make him fit. Procrustes shaped both short and tall until they were equally long and equally dead. Graded systems of school organization trap school-age travelers in much the same fashion as Procrustes' bed trapped the unwary.
>
> —J. I. Goodlad and R. H. Anderson
> *The Nongraded Elementary School*

A great deal of research has been done to evaluate various forms of the nongraded elementary school, but there are few comprehensive reviews on this topic. McLoughlin (1967), reviewing studies done up to 1966, concluded that most found no differences between graded and nongraded programs in reading, arithmetic, and language arts performance. In contrast, Pavan (1992), who limited her review of achievement to studies reported between 1968 and 1990, concluded that most comparisons favored the nongraded plan. However, both of these reviews were quite limited. They simply counted statistically significant findings favoring graded or nongraded programs, paying little attention to the particular forms of nongrading used, the methodological quality of the studies, or the size of the effects.

The purpose of this chapter is to systematically review research on the academic achievement effects of nongraded schooling, and to draw inferences from this research for applications of the nongraded ideal in today's schools.

Rationales for Nongrading

The major rationale for a nongraded approach is to provide an alternative to both retention and social promotion (i.e., promoting students regardless of performance). In the view of Goodlad and Anderson (1963) and many who have followed them (e.g., Shepard and Smith 1989), retention is harmful to students, is applied inconsistently, and fails to take into account developmental inconsistencies (e.g., late bloomers), especially among young children. A retained child repeats a whole year of content he or she failed to learn the first time. Spending a year failing to learn a body of curriculum and then spending a second year going over the same curriculum seems to be a poor practice for low achievers. Advocates of nongrading would argue that it is far better to allow such students to move more slowly through material with a high success rate and never have to repeat unlearned content.

Retention is harmful to students.

The rationale for the reemergence of the nongraded plan today is similar to that of the 1950s. In the 1980s, retention rates increased dramatically in elementary schools, especially those in large cities (Levine and Eubanks 1986–87). This was partly a result of accountability pressures, which focused on the performance of students according to grade level, not age, thereby rewarding districts for such policies as imposing grade-to-grade promotion standards and holding back low achievers (see Allington and McGill-Franzen 1992; Slavin and Madden 1991).

However, in more recent years a reaction against high retention rates has taken place because of the negative long-term effects of retention in the elementary grades. Unwilling to return to social promotion (and still under accountability pressures that discourage it), many school districts are currently experimenting with a variety of means of holding standards constant while allowing time spent in the early grades to vary. Among these is the growing trend of adding another year between kindergarten and second grade for at-risk children (such as developmental kindergarten, junior kindergarten, transitional first grade, or prefirst programs). However, research on the long-term impact of these approaches has brought their value into question (see Karweit and Wasik, 1994). The nongraded primary has been rediscovered as a means of avoiding both retention and social promotion.

Nongraded organization also offers an alternative to traditional forms of ability grouping. Goodlad and Anderson (1963) point out how nongrading can be an improvement on both between-class ability grouping (e.g., high, middle, and low self-contained second grades) and within-class ability grouping (e.g., reading groups). The problem with between-class ability grouping, they argue, is that grouping based on any one criterion (such as reading performance or general ability) cannot group students well for any particular skill. For example, a class grouped according to reading skill will have a very broad range of math levels and will even be quite diverse in performance levels on any particular reading task. As a result, the costs of ability grouping in terms of stigmatizing low achievers are not compensated for by any practically meaningful reduction in heterogeneity. Forming reading groups within heterogeneous classes is similarly flawed in their view. In order to create homogeneous groups, teachers must have many reading groups and therefore must spend much class time on follow-up activities of little instructional value.

In the nongraded plan, students are flexibly grouped for major subjects across class and age lines.

In the nongraded plan, students are flexibly grouped for major subjects (especially reading and math) across class and age lines so that the resulting groups are truly homogeneous on the skills being taught. Further, by creating multiage groups from among all students in contiguous grade levels, it is possible for teachers to create entire reading or math classes at one or, at most, two levels, so that they need not devote much class time to follow-up.

Finally, the nongraded plan is proposed as a solution to the problem of split grades. For example, in many schools with a class size of twenty-five and thirty-eight students in grades 2 and 3, principals would create one second grade class, one third grade class, and one second and third grade combination class. In a graded structure, teaching the second and third grade class is difficult, as the two portions of the class may be taught completely separately. A nongraded organization, by eliminating the designation of students as second or third graders, solves this problem.

An important factor today in the move toward the nongraded primary that was not a rationale in the 1950s is the trend toward "developmentally appropriate" practices in the early grades. Developmentally appropriate practices are instructional approaches that allow young children to develop skills at their own pace (National Association for the Education of Young Children 1989).

Review Methods

This review, adapted from a more comprehensive review by Gutiérrez and Slavin (1992), synthesizes the findings of research comparing the achievement effects of nongraded and traditional organizations in the elementary grades (K–6). The review method used is best-evidence synthesis (Slavin 1986), which combines elements of meta-analysis (Glass, McGaw, and Smith 1981) with those of narrative reviews. Briefly, a best-evidence synthesis requires locating all research on a given topic, establishing well-specified criteria of methodological adequacy and germaneness to the topic, and then reviewing this "best evidence" with attention to the substantive and methodological contributions of each study. Whenever possible, study outcomes are characterized in terms of effect sizes—the difference between the experimental and control means divided by the control group's standard deviation.

Substantive Inclusion Criteria

Every effort was made to obtain every study ever reported that could be identified as evaluating nongraded, ungraded, multiage, or Individually Guided Education programs in grades K–6. Studies spanning elementary and middle grades were included, but only data up to grade 6 were considered.

Methodological Inclusion Criteria

Studies were included if they met the following methodological criteria, which are identical to those applied in earlier reviews of ability grouping by Slavin (1987, 1990):

1. Some objective measure of achievement was used. Because of their subjective nature, grades were not included as achievement variables. In practice, all achievement outcomes were assessed using standardized measures.

2. Initial comparability of the nongraded and graded samples was established by means of random assignment of students, matching of schools or classes, or matching of individual students within classes or schools. In studies using matching, evidence had to be presented to indicate that either the groups were initially equivalent (within 20 percent of a standard deviation) or, if they were not equivalent, pretest data had to be presented to allow for adjustment of posttest scores for pretest differences. Studies that used gain scores or analyses of covariance to control for initial differences between nongraded and graded programs are listed in separate portions of each table, as statistical adjustment for pretest differences cannot be assumed to completely control for their influence on posttests (see Reichardt 1979). Results of these studies should be interpreted cautiously.

3. The nongraded program was in place for at least a semester. All studies located met this standard; in fact, only two studies were less than a year in duration.

Very few studies that used any achievement measure to compare nongraded and graded programs were excluded on the basis of these inclusion criteria. Examples of studies excluded are ones which involved nongraded secondary schools (e.g., Chalfant 1972), studies without any evidence that nongraded and control groups were initially equivalent and without adjustments for pretests (e.g., Ingram 1960), and studies of school organization plans related to but not the same as the nongraded program (e.g., Heathers 1967; Maresh 1971).

Studies were *not* excluded if they met the above criteria but failed to present data that would allow for computation of effect sizes. Instead, such studies were included in all tables with an indication of the direction and statistical significance of any differences (see table 1).

Categories of Nongraded Programs

Nongraded elementary schools have varied widely in their particulars. This variation is not surprising, given that the original conception of the nongraded idea did not pretend to touch on all aspects of school organization and instruction:

> Nongrading is a scheme for organizing schools vertically. It does not account for the many problems of organizing schools horizontally. (Goodlad and Anderson 1963, 210)

In looking at studies of nongraded elementary schools over time, an interesting pattern emerges. The earlier studies tended to apply nongrading to only one subject, usually reading. As time went on, studies began to include more than one subject, but maintained traditional curriculum and instruction. Later still, nongraded programs began to incorporate far more radical changes in curriculum and instruction along with increased use of team teaching, individualized instruction, learning stations, peer tutoring, cooperative learning, and so on. Individually Guided Education (IGE), in its Wisconsin version or in the one developed by the Kettering Foundation (through I/D/E/A), represented a full flowering of this form of nongrading (Klausmeier, Rossmiller, and Saily 1977).

It is possible to distinguish four distinct categories of nongraded programs, and this review considers each type separately. They are as follows:
1. Nongraded programs involving only one subject (Joplin-like programs)
2. Nongraded programs involving multiple subjects (comprehensive programs)

3. Nongraded programs incorporating individualized instruction
4. Individually Guided Education

In addition, we report the findings of studies of programs identified as nongraded in which it is impossible to determine what was actually implemented.

Research on Nongraded Programs

The following sections discuss the research on each of the categories of nongraded programs. The five sections contain tables summarizing the major characteristics and findings, first of randomized studies, then matched equivalent studies, and finally matched studies lacking evidence of initial equality. Within these categories the larger studies are listed first. In general, then, studies listed earlier in each table can be considered higher in methodological quality than those that come later.

In each table, effect sizes are presented for each measure or subgroup used, and then an overall effect size is presented. Asterisks by effect sizes indicate that the differences were statistically significant, according to the authors. When effect sizes could not be computed, outcomes are characterized as favoring nongraded (+), no difference (0), or favoring graded (-), with asterisks if the differences were significant. A key to all symbols and abbreviations used in all tables appears in the appendix with the tables.

Joplin-Like Nongraded Programs

Table 1 summarizes the research on nongraded programs that have as a distinctive feature the homogeneous grouping of students according to performance level in only one subject. These plans can be labeled Joplin-like programs because they share with the Joplin Plan the idea of regrouping students for just one subject (usually reading), ignoring grade levels or ages (Floyd 1954). Nine studies, all done during the 1960s, are included in this category. The subject was reading in eight studies, math in one. Most of them were described under the Joplin Plan arrangement in an earlier synthesis of ability grouping and student achievement in elementary schools (Slavin 1987). These studies appeared early in the nongraded movement, suggesting that the earlier implementations were more conservative (affecting only one subject) than those which appeared later.

Results from five of the nine studies found strong, positive effects for the nongraded plans, three studies reported no differences between them and graded plans, and one significantly favored the graded program. Overall, the findings of methodologically adequate studies of this type of nongraded program were consistent. All studies exhibiting good methodological quality (randomized and matched studies with evidence of initial equality) found substantial positive results in favor of the nongraded program. The median effect size for the four best quality studies was +.50; for all seven studies from which effect sizes could be estimated, it was +.46. The matched studies lacking evidence of initial equality that do not report positive results were characterized by similar reading programs; the biggest difference between them appeared to be their label.

> *All studies found substantial positive results in favor of the nongraded program.*

Two features were important in almost all of the successful nongraded programs evaluated: flexibility in pupil grouping, with frequent assessment of mastery at each level, and increased amounts of teaching time for the homogenous instructional groups. Because each teacher had to manage fewer groups, there was less need for independent follow-up activities such as reading worksheets. Perhaps this last characteristic is one of the most important elements favoring students in a nongraded program: more homogenous groups allow teachers to define more specific objectives for instruction, and children receive a greater amount of direct teaching.

Comprehensive Nongraded Programs

Some studies described plans in which more than one subject was nongraded. The programs in this category adhered most closely to the original conception put forward by Goodlad and Anderson (1963) in that the nongraded programs emphasized regular progress and flexible, multiage grouping but did not emphasize individualized instruction. These fourteen studies, summarized in table 2, were conducted from the late 1960s to the beginning of the 1980s.

Findings from this group of studies consistently favored the nongraded program. Only three evaluations presented small (and nonsignificant) negative total effect sizes, while eight of the ten that presented results favoring the nongraded plans reported statistically significant differences. The median effect size for the matched equivalent studies was +.34, and it was the same for all nine studies from which effect sizes could be estimated.

Among those studies that did not report any significant difference, three were conducted in university laboratory schools, and another three found equivalence in the first year of the program but started to see favorable changes in subsequent years. In the case of laboratory schools, control classes were similar to experimental ones, or they appeared to be very high quality classes. Perhaps for these reasons, significant differences did not appear in those circumstances.

Across many studies, greater duration of the program was associated with higher positive differences. Other common characteristics of academically successful nongraded plans were subjects organized by levels, use of texts written in accordance with those levels, and regrouping of students in multiage environments that allowed teachers to reduce the heterogeneity of their instructional groups.

Nongraded Programs Incorporating Individualized Instruction

Many studies of nongraded programs included indications that individualized instruction was an important part of the nongraded plan. These individualized approaches included one-to-one tutoring, programmed instruction, and learning activity packages. Following are two examples of the types of individualization adopted:

> Most students would be on contracts of work . . . [that] might last from one to five days with the student coming to the teachers only in particular moments of difficulty. (Bowman 1971, 46)

> The Individually Prescribed Instruction mathematics program . . . was used in the model school. This individualized system of instruction provided each student with the opportunity to work on undeveloped skills, to obtain a diagnosis of new learnings, and to receive a prescription for the next sequence of material to be mastered. Math specialists, instructional aides, and volunteer aides were available to pupils on a one-to-one basis. (Jeffreys 1970, 30)

All but one of the eleven studies of this type were published from 1969 to 1973, with a median of 1971. This is considerably later than the time frame in which the studies summarized in table 1 appeared. The median publication date for the Joplin-like programs is 1962, and, for the comprehensive (multiple subjects) programs, it is 1969. What this progression suggests is that individualized instruction increasingly became part of the nongraded elementary school in the late 1960s and early 1970s, at a time when individualization was gaining popularity in North American schools in general. Table 3 summarizes the characteristics and findings of the eleven studies of nongraded programs, including individualized instruction.

More positive effects were obtained with older children than with younger children.

Considered together, the results of research on these nongraded programs were remarkably consistent. No significant differences appeared in most studies. A median effect size (ES) of essentially zero (ES = +.02) was found across the nine studies from which effect sizes could be computed. These findings suggest that nongraded programs using individualized instruction were equivalent to graded plans in terms of academic achievement. As the nongraded plans became more complicated in their grouping arrangements, they apparently lost the comparative advantage of Joplin-like or comprehensive nongraded programs.

There is one interesting trend in the data on nongraded programs using individualized instruction: more positive effects were obtained with older children than with younger children. It may be that students need a certain level of maturity or self-organizational skill to profit from a continuous progress program that includes a good deal of independent work. Another indication of this is the observation that the longer the duration of the program, the better the results.

Individually Guided Education (IGE) Programs

Ten studies, most of which were done in the 1970s, met the inclusion criteria for this review. All of these evaluated the University of Wisconsin IGE program, not the Kettering model. Since nongradedness is a characteristic of IGE schools, comparisons between them and non-IGE schools cast light on the effects of programs that emphasize individualized instruction.

Although the degree of implementation of IGE processes varied from one research setting to another, IGE concepts, components, and practices were clearly established by its developers at the University of Wisconsin (Klausmeier et al. 1971). As an ideal nongraded plan, the IGE program takes into account individual differences and uses specialized curriculum materials in reading, mathematics, and other subjects. But the IGE program is far more complicated than a usual nongraded program. Most reports do not provide any description of the type of intervention actually experienced by the experimental schools; it is implied that their organization follows the structure set in the implementation guidelines of 1971.

Overall, research findings on IGE schools resembled results obtained by other studies on nongraded programs incorporating individualized instruction (see table 4). The median effect size across six studies from which effect sizes could be computed was near zero (ES = +.11). Nevertheless, four studies reported significant differences in favor of IGE schools, and all of these were evaluations of schools that clearly differ from each other. Schools closer to a full implementation of IGE concepts seemed to supply students with a wider range of instructional possibilities for their specific needs: small groups, one-to-one tutoring, or independent work. This finding supports the argument that selective use of individualized instruction can yield positive results for children's academic performance.

Studies Lacking an Explicit Description of the Nongraded Program

In addition to the four categories discussed above, twelve studies failed to state what was actually implemented in the nongraded programs they evaluated (see table 5). These were generally ex post facto studies, often with large samples in which the researchers simply accepted principals' statements that their schools were nongraded. Given the considerable diversity among implementations that were described, it would be foolish to assume anything about what the independent variable in these studies really was. Two doubts confront any reader of these reports: to what extent did the nongraded label accurately describe practices in the experimental situations, and what characteristics did control schools have that made them fit a conventional description. The value of these studies was perhaps in putting to rest the idea that simply giving a school an innovative label, in this case "nongraded," would have had some effect on student learning. These studies were included for the sake of completeness, but little can be learned from them.

This was the only group of research studies in which a trend was not evident. The median effect size was near zero (ES = +.02), but two studies found significantly positive effects, and two found significantly negative ones. The most serious limitation of these studies was the lack of descriptions that could have helped to interpret the findings.

A closer look at the four studies that presented significant differences made the argument in favor of the nongraded programs more convincing. Both positive studies had greater methodological quality: they had evidence of initial equality (students were matched on IQ), and Engel and Cooper (1971) even tested the validity of schools' labels. In contrast, each of the negative studies had some serious problems: inconsistency of findings or flaws in the experimental setting.

Interactions with Study Features

Besides differentiating results according to categories of programs, assessments were made of the interaction of nongraded versus graded organization with other features of the studies. One finding, which supports the main conclusions of this review, was that program effects for the Joplin-like and comprehensive models were particularly strong and consistent in the higher-quality studies; that is, the randomized and matched equivalent experiments. However, there were no consistent patterns with respect to effects at different grade levels (1–3 vs. 4–6) or subjects (reading, math, or language arts). Longer implementations (more than one year) were only inconsistently associated with greater effects.

Program effects declined according to the year the studies were published, but this is of course confounded with program types: the Joplin-like and comprehensive models without individualization were mostly studies in the 1960s, while most studies of nongraded programs emphasizing individualization, including studies of IGE, were reported in the 1970s.

Does Nongrading Accelerate or Decelerate Student Progress?

One of the principal rationales for nongrading is that it allows students to spend more time in the grades involved, if necessary, until they can reach a high level of performance, or to spend less time if they are able to go more quickly than other students. Surprisingly, only one study has actually assessed the degree to which nongraded students took nonnormative amounts of time to complete the primary or elementary grades. This was a study by McLoughlin (1970), which compared students in graded and nongraded primary programs in eight New York State school districts.

Nongraded programs used continuous progress curricula.

The nongraded programs used flexible cross-class and cross-age grouping, teaching to homogeneous groups, and continuous progress curricula; they would therefore probably fall into the comprehensive category defined earlier. The comparisons were made in 1964–65 and again in 1965–66.

In 1964–65, an average of 4.4 percent of students took an extra year to complete the primary grades in the nongraded schools; 4.6 percent took an extra year in the graded ones. In 1965–66, 2.9 percent of nongraded students took an extra year, while 7.3 percent of graded students were retained. No students were accelerated in either type of program in 1964–65, and one-tenth of one percent were accelerated in the nongraded schools in 1965–66.

Put another way, 95.6 percent of the nongraded students made normative progress through the primary grades in 1964–65, and 97.0 percent in 1965–66. What this means is that, at least in the time and places studied by McLoughlin (1970), nongrading was not being used as a means of altering the amount of time students spent in the primary grades. On the contrary, in 1965–66 slightly more students were decelerated by retention in the graded schools than the number that took the opportunity to spend more time in the primary grades offered by the nongraded structure.

McLoughlin (1970) also checked to see whether schools that had been implementing the nongraded plan over a longer period had more students who made nonnormative progress than newer nongraded programs. There was a slight (nonsignificant) trend, but it was in the opposite direction. First-year nongraded programs had somewhat more students making nonnormative progress than did schools that had implemented nongrading for two to seven years.

If McLoughlin's findings (1970) apply to other implementations of the nongraded concept, this result has important methodological and substantive consequences. Methodologically, there is a concern in studies of nongrading that if nongraded students take more time to complete the primary grades, their test scores will be artificially increased. That is, if "third-year" students in a nongraded school were older on average than third graders in a graded school, this could explain any test score advantage of the nongraded programs. It would be important to know this is not the case.

The pressures to have students make normative progress may be as strong in nongraded as in graded programs.

Substantively, McLoughlin's findings (1970) may be seen as questioning one assumption of many advocates of nongrading, who often paint a picture of the low-achieving child proceeding happily and successfully through the grades, never particularly aware that he or she is taking four years to accomplish what his or her classmates are completing in three years. Yet students (and, more particularly, their parents) can count, and they know who their classmates were when they entered school. The pressures to have students make normative progress may be as strong in nongraded as in graded programs.

Yet the main thrust of Goodlad and Anderson's rationale (1959) is not affected by McLoughlin's findings (1970). It is still plausible that deceleration in a continuous progress curriculum is preferable to retention. Further, in a flexible nongraded program it may be that students who would otherwise fall behind can be identified and given extra assistance so that they may catch up with their peers. The nongraded plan might be seen not as a way to give low achievers *more* time, but rather as a way to use time and other resources more flexibly. A student who is not reading at the end of first grade might well be reading at the end of second grade if he or she receives extra help (and does not have to suffer the humiliation of repeating first grade).

Discussion

As the nongraded elementary plan reappears in schools of the 1990s, it is important to learn about the history of this movement of thirty years ago. Most important, one needs to understand the achievement effects of nongraded organization and the conditions under which achievement was or was not enhanced by this innovation.

A review of research on the nongraded elementary school is particularly needed today because there was little consensus on its effects in its own time. Only two reviewers examined portions of the literature, and they came to opposite conclusions. Pavan (1973, 1977, 1992) concluded that the evidence favored the nongraded primary, while McLoughlin (1967) stated that most research showed no differences between graded and nongraded plans. We conclude that when their review methods are applied to a much larger set of studies, the evidence could be interpreted as confirming both Pavan's and McLoughlin's conclusions, contradictory though they are.

Table 6 summarizes the outcomes of the fifty-seven studies that met the inclusion standards. Looking only at the box score of significant and nonsignificant positive and negative findings, one can read the results as supporting either McLoughlin's negative conclusion or Pavan's positive one. McLoughlin argued that because nonsignificant findings outnumbered significant positive ones, the effects of the nongraded primary were equivocal. Twenty-five years later, the proportions of significantly positive findings are like those he reported; only twenty of the fifty-seven studies were significantly positive. Pavan came to the opposite conclusion in her reviews, noting that significant positive findings far outnumbered significant negative ones. This is also true in the present review—only three studies significantly favored graded programs, while twenty favored nongraded ones.

However, the conclusions of the present review, which uses a best-evidence synthesis, conform to neither McLoughlin's nor Pavan's conclusions. Instead, the evidence presented here supports a conclusion that the effects of nongraded programs depend on the type of program being implemented. Using median effect sizes rather than box scores, one sees that the effects of nongraded organization are most consistent and strongest when the program focuses on the vertical organization of the school, and when nongrading is used as a grouping strategy but not as a framework for individualized instruction.

> *The best-designed evaluations were the ones most likely to show the positive effects.*

Four categories of nongraded programs were examined, in addition to one group of studies in which the nature of the nongraded program could not be determined. Studies in two of these categories clearly supported the nongraded plans. These are the Joplin-like programs, in which students are grouped across age lines in just one subject (usually reading), and the comprehensive programs, which involve cross-age grouping in many subjects but still rely on teacher-directed instruction. The median effect sizes for studies in these categories were clearly positive (+.46 for Joplin-like programs, +.34 for comprehensive), and the best-designed evaluations were the ones most likely to show the positive effects.

In contrast, nongraded programs that incorporated a great deal of individualized instruction (and correspondingly less teacher-directed instruction), including Individually Guided Education, were less consistently associated with achievement gain. This is not to say that these approaches reduce student achievement; rather, their effects are very inconsistent, generally neither helping nor hurting student achievement, with more studies finding more positive than negative effects (especially in the case of IGE). Poorly described nongraded programs also had median effects very near zero, perhaps because experimental and control groups may not have differed in anything essential except label.

What accounts for the relatively consistent positive effects of the Joplin-like and comprehensive nongraded plans and the less consistent effects of programs incorporating individualization? Being now decades removed from the flowering of the nongraded ideal, one can only speculate, but there are many recent developments in educational research that suggest some possibilities.

Research on individualized instruction itself has generally failed to support this innovation (e.g., see Bangert, Kulik, and Kulik 1983; Horak 1981; Miller 1976; Rothrock 1982). Correlational evidence from process-product studies of more and less effective teachers has consistently found that student learning is enhanced by direct instruction from teachers, as contrasted with extensive reliance on individualization, seatwork, and written materials (see Brophy and Good 1986). As the nongraded elementary school came to resemble the open school, the research finding few achievement benefits to this approach (e.g., Giaconia and Hedges 1982) became increasingly relevant.

> Flexible cross-age grouping allows teachers to fully accommodate instruction to the needs of each child.

In its simplest forms, the nongraded elementary school has many likely benefits. By grouping students across age lines, it may allow teachers to reduce the number of within-class reading and math groups they teach at any given time, thereby reducing the need for independent seatwork and follow-up. In fact, in several of the evaluations of Joplin-like programs, it was noted that cross-age groupings made within-class groupings (i.e., reading groups) unnecessary, so teachers could spend the class period teaching the entire class with no need for seatwork.

Another factor in the success of simple nongraded plans is that flexible cross-age grouping allows teachers to fully accommodate instruction to the needs of each child in a particular subject while still delivering instruction to groups. Goodlad and Anderson's (1959, 1963) critique of traditional ability grouping is that it does not truly reduce heterogeneity in the specific skill being taught. Grouping students within classes or within grades (in all but the largest elementary schools) does not provide enough opportunity to have group instruction closely tailored to student needs. Flexible cross-age grouping does provide such an opportunity, so the instructional costs of grouping (in terms of disruption, movement, and stigma for children in low groups) can perhaps be outweighed by the greater opportunity to adapt instruction to the precise needs of students and to continue to adapt to students' needs by examining and changing groupings at frequent intervals (see Slavin 1987).

If the effectiveness of nongraded organization is due to increased direct instruction delivered at students' precise instructional levels, then it is easy to see how a move to greater individualization would undermine these effects. Learning stations, learning activity packets, and other individualized or small group activities reduce direct instruction time with little corresponding increase in making instruction appropriate to individual needs.

It is difficult to assess the impact of one of the key rationales given for the nongraded plan throughout its history—the opportunity to allow at-risk students to take as much time as they need to complete the primary or elementary grades without the use of retention. An early study by McLoughlin (1970) found that self-described nongraded programs did not generally utilize the opportunity to let low achievers take more time, but one does not know if McLoughlin's findings would apply to most nongraded programs implemented now or in the past. Clearly, however, the effectiveness of the simpler nongraded programs does not depend on the opportunity to accelerate or decelerate student progress, since most studies found positive effects in the first year of implementation—before any acceleration or deceleration could take place.

This discussion is, as noted earlier, completely speculative. There is much more we would have liked to know about how nongraded programs were actually implemented in the 1950s, 1960s, and 1970s. The return of the nongraded idea in the 1990s may answer many questions, but assessments of current forms of nongrading, as well as component analyses, are necessary to understand which elements of nongrading account for the program's effects. And studies combining qualitative and quantitative methods are needed to understand both what really changes in nongraded schools and what differences these changes make in student achievement.

Is Earlier Research on the Nongraded Elementary School Relevant Today?

How relevant is research on the nongraded elementary school to education today? Many of the problems that the nongraded elementary school was designed to solve still exist, and the reemergence of nongraded programs appears to be due in large part to concern about these problems, especially the tension between retention and social promotion and rejection of traditional forms of ability grouping. Yet there are also many differences between education today and that of thirty years ago.

The general perception that both individualized instruction (e.g., Bangert, Kulik, and Kulik 1983; Horak 1981) and the open classroom (e.g., Giaconia and Hedges 1982) failed in their attempt to increase student achievement means that it is unlikely that the nongraded elementary schools of the 1990s will, like those of the early 1970s, embrace these methods. As a result, it is more likely that the nongraded programs of the 1990s will resemble the simpler forms found in this review to be instructionally effective.

> *Instruction in nongraded primary programs will probably be more integrated and thematic than in other schools.*

Yet there are other developments in North American education today that will certainly influence the forms taken by the nongraded programs, their effects on achievement, and their ultimate impact on educational practice. The movement toward developmentally appropriate early childhood education and its association with nongrading mean that the nongraded primary school of the 1990s will often incorporate four- and five-year-olds (earlier forms rarely did so) and that instruction in nongraded primary programs will probably be more integrated and thematic, and less academically structured or hierarchical, than in other schools.

A proposal for nongraded primary programs of this type was recently made by Katz, Evangelou, and Hartman (1990). In other words, as in the early 1970s, the effectiveness of the nongraded school organization plan may become confounded with innovative instructional methods. Whether these instructional methods will have positive or negative effects on ultimate achievement is currently unknown.

Clearly, there is a need for much more research on the nongraded elementary school as it is being implemented today. Because of scientific conventions of the time, most of the earlier research reviewed here was strong in experimental design (most studies used random assignment or careful matching of experimental and control groups) but weak in description of the independent variable (i.e., the characteristics of the nongraded and graded schools). Research done today must be strong on both dimensions.

Research on the nongraded elementary school offers a fascinating glimpse into the history and ultimate fate of a compelling innovation. The return of this idea after nearly twenty years of dormancy is fascinating as well.

This review concludes that the evidence from the first cycle of research on the nongraded elementary school supports use of simpler forms of the model and certainly supports the need and potential fruitfulness of further experimentation. Yet there is also a cautionary note here. Good ideas can be undermined by becoming increasingly complex over time. A constant cycle of experimentation, research, evaluation, revision, and continued experimentation is necessary to build compelling ideas into comprehensive, effective plans for school organization and instruction.

Appendix

KEY

Abbreviations and symbols used in tables

+	Results clearly favor nongraded programs
(+)	Results generally favor nongraded programs
0	No trend in results
(−)	Results generally favor graded programs
−	Results clearly favor graded programs
AG	Ability grouping
CAT	California Achievement Test
CLTBS	California Test of Basic Skills
CRT	California Reading Test
CTBS	Canadian Test of Basic Skills
DLRT	Durrell Listening-Reading Test
G	Graded Program
GE	Grade Equivalent
GPRT	Gates Primary Reading Test
IGE	Individually Guided Education
IGI	Individually Guided Instruction
ITBS	Iowa Test of Basic Skills
KCT	Kansas Competency Test
LCRT	Lee Clark Reading Test
MAT	Metropolitan Achievement Test
MRT	Metropolitan Reading Test
NARA	Neale Analysis for Reading Ability
NG	Nongraded program
OS	Open-area school
OST	Ohio Survey Test
PT	Piaget-Type Test
SAT	Stanford Achievement Test
SES	Socioeconomic status
SRAAS	Science Research Associates Achievement Series
STEP	Sequential Test of Educational Programs

Table 1. Nongraded Programs Involving Only One Subject (Joplin-Like Programs)

ARTICLE	GRADES	LOCATION	SAMPLE SIZE	DURATION OF PROGRAM	DESIGN	TEST	EFFECT SIZES by Achievement	EFFECT SIZES by Subject	TOTAL
RANDOMIZED STUDIES									
Jones, Moore, & Van Devender (1967)	2–3	Shamokin, Pennsylvania	52 (26 NG, 26 G) (1 school)	1.5 yrs. (3 yrs. follow-up)	Students and teachers randomly assigned to NG/Joplin or heterogeneous graded classes for reading only.	SAT, LCRT		Rdg. (1.5 yrs.) +.72* Rdg. (3 yrs.) +.33	+.33
MATCHED STUDIES WITH EVIDENCE OF INITIAL EQUALITY									
Halliwell (1963)	1–3	New Jersey	295 (146 NG, 149 G) (1 school)	1 yr.	Compared NG/Joplin in reading and spelling to previous year heterogeneous grouping in the graded program. Students had comparable IQ at the beginning of the study.	CAT (gr. 1) MAT (gr. 2–3)		Rdg. +.53*	+.53*
Skapski (1960)	3	Burlington, Vermont	110 (3 schools)	3 yrs.	Students matched on IQ. Compared NG/Joplin in reading only to heterogeneous grouping in a graded program.	SAT	Su.+.91 Hi.+.48 Av.+.52	Rdg. +.57**	+.57**
Hart (1962)	4	Hillsboro, Oregon	100 (50 NG, 50 G) (1 school)	3 yrs.	Students matched on sex, mental maturity, age, and SES. Compared NG/Joplin in arithmetic only to heterogeneous grouping in a graded program.	CAT		Math +.46	+.46*

Table 1 (cont.)

ARTICLE	GRADES	LOCATION	SAMPLE SIZE	DURATION OF PROGRAM	DESIGN	TEST	EFFECT SIZES by Achievement	EFFECT SIZES by Subject	TOTAL
MATCHED STUDIES LACKING EVIDENCE OF INITIAL EQUALITY									
Bockrath (1958)	4	Archdiocese of St. Louis	3,596 (1,974 NG, 1,622 G) (50 schools)	3 yrs.	Comparison between 1956 students' reading achievement with 1953 students' scores. IQ used to adjust score medians. Stratified sample by size and location of schools.	CAT	Hi. + Lo. +	Rdg. +.51**	+.51**
Jacquette (1959)	1–6	Grand Junction, Colorado	3,517 (1,554 NG, 1,963 G) (4 schools)	5 yrs.	Schools matched on rdg. achievement and IQ. Pretest used to compute gain scores.	CAT, GPRT		Rdg. +.03	+.03
Moore (1963)	1–2	Wayne, Michigan	621 (292 NG, 329 G) (4 schools)	1 yr.	Schools matched on SES and curriculum. Change scores used to control pretest achievement significant differences. Compared NG/Joplin in reading only to conventional graded plans.	MAT	Hi. –.22 Av. –.43 Lo. –.29	Rdg. –.41**	–.41**
Enevoldsen (1961)	1–3	Lincoln, Nebraska	420 (210 NG, 210 G) (7 schools)	2 yrs. (2 sch.) 3 yrs. (1 sch.)	Students matched SES, IQ used as a covariate. Compared NG/Joplin in reading only to graded programs.	CAT		Rdg. 0	0
Kierstead (1963)	3–8	Orwell, Vermont	277 (111 NG, 166 G) (2 schools)	1 yr.	Students equated and classified by IQ and pretest. Pretest used to compute gain scores. Compared NG/Joplin in reading only to ability grouping in a graded plan.	ITBS	Hi. –.01 GE Av. +.08 GE Lo. –.14 GE	Rdg. –.02 GE	–.02 GE

* p<.05
** p<.01

Table 2: Nongraded Programs Involving Multiple Subjects (Comprehensive Programs)

ARTICLE	GRADES	LOCATION	SAMPLE SIZE	DURATION OF PROGRAM	DESIGN	TEST	EFFECT SIZES by Achievement	EFFECT SIZES by Subject	TOTAL
MATCHED STUDIES WITH EVIDENCE OF INITIAL EQUALITY									
Brody (1970)	1–2	Pennsylvania	603 (362 NG, 241 G) (3 schools)	2 yrs.	Students matched on IQ.	SAT	Hi. + Lo. +	Rdg. +.20** Math +.73**	+.46**
Otto (1969)	3–5	Austin, Texas	450 (2 upper middle-class lab schools)	2 yrs.	Students matched on pretest achievement.	MAT, ITBS		Rdg. 0 Math 0	0
Perrin (1969)	1–3	Little Rock, Arkansas	288 (144 NG, 144 G) (13 schools)	3 yrs.	Schools matched on SES. Students matched on IQ, age, sex, and race.	MAT (gr. 1–2) ITBS (gr. 3)		Rdg. +.08 Math +.14	+.11
Buffie (1962)	3	Cedar Falls, Iowa	234 (117 NG, 117 G) (8 schools)	3 yrs.	Schools matched on SES, enrollment, class size, and teachers' experience. Students matched on sex, age, and intelligence.	ITBS	Hi. +.39 Lo. +.19	Rdg. +.19 Math +.17 Lang. +.67**	+.34**
Guarino (1982)	2–5	New Jersey	162 (81 NG, 81 G) (2 schools)	5 yrs.	Schools matched on SES and ethnic mix. Students matched on age, sex, and IQ.	CAT		Rdg. +.49** Math +.19	+.34*
Ramayya (1972)	6	Darmouth, Nova Scotia	160 (80 NG, 80 G)	6 yrs.	Students matched on sex, IQ, and SES.	TBS		Rdg. +.41* Math +.25 Lang. +.59*	+.42*
Muck (1966)	1–3	Buffalo, New York	148 (1 lab school)	3 yrs.	Students matched on mental maturity.	MAT, ITBS		Rdg. +.04 Math –.36 Lang. +.15	–.06
Machiele (1965)	1	Urbana, Illinois	100 (50 NG, 50 G) (1 school)	1 yr.	Students matched on IQ, mental age, and chronological age. Compared students in NG program to students in previous year.	CAT		Rdg. +.61** Math +.38	+.49*

Table 2 (cont.)

ARTICLE	GRADES	LOCATION	SAMPLE SIZE	DURATION OF PROGRAM	DESIGN	TEST	EFFECT SIZES by Achievement	by Subject	TOTAL
MATCHED STUDIES LACKING EVIDENCE OF INITIAL EQUALITY									
Zerby (1960)	3	Morristown, Pennsylvania	394 (187 NG, 207 G) (2 schools)	3 yrs.	Schools matched on SES. IQ score used to compute achievement beyond anticipated achievement level.	CAT		Rdg. +.10 Math +.57**	+.34*
Chastain (1961)	4–6	Rangey, Colorado	360 (240 NG, 120 G) (1 school)	1 yr.	Students matched on sex and IQ. Pretest used as a covariate.	MAT		Rdg. +.01 Math –.09	–.04
Lawson (1973)	1,3,5	Kokomo, Indiana	338 (6 schools)	1, 3, & 5 yrs.	IQ used as a covariate.	CAT		Rdg. + **	+ **
Ross (1967)	1–3	Bloomington, Indiana	314 (128 NG, 186 G) (1 lab school)	6 mos.	Pretest and IQ used as covariates. Students nonrandomly assigned to NG and G programs in the school.	MAT		Rdg. +.06 GE Math +.06 GE	+.06 GE
Morris (1968)	1–3,5	Montgomery County, Pennsylvania	117 (57 NG, 60 G) (1 school)	3 yrs.	IQ used as a covariate. Compared students in NG program to students in previous year. Intervention stopped after 3 years.	ITBS, SAT		After 3 yeare. + * After 5 yrs. + **	+ **

Gumpper, Meyer, & Kaufman (1971)	1–4	Pennsylvania	(2 schools)	1 yr.	Schools matched on SES, enrollment, teachers' characteristics, and students' previous academic achievement. Pretest used to compute gain scores.	DLRT, SAT		gr. 1 Rdg. 0
								      Math (+)
								gr. 2–4 Rdg. (–)
								      Math_**
								      Lang._**
									(–)

* $p<.05$
** $p<.01$

Table 3: Nongraded Programs Incorporating Individualized Instruction

ARTICLE	GRADES	LOCATION	SAMPLE SIZE	DURATION OF PROGRAM	DESIGN	TEST	EFFECT SIZES by Achievement	EFFECT SIZES by Subject	TOTAL
RANDOMIZED STUDIES									
Higgins (1980)	3–5	Baton Rouge, Louisiana	246 (75 NG, 171 G) (3 schools)	1 yr.	Students randomly assigned to nongraded/combination or traditional reading classes. Pretest used to compute gain scores.	MRT	Hi. (+) Lo. (+)	Rdg. +.02	+.02
MATCHED STUDIES WITH EVIDENCE OF INITIAL EQUALITY									
Sie (1969)	2–4	Ames, Iowa	134 (67 NG, 67 G) (2 schools)	1 yr.	Schools matched on SES. Students matched on SAT scores. Pretest used to compute gain scores.	SAT		Rdg. +.03 Math +.14 Lang. –.11	+.02
Jeffreys (1970)	3, 5	Howard County, Maryland	96 (44 NG, 52 G) (2 schools)	1 yr.	Schools matched on SES. Students matched on pretest achievement measure. Pretest scores and parent occupation status used as covariates.	ITBS		Rdg. +.08 Math –.13	–.03
Wilt (1970)	4	Chicago Suburb, Illinois	149 (32 NG, 117 G) (8 schools)	4 yrs.	Students matched on IQ and age.	ITBS		Rdg. +.49 GE* Math +.10 GE Lang. –.27 GE	+.11 GE
MATCHED STUDIES LACKING EVIDENCE OF INITIAL EQUALITY									
Ward (1969)	1–2	Fort Worth, Texas	797 (376 NG, 421 G) (4 schools)	2 yrs.	Schools matched on SES, race, and available resources. IQ, age, and readiness scores used as covariates.	MAT		Rdg. + Math (+)	+
Burchyett (1972)	3–5	Grand Blanc, Michigan	535 (332 NG, 203 G) (2 schools)	2 yrs.	Schools matched on SES. Pretest used as a covariate.	STEP		Rdg. –.06 Math –.10	–.08

Table 3 (cont.)

ARTICLE	GRADES	LOCATION	SAMPLE SIZE	DURATION OF PROGRAM	DESIGN	TEST	EFFECT SIZES by Achievement	EFFECT SIZES by Subject	TOTAL
MATCHED STUDIES LACKING EVIDENCE OF INITIAL EQUALITY									
Bowman (1971)	1–6	Burlington, N. Carolina	457 (313 NG, 144 G) (2 schools)	1 yr.	IQ used as a covariate. Pretest used to compute gain scores.	MAT		Rdg. +.27 * Math +.28*	+.28 *
Case (1970)	5	Montgomery County, Maryland	269 (131 NG, 138 G) (4 schools)	1 yr.	Schools matched on SES. Students matched on age, sex, race, and SES (higher IQ scores for control group). Pretest used to compute gain scores.	SAT	Hi. +.18 Av. +.14 Lo. –.01	Rdg. +.01 Math +.16	+.09
Killough (1971)	1–8	Houston, Texas	267 (132 NG, 135 G) (4 schools)	3 yrs.	Schools matched on SES and ethnic distribution. IQ used as a covariate. Pretest used to compute gain scores.	SRAAS		Rdg. + * Math + *	+ *
Givens (1972)	5	St. Louis, Missouri	100 (50 NG, 50 G) (1 lab, 1 control school)	1 yr.	Students randomly selected from two populations of students that received either individualized or traditional instruction. Ex post facto experimental design. Pretest used to compute gain scores.	ITBS	Hi. (+) Av. 0 Lo. (+)	Rdg. –.11 Math +.10	.00
Walker (1973)	1–12	Kentucky	96 (32 NG, 64 G)	12 yrs.	Schools rated on an eight-dimension scale, the Nongradedness Assessment Scale. Longitudinal study to determine the long-term effects of NG and G primary school years (1–3). Rate of progress used as a covariate.	CAT		Rdg. +.24 Math +.14 Lang. +.17	+.18
Snake River School District (1972)	1–3	Blackfoot, Idaho	78 (39 NG, 39 G) (2 schools)	1 yr.	Students matched on SES. Pretest used to compute gain scores.	SRAAS		Rdg. .00 Math .00	.00

* $p<.05$
** $p<.01$

Table 4: Individually Guided Education (IGE)

ARTICLE	GRADES	LOCATION	SAMPLE SIZE	DURATION OF PROGRAM	DESIGN	TEST	EFFECT SIZES by Achievement	EFFECT SIZES by Subject	TOTAL
RANDOMIZED STUDIES									
Schneiderhan (1973)	4–6	Roseville, Minnesota	484 (206 NG, 88 IGI, 190 G) (2 schools)	1 yr.	Students randomly selected to individually guided instruction or traditional programs in the same school. IQ and pretest scores used as covarites.	ITBS	(IGI and control)	Rdg. 0 Math 0 Lang. 0	0
							(IGE & IGI and control)	Rdg. (−) Math 0 Lang. (+)	
MATCHED STUDIES LACKING EVIDENCE OF INITIAL EQUALITY									
Price (1977)	4, 6	Iowa	1,081 (637 hi, 444 lo) (14 schools)	3 yrs.	Comparison of high and low implementers of 35 processes employed in IGE. School matched on size, SES, and location. IQ used as a covariate.	ITBS		Rdg. +* Math (+)	+*
Biernacki (1976)	3–6	Toledo, Ohio	479 (174 NG, 305 G) (2 schools)	6 mos.	Schools matched on SES, race, and similar achievement in grade equivalents in reading and math for students in grade 6. Students randomly selected from chosen schools. Pretest used to compute gain scores.	MAT		Rdg. +.13 Math +.20	+.17
Klaus (1981)	4–6	LaCrosse, Wisconsin	433 (219 NG, 214 G)	3 yrs.	Pretest used to compute gain scores. IQ used as a covariate.	ITBS, SRAAS		Rdg. +.07 Math +.12 Lang. −.05	+.05
Bradford (1972)	1–3	Detroit, Michigan	394 (299 NG, 93 G) (2 schools)	1 yr.	Students matched on sex, SES, and reading and math achievement. Pretest used to compute gain scores. IQ used as a covariate.	MAT		Rdg. + Math +*	+*

Table 4 (cont.)

ARTICLE	GRADES	LOCATION	SAMPLE SIZE	DURATION OF PROGRAM	DESIGN	TEST	EFFECT SIZES by Achievement by Subject		TOTAL
MATCHED STUDIES LACKING EVIDENCE OF INITIAL EQUALITY									
Burtley (1974)	2–3	Woodberry, Illinois	302 (167 NG, 135 G)	2 yrs.	Schools matched on SES, ethnicity, size, and enrollment. Pretest used to compute gain scores.	MAT		Rdg. +.40 * Math +.55 *	+.48 *
Flowers (1977)	3	Westminster, Colorado	221 (99 NG, 122 G)	3 yrs.	Best school matches available among the remaining schools within the district based on SES. Students classified by SES.	SAT		Rdg. –.25 Math –.25	–.25
Kuhlman (1985)	2,4,6	Kansas	200 (50 OS, 50 IGE, 100 G)	2 yrs.	Students randomly selected from chosen schools. SES and number of parents used as covariates.	KCT		Rdg. 0 Math 0	0
Soumokil (1977)	3,5	Columbia, Missouri	102 (2 schools)	2 yrs. (gr. 3) 3 yrs. (gr. 5)	Pretest and IQ used as covariates.	ITBS		Rdg. +.79 ** Math +.80 **	+.80 **
Henn (1974)	4	Ohio	14,030 (7,072 NG, 6,958 G) (24 schools)	2 yrs.	Schools matched on SES, available resources, and teachers' qualifications.	MAT, OST		Rdg. +.05 Math +.01	+.03

* p<.05
** p<.01

Table 5: Studies Lacking an Explicit Description of the Nongraded Program

ARTICLE	GRADES	LOCATION	SAMPLE SIZE	DURATION OF PROGRAM	DESIGN	TEST	EFFECT SIZES by Achievement	EFFECT SIZES by Subject	TOTAL
MATCHED STUDIES WITH EVIDENCE OF INITIAL EQUALITY									
Hickey (1962)	3	Diocese of Pittsburgh	1,348 (745 NG, 603 G) (14 schools)	3 yrs.	Schools matched on SES. Students matched on IQ.	MAT	Hi. +.31 * Av. +.18 Lo. −.01	Rdg. +.24 * Math +.68 ** Lang. 0	+.46 **
Lair (1975)	3	Richardson, Texas	463 (183 NG, 280 G) (12 schools)	3 yrs.	Random selection of 6 G and 2 NG schools. Students matched on readiness for learning scores.	CLTBS	Su. −.12 Hi. −.21 Av. −.36	Lang. −.09	−.09
Aigner (1961)	4	Bellevue, Washington	428 (214 NG, 214 G)	3 yrs.	Groups equated with the School and College Abilities Total test.	STEP	Hi. 0 Av. 0 Lo. 0	Rdg. (−) Math (−)	(−)
Mycock (1966)	1	Manchester, England	108 (4 schools)	1 yr.	School matched on size, resources, and staff ratio and quality. Students matched on age, sex, and intelligence.	NARA, PT		Rdg. 0 Math 0	0
Reid (1973)	4	Alabama	100 (50 NG, 50 G)	3 yrs.	Students matched on age, sex, and mental ability.	SAT	Hi. −.11 Av. −.01 Lo. −.05	Rdg. +.01 Math −.05 Lang. +.01	−.01
Williams (1966)	3	Hammond, Indiana	76 (38 NG, 38 G)	3 yrs.	Students matched on age, sex, and IQ.	SAT	Hi. +1.29 * Lo. −1.30 *	Rdg. −.46 * Math −.23	−.34
Engel and Cooper (1971)	6	Darmouth, Nova Scotia	40 (20 NG, 20 G) (2 schools)	6 yrs.	Schools selected according to an index for nongradedness. Students matched on IQ.	CAT		Rdg. +1.20 ** Lang. +1.02 **	+1.10 **

Table 5 (cont.)

ARTICLE	GRADES	LOCATION	SAMPLE SIZE	DURATION OF PROGRAM	DESIGN	TEST	EFFECT SIZES by Achievement	EFFECT SIZES by Subject	TOTAL
MATCHED STUDIES LACKING EVIDENCE OF INITIAL EQUALITY									
Herrington (1973)	6	Dade County, Florida	951 (16 schools)	1 yr.	Schools randomly selected from SES ranked lists. Classes randomly selected. Pretest used as covariate.	SAT		Rdg. (+) Math +	(+)
Vogel and Bowers (1972)	K–6	Evanston, Illinois	473 (224 NG, 249 G)	1 yr.	Teachers matched on sex, training, experience, and age level taught. Pretest used as covariate.	SAT		Composite –**	–**
Hopkins, Oldridge, & Williamson (1965)	3–4	Los Angeles County, California	330 (139 NG, 191 G) (4 schools)	3 yrs.	IQ used as covariate.	CRT		Rdg. +.02	+.02
Carbone (1961)	4–6		244 (122 NG, 122 G) (6 schools)	At least 3 yrs.	Schools matched on SES. Classes randomly selected. Students matched on sex and age. IQ used as covariate.	ITBS		Rdg. –** Math –** Lang. –**	–**
Remacle (1970)	5–6	Brookings, South Dakota	128 (64 NG, 64 G) (1 school)	2 yrs. (gr. 5) 1 yr. (gr. 6)	Random selection of students in control group. IQ used as covariate.	ITBS		Rdg. +.24 GE Math +.37 GE* Lang. +.33 GE	+.31 GE

* $p<.05$
** $p<.01$

Table 6: Summary of Effects by Type of Nongraded Plan

TYPE OF PROGRAM	TOTAL STUDIES	SIGNIFICANT POSITIVE	NONSIGNIFICANT POSITIVE	NO DIFFERENCE	NONSIGNIFICANT NEGATIVE	SIGNIFICANT NEGATIVE	MEDIAN EFFECT SIZE*
Joplin-Like	9	4	2	1	1	1	+.46 (7)
Comprehensive	14	8	2	1	3	0	+.34 (9)
Individualized	12	2	6	2	2	0	+.02 (9)
IGE	10	4	3	2	1	0	+.11 (6)
Unspecified	12	2	3	1	4	2	+.01 (6)

*Number of studies in which an effect size could be computed is presented in parenthesis.

References

Aigner, B. W. 1961. *A statistical analysis of achievement differences of children in a nongraded primary program and traditional classrooms.* Unpublished doctoral dissertation, Colorado State College.

Allington, R. L., and A. McGill-Franzen. 1992. Does high-stakes testing improve school effectiveness? *ERS Spectrum* 10 (2): 3–12.

Bangert, R., J. Kulik, and C. Kulik. 1983. Individualized systems of instruction in secondary schools. *Review of Educational Research* 53:143–58.

Biernacki, G. J. 1976. *An evaluation of an IGE/MUS-E inner-city elementary school based on selected criteria.* Unpublished doctoral dissertation, The University of Toledo.

Bockrath, S. M. B. 1958. *An evaluation of the ungraded primary as an organizational device for improving learning in Saint Louis Archdiocesan Schools.* Unpublished doctoral dissertation, St. Louis University.

Bowman, B. L. 1971. *A comparison of pupil achievement and attitude in a graded school with pupil achievement and attitude in a nongraded school 1968–69.* Unpublished doctoral dissertation, University of North Carolina, Chapel Hill.

Bradford, E. F. 1972. *A comparison of two methods of teaching in the elementary school as related to achievement in reading, mathematics, and self-concept of children.* Unpublished doctoral dissertation, Michigan State University.

Brody, E. B. 1970. Achievement of first- and second-year pupils in graded and nongraded classrooms. *Elementary School Journal* 70:391–94.

Brophy, J. E., and T. L. Good. 1986. Teacher behavior and student achievement. In *Handbook of research on teaching,* edited by M. C. Wittrock. New York: Macmillan.

Buffie, E. G. W. 1962. *A comparison of mental health and academic achievement: The nongraded school vs. the graded school.* Unpublished doctoral dissertation, Indiana University.

Burchyett, J. A. 1972. *A comparison of the effects of non-graded, multi-age, team-teaching vs. the modified self-contained classroom at the elementary school level.* Unpublished doctoral dissertation, Michigan State University.

Burtley, N. 1974. *A comparison of teacher characteristics and student achievement in individually guided education (IGE) and traditional inner city elementary schools.* Unpublished doctoral dissertation, Michigan State University.

Carbone, R. F. 1961. A comparison of graded and non-graded elementary schools. *Elementary School Journal* 61:82–88.

Case, D. A. 1970. *A comparative study of fifth graders in a new middle school with fifth graders in elementary self-contained classrooms.* Unpublished doctoral dissertation, The University of Florida.

Chalfant, L. S. 1972. *A three-year comparative study between students in a graded and nongraded secondary school.* Unpublished doctoral dissertation, Utah State University.

Chastain, C. S. 1961. *An experimental study of the gains in achievement in arithmetic and reading made by the pupils in the intermediate grades in the Rangely, Colorado, Elementary School who were instructed in traditional classrooms, in achievement platoons, and in nongraded classrooms.* Unpublished doctoral dissertation, Colorado State College.

Enevoldsen, C. L. 1961. *An evaluation of the ungraded primary program in selected schools in the Lincoln, Nebraska, Public School system.* Unpublished doctoral dissertation, University of Nebraska.

Engel, B. M., and M. Cooper. 1971. Academic achievement and nongradedness. *The Journal of Experimental Education* 40:24–26.

Flowers, J. R. 1977. *A comparative study of students in open space individually guided education (IGE) and traditional schools.* Unpublished doctoral dissertation, University of Northern Colorado.

Floyd, C. 1954. Meeting children's reading needs in the middle grades: A preliminary report. *Elementary School Journal* 55:99–103.

Giaconia, R. M., and L. V. Hedges. 1982. Identifying features of open education. *Review of Educational Research* 52:579–602.

Givens, H., Jr. 1972. *A comparative study of achievement and attitudinal characteristics of black and white intermediate pupils in individualized, multigrade and self-contained instructional programs.* Unpublished doctoral dissertation, St. Louis University.

Glass, G. V., B. McGaw, and M. L. Smith. 1981. *Meta-analysis in social research.* Beverly Hills: Sage Publications.

Goodlad, J. I., and R. H. Anderson. 1959. *The nongraded elementary school.* New York: Harcourt, Brace and Company.

———. 1963. *The nongraded elementary school* (rev. ed.). New York: Harcourt, Brace, & World.

———. 1987. *The nongraded elementary school* (reprint ed.). New York: Teachers College Press.

Guarino, A. R. 1982. *An investigation of achievement, self-concept, and school related anxiety in graded and nongraded elementary schools.* Unpublished doctoral dissertation, The State University of New Jersey at Rutgers.

Gumpper, D. C., J. H. Meyer, and J. J. Kaufman. 1971. *Nongraded elementary education: individualized learning—teacher leadership—student responsibility.* University Park: The Pennsylvania State University Institute for Research on Human Resources.

Gutiérrez, R., and R. E. Slavin. 1992. Achievement effects of the nongraded elementary school: A best evidence synthesis analysis. *Review of Educational Research* 62: 333–76.

Halliwell, J. W. 1963. A comparison of pupil achievement in graded and nongraded primary classrooms. *The Journal of Experimental Education* 32:59–64.

Hart, R. H. 1962. The nongraded primary school and arithmetic. *The Arithmetic Teacher* 9:130–33.

Heathers, G. 1967. *Organizing schools through the dual progress plan.* Danville, Ill.: Interstate.

Henn, D. C. 1974. *A comparative analysis of language arts and mathematics achievement in selected IGE/MUS-E and non-IGE/MUS-E programs in Ohio.* Unpublished doctoral dissertation, University of Cincinnati.

Herrington, A. F. 1973. *Perceived attitudes and academic achievement of reported graded and nongraded sixth-year students.* Unpublished doctoral dissertation, University of Miami.

Hickey, S. M. P. 1962. *An analysis and evaluation of the ungraded primary program in the diocese of Pittsburgh.* Unpublished doctoral dissertation, Fordham University.

Higgins, J. J. 1980. *A comparative study between the reading achievement levels of students in a combination/ungraded class and students in a graded class.* Unpublished doctoral dissertation, George Peabody College for Teachers of Vanderbilt University.

Hopkins, K. D., O. A. Oldridge, and M. L. Williamson. 1965. An empirical comparison of pupil achievement and other variables in graded and ungraded classes. *American Educational Research Journal* 2:207–15.

Horak, V. M. 1981. A meta-analysis of research findings on individualized instruction in mathematics. *Journal of Educational Research* 74:249–53.

Ingram, V. 1960. Flint evaluates its primary cycle. *Elementary School Journal* 61:76–80.

Jacquette, F. C. 1959. *A five-year study to determine the effects of the ungraded classroom organization on reading achievement in Grand Junction, Colorado.* Unpublished Field Study, Colorado State College.

Jeffreys, J. S. 1970. *An investigation of the effects of innovative educational practices on pupil-centeredness of observed behaviors and on learner outcome variables.* Unpublished doctoral dissertation, University of Maryland.

Jones, J. C., J. W. Moore, and F. Van Devender. 1967. A comparison of pupil achievement after one and one-half and three years in a nongraded program. *The Journal of Educational Research* 61:75–77.

Karweit, N. L., and B. A. Wasik. 1994. Extra-year kindergarten programs and transitional first grades. In *Preventing early school failure: Research on effective strategies,* edited by R. E. Slavin, N. L. Karweit, and B. A. Wasik. Boston: Allyn & Bacon.

Katz, L. G., D. Evangelou, and A. Hartman. 1990. *The case for mixed-age grouping in early education.* Washington, D.C.: National Association for the Education of Young Children.

Kierstead, R. 1963. A comparison and evaluation of two methods of organization for the teaching of reading. *The Journal of Educational Research* 56:317–21.

Killough, C. K. 1971. *An analysis of the longitudinal effects that a nongraded elementary program, conducted in an open-space school, had on the cognitive achievement of pupils.* Unpublished doctoral dissertation, University of Houston.

Klaus, W. D. 1981. *A comparison of student achievement in individually guided education programs and non-individually guided education elementary school programs.* Unpublished doctoral dissertation, University of Missouri-Columbia.

Klausmeier, H. J., M. R. Quilling, J. S. Sorenson, R. S. Way, and G. R. Glasrud. 1971. *Individually guided education and the multiunit elementary school: Guidelines for implementation.* Madison: University of Wisconsin, Wisconsin Research and Development Center for Cognitive Learning.

Klausmeier, H. J., R. A. Rossmiller, and M. Saily, eds. 1977. *Individually guided elementary education: Concepts and practices.* New York: Academic Press.

Kuhlman, C. L. 1985. *A study of the relationship between organizational characteristics of elementary schools, student characteristics, and elementary competency test results.* Unpublished doctoral dissertation, University of Kansas.

Lair, D. P. 1975. *The effects of graded and nongraded schools on student growth.* Unpublished doctoral dissertation, Baylor University.

Lawson, R. E. 1973. *A comparison of the development of self-concept and achievement in reading of students in the first, third, and fifth year of attendance.* Unpublished doctoral dissertation, Ball State University.

Levine, D. U., and E. E. Eubanks. 1986–87. Achievement improvement and non-improvement at concentrated poverty schools in big cities. *Metropolitan Education* 3:92–107.

Machiele, R. B. 1965. A preliminary evaluation of the non-graded primary at Leal School, Urbana. *Illinois School Research* 1:20–24.

Maresh, R. T. 1971. *An analysis of the effects of vertical grade groups on reading achievement and attitudes in elementary schools.* Unpublished doctoral dissertation, University of North Dakota.

McLoughlin, W. P. 1967. *The nongraded school: A critical assessment.* New York: State Education Department.

———. 1970. Continuous pupil progress in the non-graded school: Hope or hoax? *Elementary School Journal,* 90–96.

Miller, R. L. 1976. Individualized instruction in mathematics: A review of research. *The Mathematics Teacher* 69:345–51.

Moore, D. I. 1963. *Pupil achievement and grouping practices in graded and ungraded primary schools.* Unpublished doctoral dissertation, University of Michigan.

Morris, V. R. 1968. *An evaluation of pupil achievement in a nongraded primary plan after three, and also five years of instruction.* Unpublished doctoral dissertation, Lehigh University.

Muck, R. E. S. 1966. *The effect of classroom organization on academic achievement in graded and nongraded classes.* Unpublished doctoral dissertation, State University of New York at Buffalo.

Mycock, M. A. 1966. *A comparison of vertical grouping and horizontal grouping in the infant school.* Unpublished master's thesis, University of Manchester.

National Association for the Education of Young Children. 1989. *Appropriate education in the primary grades.* Washington, D.C.: Author.

Otto, H. J. 1969. *Nongradedness: An elementary school evaluation.* Austin: University of Texas.

Pavan, B. N. 1973. Good news: Research on the nongraded elementary school. *Elementary School Journal,* 333–42.

———. 1977. The nongraded elementary school: Research on academic and mental health. *Texas Tech Journal of Education* 4:91–107.

———. 1992. The benefits of nongraded schools. *Educational Leadership* 50 (2): 22–25.

Perrin, J. D. 1969. *A statistical and time change analysis of achievement differences of children in a nongraded and a graded program in selected schools in the Little Rock Public Schools.* Unpublished doctoral dissertation, University of Arkansas.

Price, D. A. 1977. *The effects of individually guided education (IGE) processes on achievement and attitudes of elementary school students.* Unpublished doctoral dissertation, University of Missouri-Columbia.

Ramayya, D. P. 1972. *Achievement skills, personality variables, and classroom climate in graded and nongraded elementary schools.* Dartmouth, N.S.: Dartmouth Public Schools.

Reichardt, C. S. 1979. The statistical analysis of data from nonequivalent group designs. In *Quasi-experimentation: Design and analysis issues for field settings,* edited by T. C. Cook and D. T. Campbell. Chicago: Rand McNally.

Reid, B. C. 1973. *A comparative analysis of a nongraded and graded primary program.* Unpublished doctoral dissertation, University of Alabama.

Remacle, L. F. 1970. *A comparative study of the differences in attitudes, self-concept, and achievement of children in graded and nongraded elementary schools.* Unpublished doctoral dissertation, University of South Dakota.

Ross, G. A. 1967. *A comparative study of pupil progress in ungraded and graded primary programs.* Unpublished doctoral dissertation, Indiana University.

Rothrock, D. 1982. The rise and decline of individualized instruction. *Educational Leadership* 39:528–31.

Schneiderhan, R. M. 1973. *A comparison of an individually guided education (IGE) program, an individually guided instruction (IGI) program, and a traditional elementary educational program at the intermediate level.* Unpublished doctoral dissertation, University of Minnesota.

Shepard, L. A., and M. L. Smith, eds. 1989. *Flunking grades: Research and policies on retention.* New York: Falmer.

Sie, M. S. 1969. *Pupil achievement in an experimental nongraded elementary school.* Unpublished doctoral dissertation, Iowa State University.

Skapski, M. K. 1960. Ungraded primary reading program: An objective evaluation. *Elementary School Journal* 61:41–45.

Slavin, R. E. 1986. Best-evidence synthesis: An alternative to meta-analytic and traditional reviews. *Educational Researcher* 15 (9): 5–11.

———. 1987. Ability grouping and student achievement in elementary schools: A best-evidence synthesis. *Review of Educational Research* 57:293–336.

———. 1990. Ability grouping and student achievement in secondary schools: A best-evidence synthesis. *Review of Educational Research* 60: 471–99.

Slavin, R. E., and N. A. Madden. 1991. Modifying Chapter 1 program improvement guidelines to reward appropriate practices. *Educational Evaluation and Policy Analysis* 13:369–79.

Snake River School District. 1972. *Curriculum change through nongraded individualization.* Blackfoot, Idaho: School District 52.

Soumokil, P. O. 1977. *Comparison of cognitive and affective dimensions of individually guided education (IGE) and standard elementary school programs.* Unpublished doctoral dissertation, University of Missouri-Columbia.

Vogel, F. S., and N. D. Bowers. 1972. Pupil behavior in a multiage nongraded school. *The Journal of Experimental Education* 41:78–86.

Walker, W. E. 1973. *Long term effects of graded and nongraded primary programs.* Unpublished doctoral dissertation, George Peabody College for Teachers.

Ward, D. N. 1969. *An evaluation of a nongraded school program in grades one and two.* Unpublished doctoral dissertation, The University of Texas at Austin.

Williams, W. 1966. Academic achievement in a graded school and in a non-graded school. *Elementary School Journal* 66:135–39.

Willis, S. 1991. Breaking down grade barriers: Interest in nongraded classrooms on the rise. *ASCD Update* 33 (3): 1, 4.

Wilt, H. J. 1970. *A comparison of student attitudes toward school, academic achievement, internal structures and procedures: The nongraded school vs. the graded school.* Unpublished doctoral dissertation, University of Missouri.

Zerby, J. R. 1960. *A comparison of academic achievement and social adjustment of primary school children in the graded and nongraded school programs.* Unpublished doctoral dissertation, The Pennsylvania State University.

Portions of this article were adapted from Gutiérrez and Slavin, 1992. Preparation of this article was supported by a grant from the Office of Educational Research and Improvement (OERI), U.S. Department of Education (No. OERI-R-117-R90002). However, any opinions expressed are those of the authors and do not necessarily represent OERI positions or policies.

Reinventing School
Teachers' Perspectives on Multiage Classrooms

David Marshak

> We don't act like fourth, fifth, and sixth graders. We just act like kids at school, learning. We get to make a lot of choices by ourselves. Mostly everybody gets along. The teachers are the best. What I mean is, they are nice and they trust our opinions.
> —A fifth grade student in a grades 4–6 multiage classroom

A few years ago, a teacher of a grades 4–6 multiage classroom told me that he was tired of all the attention high schools were receiving for their first small steps toward restructuring. "They're just nibbling at the edges," he said. "We've gone far beyond that. We've changed just about everything that we do, starting with putting three age levels together and keeping kids with the same teacher for three years, and on to integrative curriculum, a lot more student-directed learning and student responsibility, interdisciplinary projects, and more. Doesn't that count as restructuring?"

"Yes," I told him. And I believe it even more today. The movement in elementary schools known primarily as multiage classrooms certainly counts. And it is probably more than restructuring—it could become the beginning of the reinvention of schooling in the elementary grades.

Multiage classrooms begin with a teacher's philosophical commitment and require that teachers—and schools—maintain this commitment over time. "It can't be just a way to solve a numbers problem," explained Alice Leeds, who teaches a grades 4–6 class at the Lincoln Community School in Lincoln, Vermont. "The teacher has to believe in and understand its value. Then you need school leadership and policy to support multiage, so they don't toss it away whenever the numbers shift a bit."

I interviewed seven teachers who shared among them seventy-five years of elementary school teaching. Thirty-nine of those years had been spent in multiage classrooms that they had designed and operated. These teachers were Alice Leeds (gr. 4–6) from Lincoln Community School in Lincoln Vermont; Pat Minor (gr. 2–3), Debbie Cross (gr. 4–6), John Bourgoin (gr. 4–6), and Arnell Paquette (gr. 4–6) from Beeman Elementary School in New Haven, Vermont; and Carol Hasson (gr. 4–5) and Jodi Lane (gr. 1–2) from Robinson School in Starksboro, Vermont.

What they articulated offers the first steps toward a systemic understanding of (1) the defining qualities of multiage classrooms and (2) the benefits of such classrooms for students, teachers, and parents.

The Defining Qualities of Multiage Classrooms

> I stayed with Ms. (teacher's name) three years, and she was nice. I got where I knew everything she would say. I could almost say it before she said it. She would look at me and she'd go, "You've been with me in this class so long!" That was really nice.
> —A sixth grade student in a grades 4–6 multiage classroom

> The younger kids depend on the older kids a lot. And sometimes the older kids depend on the younger ones, because it's pretty amazing what some of them can do. Some of them, you think, "Oh man, they don't know that question"—but then a lot of them know it. That's pretty amazing. . . . The younger kids really do look up to us, because if they need help or something, they're always asking an older kid.
> —A sixth grade student in a grades 4–6 multiage classroom

All of these teachers agreed that multiage classrooms are defined by a set of qualities that begin with at least a two-year span in the ages of students within the class. The other defining qualities evolve from this multiplicity of students' ages. They are as follows:

1. Multiage classrooms include students who cover a two-year span in chronological age and would otherwise be placed in different grades.
2. Each student remains in the same classroom with the same teacher(s) for at least two school years, often longer.
3. The teacher learns to perceive each student not as a member of a grade grouping but as the individual he or she is, with several qualities and capabilities, not all of which are at the same level of development.

    MINOR: You have technically more than one grade in the classroom. But once they've walked through the door, I don't think about them as second graders or third graders. They're kids, and they have varying degrees of abilities. You take them where they are, see what skills they have, and what they need to work on. In this class, we have kids who are from six years old to ten years old. Multiage is exactly what these kids are.

4. The children learn to perceive each other less and less in terms of grade membership and more in terms of specific personal qualities and capabilities. Chronological age becomes less important as a determinant of children's relationships, while developmental age becomes more important.

    CROSS: In the multiage classroom there's a place for everybody; everybody fits somewhere. It's okay for a sixth grader, say, to be friends with a fourth grader. They care for each other, and they help each other.

5. A multiage classroom generates more profound relationships between teacher and students, among students, and between teacher and parents. Indeed, each of these seven teachers used the metaphor of family to characterize the social qualities of his or her classroom.

    CROSS: It's a family, and a community. It's a feeling that you foster and that you look for.

    HASSON: In a multiage classroom the students, along with the teacher, take on roles similar to those in a family. The atmosphere is like a family. Comfort and trust are two key characteristics. Dependence, or interdependence, is also really important. Knowing that you will all be together for more than one year allows you to invest in really getting to know and trust each other. And you are more likely to know personal things about each other. Parents are more likely to share problems that are going on at home. You're just all working together more. That's what I think of as a family: everybody works together.

6. The qualities of the multiage classroom encourage the teacher to begin a transformation of his or her pedagogy. In this work the teacher moves from "teaching to an imaginary middle of the class" to conceiving and structuring learning activities that meet the needs of diverse individuals.

> LANE: There are a lot of different levels in a multiage classroom, and you're able to individualize and have kids working at their own level, at their own pace. But you're also able to do a lot of small group activities, and some whole group ones, too, that are more open ended—that meet all those different levels.
>
> BOURGOIN: Units or activities are planned for participation by the whole group much of the time. But the individual student's work may be more individualized; the expectations will vary, depending on the individual's needs.

In conversations I've had with not only these seven multiage teachers but with several dozen others, each has articulated a similar perceptual and conceptual shift that is generated by the defining element of the multiage classroom: a wider age range. Almost all teachers know that every single-grade classroom contains students with a wide range of developmental levels, and that each child embodies his or her own wide range of developmental variety. Yet the very structure of age grading encourages most teachers to perceive their students as similar and to conceive of teaching as an activity directed toward the whole class.

A multiage classroom is obviously different, and this difference encourages teachers to begin to reinvent their teaching activities. Teachers are freed to perceive students as diverse, both in relation to each other and to their own set of qualities and capacities. This perceptual shift leads teachers toward reconceiving the nature of instruction and relationships within their classrooms.

The Benefits of Multiage Classrooms for Students

> There's one (fourth grade) kid in my class, he's very skilled, and he's in most of my groups. He does a lot with me because he's smart for his age, and we always work together because he's fun. . . . If the other younger kids need help with something, I can help them—you know, spelling or figuring out a math problem.
> —A sixth grade student in a grades 4–6 multiage classroom

> I think you learn to work with the younger kids and not to feel like you're better than them because you're older. . . . When we mix the classes together, everyone seems to be more friendly to each other than when we were in separate grades. You really have to learn to work with all different kids. You have to learn to work with them instead of thinking you're better.
> —A sixth grade student in a grades 4-6 multiage classroom

From the perspective of these seven experienced teachers, what are the benefits for students? All of these teachers perceived an improved relationship between themselves and students. For students this meant the teacher had greater knowledge of their individual capacities and needs; there was greater consistency of teacher behavior and expectations, greater felt comfort and security in the classroom, and greater mutual caring and concern.

MINOR: There is the possibility of continuity with teachers. For some children that is absolutely essential for them to be comfortable, to feel secure. Nobody, if they're uncomfortable or are not settled, will learn to their best potential. And when the kids come in after I've had them for one year, they come back and they're really on top of it. They really understand what's expected, and they're ready to work the first day.

LEEDS: The benefits are, they get to evolve over a two- or three-year period, so they don't have to get to know the teacher again. Once they're integrated with the classroom, they're going to be there awhile, and they can feel comfortable and really settle in. So it builds a certain amount of confidence and continuity.

HASSON: For students I think the consistency of having the same teacher for more than one year is the biggest benefit of multiage classrooms. The consistency—knowing the expectations and the routine—allows kids to feel safe, and you see fewer behavior problems and less acting out to get attention. Kids who come in labeled as behavior problem kids—usually by the second year—those behaviors are minimized because they're into the routine, they know the expectations, and it's consistent for them. Shy kids tend to become more relaxed and come out of their shells. Followers tend to feel safe to explore being leaders.

Each teacher noted that the social climate of a multiage classroom is more positive in a variety of ways. One element of this involves the recognition of diversity by the students and their increased acceptance and even valuing of the differences among their peers.

MINOR: I think the kids are much more accepting of each other. They're not so judgmental because there is a huge range. I think they've come to realize that everybody is not always going to be good at everything—that "So-and-so can do this really well, while this other area they really need to work a lot harder in"— and they're much more accepting of that. I think it's far more motivating when they don't feel out of place, put down. And their self-images are much more positive by the end of the year. They're more eager to go on and to work harder because of how they feel about themselves.

BOURGOIN: It's almost like there's more opportunity for a greater number of kids to be able to have individual strengths and responsibilities. Whereas in a single-grade situation things always leveled off, I think there's more flexibility in multiage grouping for a greater number of kids to be able to stretch.

PAQUETTE: It's just so safe in the multiage setting for the kids to work at whatever level they need to be on. I think it's rewarding academically for a younger child to be able to work with a sixth grader, but also for a fourth grader who is perhaps really needy to see that, "Gee, there's a fifth grader doing the same thing, or a sixth grader doing the same thing that I'm doing, and it's okay." I think it's just a safer environment emotionally for kids.

LEEDS: So if they're a slow student or an accelerated student, it's not like, "Oh gee, of all the fifth grade, this kid can't do fractions yet, or this kid is way, way ahead." Where they're at is not so crucial. It's not such a visible thing because it's a given that they're all over the place in ability levels, so they get to be where they are. Other students notice, of course, but it doesn't seem to be such a stigma or a big deal.

Another element of the improved social environment of the classroom is the reduction of negative norms.

CROSS: One of the biggest things I see . . . is all that cockiness, that "I'm cool" stuff that sixth grade students demonstrate—it was virtually eliminated the first year [we went to multiage] because they have to be role models. . . . All that preadolescent stuff, twenty-five of them in the classroom at one time. It's awful. And to split them up and have them be role models and mix with other kids, it's a joy.

BOURGOIN: To see or hear a child judge another one based on whether they're a good student or not—that's a rarity. . . . They're aware of differences, though, and I think because of that awareness, they are much more inclined to try and remedy the situation by helping another kid, as opposed to using it against them.

Each teacher mentioned that students of different ages become increasingly interdependent within a multiage setting, because they often teach each other. This peer tutoring and interdependence leads to better learning and enhanced self-esteem.

LEEDS: [Teaching a peer] builds confidence that you really know something. If you know something well, you can explain it to another child. And students have to know things well enough that they can explain them to someone else. They're constantly in that situation of explaining information to someone else.

LANE: You have to really know something in order to teach it to another child. Putting kids together with partners allows them to teach something so they can learn it even better. They all like to do that for each other. Not just the older kids, the younger ones, too.

CROSS: Kids are more apt to offer help to each other in a multiage. They see somebody working on something and go, "Oh, I know how to do that; let me show you." They take it upon themselves.

BOURGOIN: What's happened as time has gone on is that the younger kids have discovered that they have some things that they can help somebody else with, too. So there's a constant asking, "Can so-and-so help me?" and much more of a seeking each other out for assistance, not a direct relying on the teacher all the time. They begin to see each other as having something to offer in terms of knowledge as well as social things.

A related outcome to the greater interdependence is the increased independence of children from the teacher as they learn to rely on each other as facilitators of learning.

LEEDS: I see students in my classroom become more willing to take care of questions or problems for themselves as the year, or years, go on. They ask me less often as the first option and try to figure it out for themselves, either with a peer or alone. Then, if they're still stuck, they come to me.

Every teacher noted that children in a multiage classroom experience a much wider range of group roles than in a single-grade experience. Each child has the opportunity to be an "elder," a leader, and a role model in the classroom.

LANE: For many older kids, being able to be the person who is the role model is extremely important and encourages them to become responsible leaders. I have very few behavior problems this year, none really. And I think that a lot of that comes from being able to be the older kid in charge.

MINOR: [Children in their second year in the class] . . . are really the leaders. If they have been in a class for a year they take a leadership role, and for some of these kids, this is the first time this has ever happened to them. . . . Also, they become role models for the younger kids; buddies and instructors in a lot of ways, helping the [new] kids to get settled in.

LEEDS: As they get older, they get to become leaders and role models, and they become sort of assistants to the teacher. I don't mean that it takes them away from their own work. I think sometimes parents worry about this, about children taking on responsibilities. I see it as very positive. It builds confidence, and they develop leadership skills and group skills.

HASSON: I was worried entering this school year because, looking at my fourth graders, I couldn't see any strong leaders emerging among them as they turned into fifth graders. I was concerned about this since I depend on the students I've already had in class to set the stage and become role models for the younger kids. Thankfully, I was pleasantly surprised to see kids who'd been followers take on leadership roles and blossom into strong leaders and role models. I don't think this would have happened for these kids had this not been a multiage classroom.

Many children also experience a role that differs from their role at home, which is often strongly influenced by their birth order.

HASSON: Multiage gives kids an opportunity to experience roles different from those they have in their family. For instance, a child who is the youngest at home will get a chance to reverse that role and become an older child. She'll get to feel what that's like and have that kind of responsibility. She'll have the opportunities that go along with being an older child as well as the negatives. And if you're an older child in your family, it's vice versa. Experiencing these different roles can help kids gain a better understanding of themselves and of their relationships with siblings.

Each teacher explained that a multiage classroom eases the stress of entering a new classroom for the child and allows the teacher to pay more attention to each new student.

LEEDS: When students come in, they're not part of a huge group of kids that are all new. Maybe half or two-thirds have already been there and help them adjust. It's not just one teacher getting them ready; they have a lot of students who are helping them adapt. In fact, in our classroom we have a peer partner program. They all have peer partners, so they don't have to wait every time they have a question on procedure or content or whatever. There's always a student right there who can help them answer a question. . . . And I can get to know each new student much more quickly because there's a manageable number of them.

Several teachers noted that multiage classrooms help children focus on learning just by reducing the number of transitions in their school career.

CROSS: Another benefit for the kids is the continuity from year to year. One fourth grader was saying how hard fourth grade was because it was such a change. And I said, "Well, you should talk to Jonathan about fifth grade and how it's different." And he had already, and Jonathan had said that fifth grade is so much better because you know the teacher, you know what needs to happen. When they go into fifth grade, there's that familiarity and that comfort. They don't have to worry, and therefore, often, the academics take over.

Several teachers reflected that multiage classrooms may help to resolve the dilemma of failing a student during the elementary years.

MINOR: If kids need an extra year in the class, they can have it. Instead of spending two years they can spend three years. And since half of the class that they've been with will be there, the stigma that has always been associated with repeating a year isn't there. We've done this with a few kids, and they do better with the extra time. And nobody calls them a failure.

The Benefits of Multiage Classrooms for Teachers

> Yeah, if you stay with a teacher for three years, well, she knows what you're good at and what you can do. And it makes you work harder. . . . And when we're the oldest, we can help the fourth graders and be role models. They take on what you do. Like, if you act good, that's probably what they'll act like, because you set good examples.
> —A sixth grade student in a grades 4–6 multiage classroom

> Question: Do you remember what the older kids did when you were in fourth grade?
> Answer: I remember some of it. They were always getting their work done and stuff, and acting pretty good.
> —A sixth grade student in a grades 4–6 multiage classroom

All seven teachers spoke with conviction about the benefits of multiage classrooms for teachers. Obviously some of the benefits for teachers complement the benefits for students.

When asked to rank order the benefits of multiage classrooms for teachers, each teacher listed "deeper, more profound relationships with kids" and "greater personal rewards in seeing students' growth and learning" as the most significant. Teachers consistently spoke of these two outcomes in the same paragraphs, identifying them as interrelated phenomena.

LEEDS: I think the biggest benefit is that you get to work with the child over two or three years, and when the child comes back you can pretty much pick up where you left off. You can set very long-term goals for children; you don't have to say, "By the end of the year I've got to get them here." You take a longer and broader vision with the child, and I think in that way your goals are not as superficial. You don't just say, "I've got to get them to know their times tables." So you think in terms of, "I'd like to see this child develop more social confidence; I'd like to see this child be willing to take on more leadership or take on more challenge, and I'd like to see them be able to follow through." You start to see each child more as a person rather than just as somebody you've got to give so many skills to, and you work on things in a broader way. I used to say that you have a second and a third chance, but now I see it as much more than that. You take a look at the person; you develop a relationship with them; you develop a relationship with their family; so you see them in a wider context, not just as a kid who is in your classroom. You develop more compassion; you develop a relationship, because you care. You grow to love the children. That, I think, is the big one—you get to know those kids and work with them and see them progress over a long period of time. It's always wonderful to witness their growth.

LANE: Being able to know right where they are at the beginning of the second year is great. If I were to send kids on after one year, I just wouldn't see their continued growth. And there are some kids who really need that second year to grow. It gives me wonderful feedback when I have kids for two years, and they didn't quite get it that first year; but by the end of that second year, wow, look how much they've got. That's really rewarding for me.

HASSON: I think you become more invested in a child's education when you teach that child for two years or more. You know the child is going to be with you, and you know that you're playing a big role in this person's education. And I think you care more because you get to know the child more. Sometimes you might go through a whole year having a child in your class and not ever really get to know her. That child goes on, and you always wonder, "Did I do enough?" In a multiage you always have that second year to do even more.

BOURGOIN: Time makes the big difference as far as being able to have a kid from one year to the next. There were always certain children of whom I would say, "This kid's going to get there, but just needs some time." And I would never see it happen, because they would leave. Whereas now I could say, "I'm not going to get too uptight about this kid this year. I know what he or she needs; the kid isn't really ready; the kid needs some time. I'm not going to get on his or her case right now. I don't need to; it's just going to make them anxious." And then the following year it's like, "I knew this kid needed some time. That's all it took."

CROSS: For myself, it's much more rewarding to have a child for more than one year because you see the blossoming. I've had some of my kids in this class for three years, and it's just incredible to look back and see them. My colleague had one student for three years, and he kept him for a fourth year because he needed it. And just to see how that child has grown is really rewarding, much more so than straight grades.

Every teacher described the ways in which multiage classrooms minimize the stress of starting a new school year and support productive use of school time right from the first week of school.

MINOR: It takes a good two months to settle a new class in: to find out where they're at, to get them to understand the routine and expectations, and for me to get to know where they were and how they work so I'm comfortable with them. But with a multiage, we're rolling the first week of school. I mean, I never had that before. The first year of multiage I was shocked; I was absolutely blown away. I went home saying, "This is too easy." It was so much less stressful than it had ever been before. Now when I start the year I know half the kids already, their strengths and weaknesses. I know what they missed last year and where the holes are. I know where I can go with them. And the [new] kids seem to fit right in.

HASSON: There's none of that time in the beginning of the year where the teacher has to get to know the students and the students get to know the teacher, and all that's wasted in that process, especially for kids who have a difficult time with transitions and new environments.

LEEDS: One thing is that every year you don't have to integrate a whole new class of kids. You really can integrate the new kids more easily into the room, and the other children help you do that. A couple of years ago, when one girl became a fifth grader and the new fourth graders came in, she said, "You know, it's much easier when you come back." The kids really help get each other going.

LANE: At the end of the year I know exactly where they left off. When they come back in, it's just amazing how much things fly from that point on.

❖ ❖ ❖ ❖ ❖

Each teacher explained that a key benefit of multiage classrooms is the development of stronger and more productive relationships with the parents of their students.

HASSON: Kids know that I've gotten a relationship going with their parents, and the communication is much more frequent and comfortable. I feel like I develop a really intimate relationship with my parents over the two years, and I think that's really good for kids to know.

MINOR: You have to get to know the parents in order for them to help their kids and be supportive of the school system and know what we're doing and where we're going. After one year they get to know me, and so they know how I'm handling their kid. We can work together through problems that their kid has, maybe concerns they have. We have to work together to do this. They get so that if they have concerns, they call me or write me, and I can talk to them; call them and say, "I really think your child will benefit from summer school to keep him or her going," or "They really need to be worked with on this or that behavior. This is what we're working on." Or maybe there's been some stress in the family for some reason. We can talk about it, work it through and help their child.

LEEDS: I really think parents make more of a commitment to their relationship with me as their kid's teacher in a multiage than they did in a straight grade. It's like they know they're stuck with me for a long time, and I'm going to be important to their kid, so they're more willing to work at it, to put more effort into things.

LANE: I think the relationship that I am able to develop with the parents is incredible. Even parents who tend to be a little hard to get to know—when you have them for two years, you see them twice as much as you would see them in one year, and by the end of those two years you really know them well.

PAQUETTE: When you have kids more than one year, you begin to build a relationship with the parents, and it builds. The first year it might be kind of sketchy, but after a year, in the second and maybe the third year even, it's different. It's not your typical parent-teacher relationship; it can be more of a partnership because it builds from year to year. It makes it easier to deal with kids because you've got two or three adults working for the kid.

CROSS: I find them [parents] much easier to approach, and they approach me more often. I get phone calls at home, or notes, or whatever. I think that there's a comfort for them, too. It isn't formal at all after the first year; it really is quite different.

BOURGOIN: There used to be a formality to the parent-teacher conferencing or the getting together for whatever reason. And now, [with multiage] it's become much more of an open dialogue that you can have with the parent about their child. I find myself being a lot more candid than I used to be.

CROSS: We originally had said that we'd only keep the child for two years because we didn't think it would be wise to keep them for three years. And now we're getting more and more requests from parents to keep the child for three years.

Several teachers identified the year-to-year continuity that multiage classes create as a significant benefit.

CROSS: You start thinking and planning in cycles of several years, and once you get the hang of it, it seems to make things easier.

HASSON: Planning instruction is a lot easier in a multiage classroom. You know the kids, their needs, likes, and dislikes. You aren't spending all that time trying to figure out what they need, so your units are better. The following year, you know where they've been and where they need to go.

Finally, every teacher expressed a philosophical commitment to multiage classrooms and in one way or another noted that such a commitment brought focus and renewed purpose to their professional lives.

BOURGOIN: I think one of the benefits for me on a personal level has been that I've always felt that this [multiage] was what teaching should really be. That this was the natural, if you want to call it that, way to teach. I felt it was very unnatural to take children from a natural setting like a family and then put them into this building or space and work under the assumption that because you are a nine-year-old you have this bulk of information that you have to learn because the textbook publisher says that that's what nine-year-olds need to know. It just went against a lot of my instincts about how kids learn and how I should be teaching them. It's a lot more work in one sense, but on the other hand it's much more rewarding because I feel that I'm doing what children need me to do as a teacher.

The Benefits of Multiage Classrooms for Parents

> Your parents get to know your teacher after awhile. They're not afraid to talk to them and tell them stuff. So sometimes I don't like it that much, but most of the time it's pretty good, you know, that your parents and the teacher can talk and get along and help you and stuff.
> —A sixth grade student in a grades 4–6 multiage classroom

The teachers also saw several clear benefits for parents in the multiage classrooms of their children. These benefits focus on the increase in comfort that parents feel when they can get to know a teacher over more than a year and the greater likelihood that parent and teacher can work together to support a child's growth and learning.

HASSON: I think some parents are really afraid to come into school and are intimidated; they feel a lot more comfortable not having to get to know another person the next year. Both [a colleague] and I had a parent who last year hardly ever came to conferences. She started coming halfway through the year, and then she came for the rest of the year. This year she started out the year coming, and I know that wouldn't have happened if she'd had totally new teachers. I think she would have still felt that intimidation. So I feel like they are more comfortable with you, and they're used to your routines. All my parents know the routines for their child's homework. So the next year it's a lot easier because they know what to expect. For instance, all my kids buy binders to organize themselves. They know that in fourth grade they're going to use them, and in fifth grade they're going to use them. And the parents get into the routine. I think routines in people's crazy lives are really important, and that's one important thing that multiage gives parents.

LANE: Every time a child goes to a new teacher, there's a certain amount of stress for the child and for the parent. [Multiage] takes away that stress for a year. They think, "Oh, yeah, we know how it's going to be"—I think it makes life a little easier sometimes. I have such strong parent support in the classroom. At the beginning of this year, right from the first week of school, I had parents from last year say, "When can we come in?" And they were able to start coming in that first and second week, whereas with the parents that I didn't quite know yet, I wanted to wait until we had an opportunity to talk and discuss what their role would be in the classroom. For those ["returning"] parents there wasn't that lag time—for the kids either. They were able to get right back into it and not have to wait around for anything.

LEEDS: For parents, they really get to know the teacher. I think that's a big plus. They know who is with their kid every day, all day long. And they get to develop a certain comfort level so if there is a touchy subject, or if they're concerned about something, we can talk. I've had parents talk to me about things that were good for me to be aware of but that may have been difficult for them to talk about. You just develop more of an ease. I've worked with parents over three years who've had challenging situations at home, and you develop a whole rapport around their kid. They don't have to readjust every year and think, "Well, how is it going to be for my child this year and what's the teacher going to expect? What kind of homework is there going to be? What are they going to do about this, that, and the other?" They get to know what the story is. So just the way the child gets comfortable, the parents can get comfortable. And if there are some things that they're not comfortable with, usually they're worked out in the first year, and from there it's smooth sailing.

HASSON: I think that when you only have a student for one year, it's hard to see where kids started and where they ended unless you really document it all along the way. And even then, in one year it's hard to see a lot of progress. Sometimes parents notice their child making that progress more than teachers do, and parents are feeling more positive than teachers do at the end of certain periods of time in the kid's life. They can say, "Wow, this is where they were, and this is where they are." Having a child for more than one year, you can share the parents' enthusiasm and say, "Gosh, remember two years ago when so-and-so came in my room? Here's a piece of work that they were doing then. And now here it is two years later, and, wow, look at this book that they started reading! Look what kind of books they can read!" I think that is really positive, because parents know now that you can see [the progress] and appreciate it more than you could when you only had their child for one year.

Disadvantages of Multiage Classrooms

> It's a lot of work. It's a tremendous amount of work.
> —A teacher of a grades 4–6 multiage classroom

Are there disadvantages in multiage classrooms for children? Absolutely none, each of these teachers said. But what about for *teachers*?

CROSS: It's a lot more work at the start. And later on it's still more work than straight grades are.

PAQUETTE: Every year is different. We thought after the third year we'd go into our fourth year—which would be repeating the first year—and we'd have it made. Well, it wasn't anything like our first year. So every year has been different, and that's because of the makeup of the class. And that's both a challenge and a lot of work.

MINOR: It does take a lot of preparation time. And the first year I worked on this, it took awhile. I guess any time you switch grade levels or add a grade, you don't necessarily have the materials that you might need for extending the ranges. So it takes awhile to build up the reading books and the manipulatives, that kind of thing. Sometimes having to extend, having things be open ended so they will take in all of the ranges of ability, takes some work. This is the fourth year, so I'm finding fewer problems pulling out materials that I've used and adding to them. After the initial shock of trying to figure out how to deal with the ranges that you've got, I don't think it's that much different in a lot of ways.

LEEDS: Parents don't always understand the benefits at first. So I think it's important to share with parents and encourage their understanding of the benefits. That can be somewhat challenging. On the positive side, parents sell the idea of multiage to each other just as the children do. This year a group of concerned parents worked with a couple of teachers in our school to evaluate our multiage program, and they were really turned around. They've become our best spokespeople for multiage.

You do feel more of a commitment to your kids. If I ever left, I would be leaving some kids midstream. I would always feel like I was leaving in the middle of the year. So you make a bigger commitment to a school when you become a multiage teacher. You're making a bigger commitment to a group of children. You really feel like if you leave, you need to help bridge that transition. It's never a great time to leave.

Are there disadvantages in multiage classrooms for parents? None of these teachers articulated any.

LANE: I know concerns that parents have, but I haven't seen any negatives or had any parents tell me about anything like that.

LEEDS: Of course, if a parent is having a problem with the teacher, then they get more anxious. They think, "Oh, gosh, I'm going to have to deal with this teacher for two or three years." Parents, I think, are more likely to come up early on and try to get it worked out. They're not as likely to wait it out. So it might seem negative, but my experience is that it ends up being positive.

Final Thoughts

> I was in a regular fourth grade . . . I like the multiage better. It's more like different people . . . have to learn to get along good, and they do!
> —A sixth grade student in a grades 4–6 multiage classroom

It is much too soon to understand where this reinvention of the elementary classroom will lead. But it is fair to say that the paradigm of the multiage classroom—in its definition, its nurturing of relationships, and the directions it propels teachers to explore, particularly in terms of children's diverse capabilities, curriculum, instruction, and self-direction in learning—finally shatters the egg-carton, industrial model of schooling. The multiage model offers insight into what twenty-first century schools might become if they are designed first and foremost to promote the health, growth, and learning of children as whole persons.

References

Anderson, R., and B. N. Pavan. 1993. *Nongradedness: Helping it to happen.* Lancaster, Pa.: Technomic Publishing.

Banks, J. C. 1995. *Creating the multi-age classroom.* Edmonds, Wash.: CATS Publications.

Charney, R. S. 1992. *Teaching children to care: Management in the responsive classroom.* Greenfield, Mass.: Northeast Foundation for Children.

Chase, P., and J. Doan. 1994. *Full circle: A new look at multiage education.* Portsmouth, N.H.: Heinemann.

Gamberg, R., et al. 1988. *Learning and loving it: Theme studies in the classroom.* Toronto: OISE Press.

Gaustad, J. 1992. Nongraded education: Mixed-age, integrated, and developmentally appropriate education for primary children. *Oregon School Study Council Bulletin* 35:7.

———. 1992. Making the transition from graded to nongraded primary education. *Oregon School Study Council Bulletin* 35:8.

———. 1994. Nongraded education: Overcoming obstacles to implementing the multiage classroom. *Oregon School Study Council Bulletin* 38:3, 4.

Maeda, B. 1995. *The multi-age classroom: An inside look at one community of learners.* Cypress, Calif.: Creative Teaching Press.

Miller, B. A. 1994. *Children at the center: Implementing the multiage classroom.* Portland, Ore.: Northwest Regional Educational Laboratory.

Rathbone, C., et al. 1993. *Multiage portraits: Teaching and learning in mixed age classrooms.* Peterborough, N.H.: Crystal Springs Books.

Wood, C. 1994. *Yardsticks: Children in the classroom ages 4–12.* Greenfield, Mass.: Northeast Foundation for Children.

SECTION III

Implementation

I shall tell you a great secret, my friend. Do not wait for the Last Judgement—it takes place every day.

—Albert Camus

SECTION III

Implementation

Inundated with rich images and armed with solid information about the historical foundation, the research base, and the benefits of multiage groupings, the next phase of discussion moves from the "what" and the "why" to the "how." How is the multiage classroom actually implemented in schools? What are the processes that ensure success for all students, teachers, and parents?

To inform the reader about implementation issues, three distinguished practitioners offer their opinions from the "trenches." Immersed in nongraded education, Marilyn Hughes provides an invaluable overview of the transition process in her essay, "Nongraded Education: A Report from Aspen, Colorado." She shares the master plan that she and a colleague developed and used in their pursuit of a multiage educational format. Hughes also discusses her philosophy, delineates expected student outcomes, and elaborates on ways to empower change. She then focuses on the design phase, which addresses academic concerns such as assessment, instruction, and student contracts, and to practical issues of scheduling and the physical environment.

Kathy Magee's article, "Instructional Strategies in a Multiage Primary Classroom," takes us directly into the multiage classroom and focuses intensely on instructional concerns. In this enlightening piece with a practical emphasis, readers learn about the techniques and methodologies used to "read and teach" all students in the multiage setting, including cooperative learning, thematic instruction, literacy strategies, and computer use. The discussion concludes with a mention of several overriding issues: parents and parent questions, as well as the unending concerns about assessment.

Finally, in an especially timely essay for schools today, Frank Betts discusses technology for teaching and learning. Clearly defining what technology is, the author looks at its appropriate use in the multiage classroom. He also goes on to identify specific software programs for the traditional disciplines such as language arts, science, math, social studies, and art, as well as other instructional arenas such as planning.

Nongraded Education
A Report from Aspen, Colorado

Marilyn Hughes

> In the best of all worlds, elementary-age children would be educated within a team-taught, multiage, nongraded framework.
> —J. Goodlad and R. Anderson, *The Nongraded Elementary School*

While I was a student at Berkeley in the 1960s, it became eminently clear to me that the old graded systems of education were bankrupt. You may recall that this opinion, widely held by young people and largely ignored by members of the establishment, was not very popular. With the arrival of the 1990s, however, there is a respectable body of evidence about the ways in which children learn. This research suggests I was right, although my justification may have been misguided.

Today I am teaching and learning in Aspen, Colorado. I team with my partners, Betsy Ann Anastas and Mimi Hauenstein, in a nongraded, multiage, family grouped classroom where students spend up to four years in continuous progress with the same teachers and classmates. Our working definition of nongraded education is quite simple. For us it means providing our students with individualized, developmentally appropriate education in which students define the programs, and artificial grade

---

© 1992 by Marilyn Hughes. Marilyn Hughes is also the creator of the process for systemic change referred to in this chapter. All rights reserved.

labels never define the students. It means rich, authentic learning experiences through which students learn how to inquire, produce, perform, and problem solve. Mostly it means providing the most nondiscriminatory context within which all members of the learning community have an equal opportunity to reach their individual potentials.

Our nongraded classroom began in the 1989–90 school year with thirty-eight kindergarten and first grade students. (Our district is still graded even though we're not!) The following year, 1990–91, we continued with thirty-six of the same students, now in grades 1 and 2, plus six new students, including students in the English-as-a-Second-Language (ESL), gifted, special education, and severe needs programs. This family grouping, as we have come to think of it, continued in 1991–92 as a grades 2–3 cluster and remained as such in the 1992–93 school year, having graduated our oldest students while gaining our first set of siblings. That was also the year that Mimi joined our staff as a rotating teacher, providing me with time out of class to research and write.

Artificial grade labels never define the students.

Our program is implemented through concept-based units of study that are fully integrated, infused with thinking skills, and authenticated through a focus on current issues and questions. Our days vary with the needs of our students and are structured upon a balance of direct instruction, independent study in twenty hands-on learning centers, and a variety of guided learning experiences. At the center of everything are six student outcomes that are the driving force behind every action we take.

This program didn't happen overnight. Rather, it was the product of a twenty-year evolution filled with questions, research, practice, reflection, and more questions. It began with the realization that if I was ever going to effect any significant change in education, I needed to begin with a valid change process. Through this process I would eventually develop a blueprint for nongraded education. And from that blueprint, my partners and I would construct the Aspen Nongraded Learning Community.

In this chapter I will describe my change process and how it was used to design the philosophy and outcomes, curriculum content, assessment, instruction, scheduling, physical environment, and context for our own nongraded learning community. I will then outline a specific unit of study, "Life, Liberty, and the Pursuit of Happiness," which I coauthored with my partners and which demonstrates our program in action. It is my hope that the excerpts in this chapter may help other educators design nongraded programs that will endure well into the twenty-first century.

Constructing a Valid Change Process

> Nearly a century of change has left schools playing catch-up, and it will take a whole-system approach to meet society's evolving needs.
> —Frank M. Betts, *How Systems Thinking Applies to Education*

The futurists have painted a picture of the twenty-first century as an era of rapid change in which resolution of complex global issues will require all citizens to produce, perform, and problem solve. There can be no dead weight, no individuals who continue the wasteful habits of mind from the past. We desperately need the collaborative efforts of all our citizens to meet future challenges. That is why educators of vision are supporting a reemergence of nongraded education in the 1990s. But nongraded education was a great idea twenty years ago and we couldn't make it stick. If we're going to have any better luck this time we must reflect on our past efforts and discover what went wrong.

Educators of vision are supporting a reemergence of nongraded education in the 1990s.

My own reflections had brought me to one conclusion: educators had invested far too much time and money in piecemeal change efforts, endlessly searching for the "quick-fix" package that would heal an ailing educational system. If we had wanted to make a systemic change—from graded to nongraded, or to any new system—we should have employed a "whole-system" approach, a process that would carry us continually forward from the inception of our new idea all the way to implementation in the classroom.

A valid systemic change process must do three things: (1) justify the change, (2) empower the change, and (3) implement the change. (Table 1 describes the underlying assumptions and procedures for this process.)

Table 1. Systemic Change Process

UNDERLYING ASSUMPTIONS	PROCEDURES
1. **Justifying Change:** The change must be based on a philosophy and a set of specific student outcomes that reflect the changing world into which our students will graduate.	1. Identify both a statement of philosophy about the current role of education and a set of student outcomes that responds to future trends. 1A. **Audit:** Match outcomes to future trends.

2. **Empowering Change:** All educational components must be designed specifically for the achievement of stated outcomes, such that together they run in perfect synchronization.	1. Examine and design each program component—curriculum content, assessment, instructional methods, scheduling, and physical environment. Use the statements of philosophy and outcomes as a metacontext for program design.
	   a. Formulate questions
	   b. Reflect
	   c. Write design principles for each component in answer to questions
	
	1A. **Audit:** Check design principles for direct contribution to achievement of outcomes.
	
	2. Using the design principles, develop the structure and format for each component for use in writing units of study and recordkeeping.

3. **Implementing Change:** Any systemic change in education must result in an action plan for teachers to take back to their classrooms.	1. Write the units of study.
	
	1A. **Audit:** Balance instruction
	
	2. Make administrative decisions about program context:
	    staffing
	    budgets
	    student grouping
	    staff evaluations
	    management system
	    staff development
	    resources
	    parent participation

With the above process in hand, I was ready to make a change to nongraded education, and this time I was going to do it right!

Justifying the Change

Did you ever ask yourself, what is so important about education that it should consume thirteen years of a person's life? What could possibly justify such an intrusion? Whatever the justification may be, it must be clearly expressed in our philosophy and student outcomes. Thereafter, every decision we make, from the content of our curriculum to the arrangement of classroom furniture, must be evaluated for its contribution to the achievement of those outcomes.

I believe that the only way to justify years of schooling is to demonstrate how those years can make a significant contribution toward the preparation of young people for the future. It follows then that, as an educator, I must have a strong sense of the future into which my students will graduate. For that sense I looked to the futurists who generally characterized the next century as one of rapid change. Table 2 lists some specific changes and the categories into which they most commonly fall.

When I first looked at these future trends I wondered what education could possibly do to prepare young people for a world in which knowledge obsolescence is so rapid that a predicted 80 percent of the jobs that will exist in the year 2000 haven't even been invented yet (Wurman 1989). Surely, spending thirteen years memorizing disjointed bits of information with a career day thrown in would be of little value. So I went looking for the "big idea" that would justify all the time, effort, and money expended on education, and I found it in a most unexpected place—the *T.V. Guide!*

The Public Broadcasting Station was running a series by James Burke called *The Day the Universe Changed*. In it, Burke made a stand for the power of knowledge and for the value of spending years attaining that power. His words became the driving force behind the philosophy and student outcomes for my nongraded classroom. I had found my justification. I was ready to write my philosophy statement.

Table 2. Future Trends

KNOWLEDGE BASE	FAMILY STRUCTURE	WORKPLACE
• Current knowledge will become obsolete at an increasingly rapid rate. • The amount of new knowledge generated will require the generalization of knowledge. • Knowledge obsolescence will make lifelong learning essential.	• The number of working mothers will increase dramatically. • The number of single-parent homes will also increase. • With changes in family structure, the home will no longer be a center for learning.	• There will be a shift from the production of the industrial age to service/information industries. • Industries will be created and will function and die in a ten-year span. • Workers must anticipate at least four career changes in one lifetime. • Individual workers and whole nations must prepare for new business collaborations.

TECHNOLOGY	CULTURAL DEMOGRAPHICS	GLOBAL INTERDEPENDENCE
• New technologies will make all forms of communication instant. • Biogenetics will change life and even value systems as we know them. • Technological obsolescence will be rapid and dramatic.	• There will be a graying of the world's population. • Minorities will increase. • Mass migrations of populations will occur. • There will be a new emphasis on the aesthetic and spiritual aspects of life.	• Borders will change. • Currency systems within and between nations will change. • New trade partnerships will surface. • Governments will change dramatically. • Environmental and health issues will take on global proportions.

Philosophy Statement: The Current Role of Education

What you believe the Universe to be and how you react to that belief, in everything you do, depends on what you know. And when that knowledge changes, for you the Universe changes.
—James Burke, *The Day the Universe Changed*

Today's students will be handed the stewardship of a fragile universe in the twenty-first century. They will be asked to make thoughtful, intelligent decisions about crucial political, economic, and environmental issues. As participatory citizens in a rapidly changing world, they will face global challenges unheard of in the industrial age. It is imperative that these students acquire an understanding of the power of knowledge and of their responsibility to act on that knowledge with the highest degree of human intelligence.

If the experience of human intelligence can restructure our universe, as Burke's statement suggests, then the development of the knowledge, skills, behaviors, and attitudes of human intelligence should most certainly be the prime directive of education. Therefore, we can no longer tolerate the belief that if students spend thirteen years of their lives memorizing disjointed bits of information in nine-month segments, they will somehow gain the knowledge and skills necessary to face future challenges.

> *The knowledge, skills, behaviors, and attitudes of human intelligence should most certainly be the prime directive of education.*

Instead, educators, parents, students, and others must collaborate to form a learning community in which children can actively practice the art of intelligent participatory citizenship. Furthermore, to ensure that all students have an equal opportunity to reach their personal intellectual potentials, the notion of nongraded education must be revisited as the best, most nondiscriminatory context for learning. Within this context, the educational programs will provide for the following:

1. The acquisition of broad-based knowledge and basic skills through individualized, developmentally appropriate programs
2. The development of the thinking, production, technological, and communication skills necessary to solve real-life problems in the future world

3. The nurturing of emotional and physical wellness, humaneness, and aesthetic sense to make decisions about personal, social, and global relationships and responsibilities
4. The cultivation of the innate curiosity, creativity, courage, and joy within children to become lifelong learners

Student Outcomes: A Model of Intelligence

Now I had my philosophy statement about education's role in the development of human intelligence. That was all well and good, but I knew my philosophy was of little value unless it was accompanied by a specific model of intelligence toward which to aim all my efforts. This model needed to be constructed within the context of the twenty-first century world into which my students would graduate. So I constructed a model based upon all the knowledge, skills, attitudes, and behaviors of intelligence. Eventually, this model evolved into the six student outcomes listed in table 3.

In their complete form, these outcomes had four parts: (1) the outcome; (2) a set of concepts—major understandings that students must demonstrate in order to have achieved the outcome; (3) a set of proficiencies that tell what the student can do when the outcome has been achieved; and (4) an evaluation system for knowing how well the outcome has been achieved. Furthermore, for the "knowledgeable person outcome," a specific list of critical content was designated for mastery, including skills in communicating knowledge, creating knowledge, and reflecting on knowledge. There was also a specific list of thinking skills in five categories that define the proficiencies of a complex thinker. They include skills in (1) foundations of thinking, (2) logical reasoning, (3) critical thinking, (4) decision making, and (5) strategic problem solving.

Table 4 illustrates the six outcomes, their proficiency categories, and one concept from each outcome. (The specific proficiencies have not been included here.)

This completed the first phase of the systemic change process—justifying the change to a new educational system. I had looked to the future, to the past, and back to the future again. I'd written my philoso-

Table 3. Future-Oriented Student Outcomes

FUTURE TREND	STUDENT OUTCOME
1. Changing Knowledge Base requires . . .	a *Knowledgeable Person* who continues to learn throughout his or her lifetime.
2. Changing Family Structure requires . . .	a *Reflective Individual* who can draw strength from within in the absence of the traditional nuclear family structure.
3. Changing Workplace requires . . .	a *Quality Producer* who has the organizational abilities and creative imagination to produce, perform, and problem solve in a variety of situations.
4. Changing Technology requires . . .	a *Technologically Literate Person* who understands the nature and uses of technology and acquires skills in keeping with evolving technologies.
5. Changing Cultural Demographics and Global Interdependence requires...	a *Community Member* who can communicate to others, collaborate with others, and be a citizen among others.
6. All future trends require...	a *Complex Thinker* who applies higher-order thinking skills to a variety of situations, demonstrating an understanding of the patterns and connections of all living things.

phy statement about the role of education and was secure in the knowledge that education is even more important in a child's life than ever before. I had designated my student outcomes and was ready to design the educational components that would offer every individual student an equal opportunity to reach those outcomes.

Empowering the Change

While the justification for my nongraded classroom model came from its future-oriented philosophy and student outcomes, the power to reach those outcomes arose from the careful design of each program component. Here's the "whole-system" thinking in action.

Table 4. Student Outcomes

KNOWLEDGEABLE PERSON	COMPLEX THINKER	TECHNOLOGICALLY LITERATE PERSON
Concept: The lifelong pursuit of knowledge creates infinite possibilities.	*Concept:* To acquire wisdom one must understand that there is a pattern to our universe and a connection between all living things.	*Concept:* Throughout time communication has been a factor of change but technology has made those changes more rapid and powerful.
Proficiency categories: • Critical content • General knowledge • Ways of knowing	*Proficiency categories:* • Foundations • Logic • Critical thinking • Decision making • Strategic problem solving	*Proficiency categories:* • History of technology • Research • Telecommunications • Writing/Publishing

QUALITY PRODUCER	REFLECTIVE INDIVIDUAL	COMMUNITY MEMBER
Concept: Civilizations flourish in the celebration of their producers, contributors, problem solvers, and creators.	*Concept:* Freedom is both a right and a responsibility.	*Concept:* Our future survival is dependent upon the intelligence of our decisions as to how and when to intervene in the natural evolution of the universe.
Proficiency categories: • Goal setting • Organization • Resource finding • Self-regulation • Creation	*Proficiency categories:* • Emotional self • Physical self • Social self • Intellectual self • Aesthetic self	*Proficiency categories:* • Communication • Collaboration • Citizen among others in the educational, cultural, local, national, global, and natural communities.

Imagine a clock, one of those big old clocks with all the gears ticking away in perfect synchronization. Day after day they move in continuous progress toward the next day and the next and the next. That's the vision I have of the perfect educational system. Each gear is a different component of the program, finely crafted to work in perfect harmony with all the other gears. There's a large gear in the very center of the clock that houses the philosophy and student outcomes. This gear drives a series of five slightly smaller gears—those housing the curriculum content, the assessment, the instructional methods, the scheduling, and the physical environment of the program. Attached to those gears are a series of administrative gears that define how the system will be staffed and budgeted, how students will be grouped, etc. The clock runs perfectly until one tiny little gear gets out of sync. Then the whole system grinds to a halt. (This is what happened to nongraded education all those years ago. Someone forgot to properly design all the gears.)

> *I wanted to know how to design instructional methods around the ways individual children learn.*

To empower my educational master plan to create a nongraded system, I began asking myself questions about each component in relationship to the philosophy and six student outcomes. For example, I wanted to know how to design curriculum content that would reflect a change in goals from the mastery of finite content to the development of human intelligence. I wanted to know how to design instructional methods around the ways individual children learn, to ensure all students an equal opportunity for success. I had many more questions about authenticity, performance assessment, and constructing interactive environments. In answer to those questions I came up with approximately thirty design principles for constructing each component of the classroom. Then Betsy Ann and I took those design principles and created the structure and format for our nongraded learning community. What follows is an abbreviated look at the design principles and samples from the format and structure that arose from them.

Designing the Components of Curriculum Content

Design Principles

The curriculum content will:
- be integrated across the disciplines using multiple viewpoints and current issues and questions as structural organizers.

- be concept based using the same concepts as those stated in the student outcomes.

- have objectives written as thinking skills applied to content.

- recognize the importance of technology through a balance of old and new basics.

- include a balance of aesthetics and technology.

Structure and Format

The curriculum content section of our units of study begins with a philosophy statement informing students why the study of this unit is essential to the achievement of one or all of the student outcomes. Here, the concepts, as well as the current issues or questions through which the unit will be studied, are designated. Next comes the curriculum content that has been selected for the unit. All content is written through five viewpoints—the sociological, scientific, aesthetic, linguistic, and personal viewpoints. "Viewpoints" here goes beyond the notion of bias to mean looking at knowledge through the eyes of a historian or a scientist, an artist or a writer.

For example, if you asked a historian to tell you about World War II, he would describe the treaties made and broken and the other historical events leading to the struggle between the Axis and Allied Powers. If you then asked a scientist about World War II, she would tell you about the development of radar, the race for the atomic bomb, and the part weather played in the outcome of the war. A writer might offer a viewpoint of the war through the lives of people who lived and perhaps died in the war. An artist would tell you about the threatened burning of Paris. And a soldier might tell you the war was all about jungles, mosquitoes, and the Japanese. In other words, there is no way to fully "know" World War II when seen through only one pair of eyes.

Each viewpoint has concepts taken from the six student outcomes, creating a strong link between outcomes and content. Additionally, each viewpoint has a number of designated critical content categories that arose from one question: "What does an individual have to know in order to be a knowledgeable person, complex thinker, technologically literate person, a quality producer, reflective individual, and a community member?" Table 5 illustrates one concept and the critical content categories for each of the five viewpoints.

The final step in writing curriculum content for the unit is to write curricular objectives. We use a Curricular Objectives Matrix form to record the objectives for the five categories of thinking about knowledge, and for communicating knowledge, creating knowledge, and reflecting on knowledge. Examples from this form are seen later in the examination of the unit, "Life, Liberty, and the Pursuit of Happiness."

Assessment

Design Principles

The assessment will:

- use a specific model of intelligence as defined by student outcomes for evaluation criteria.

- include an authentic performance task assessment.

- be multidimensional to reflect the individual learning styles of students.

- include numerous opportunities for self-assessment.

- include consistent opportunities for students to be familiarized with assessment procedures well in advance of their implementation.

Structure and Format

We assume that all our students are brilliant, but that they have different ways of showing their brilliance. Some are better at telling us what they know while others are better at writing it. So we offer a variety of ways for children to be evaluated. We begin by letting them show us the best they can be in the manner they choose and then teach them how to demonstrate their brilliance in other ways. When writing units of study (and when instructing our basic skills program), we designate specific

Table 5. Curriculum Content

SOCIOLOGICAL VIEWPOINT	SCIENTIFIC VIEWPOINT
Concept: Freedom is both a right and a responsibility.	*Concept:* Our future survival is dependent upon the intelligence of our decisions as to how and when to intervene in the natural evolution of the universe.
Content Areas: • Geography • History • Social/civic institutions • Cultural studies • Global citizenship	*Content Areas:* • Physical science • Life science • Earth science • Mathematics • Technology • General science

LINGUISTIC VIEWPOINT	AESTHETIC VIEWPOINT	PERSONAL VIEWPOINT
Concept: The power of great literature and oratory to influence choice and effect change makes the preservation of the freedom of speech essential to the well-being of democratic societies.	*Concept:* The images, emotions, and beauty produced through aesthetic communication are essential to the development of the intellect and the quality of human life.	*Concept:* Civilizations flourish in the celebration of their producers, contributors, problem solvers, and creators.
Content Areas: • Oral language • Written language • Systems/mass media • Systems/languages	*Content Areas:* • Visual arts • Performing arts • Cultural arts • Natural arts	*Content Areas:* • Intrapersonal • Interpersonal • Eminent people • Philosophy

assessment tools in a broad spectrum of categories, including (1) written test, curriculum based; (2) written test, standardized; (3) oral test/interview; (4) observed performance; (5) simple product; (6) spatial/visual; (7) kinesthetic; and (8) authentic performance task. (An example of a performance task outline is included in the "Life, Liberty, and Pursuit of Happiness" forms.)

Most of our assessment is part of our actual instruction, giving us a variety of settings in which to evaluate a child. We keep accordian-file portfolios on each child with each pocket designated for artifacts we collect from a different instructional setting. These settings include basic skills instruction, unit instruction, unit rehearsal, unit performance, and random anecdotal observations that we record on a roll of sticky labels, which we carry with us throughout the day.

We gather all this information together, and with additional information supplied by parents and the students themselves, we create a complete profile of each child.

Instructional Methods

Design Principles

Instructional methods will:

- accommodate a variety of learning styles and individual needs by offering a broad range of activities from teacher-directed to independent study.

- be individualized by pace, breadth, depth, level, and interest, as appropriate.

- include numerous opportunities for experiential learning.

- include numerous opportunities to examine open-ended questions.

- include numerous experiences using and examining current technologies.

- offer many opportunities to develop literacy in all forms of communication—linguistic, technological, aesthetic, and cultural.

- be directly linked to assessment through a carefully balanced program of basic skills instruction, unit instruction, unit rehearsal, and unit performance.

Structure and Format

The balanced program of basic skills instruction, unit instruction, unit rehearsal, and unit performance arose out of the current focus in education on performance skills. Before an actor can perform a role on stage, he must have basic instruction in acting, specific instruction from the director in the role he is going to play, a lot of rehearsal, and then, finally, he's ready for the performance. This metaphor also holds true for educating students in the performance of intellectual tasks.

Although much of our basic skills instruction happens through our units of study, we still conduct skill groups, as appropriate, to ensure a high level of academic excellence. In addition to the typical language arts and math skills, we consider thinking, technology, and cooperative problem-solving skills to be part of the basics as well.

All our instruction is multidimensional and includes activities in the following ten categories: (1) large group, teacher directed; (2) small group, teacher directed; (3) cooperative problem solving; (4) individual problem solving; (5) independent study; (6) technology; (7) mentors, presenters, field studies; (8) simulations and other games; (9) family studies; and (10) open-ended questions. This broad spectrum of activities reflects our intent to respond to the individual needs and learning styles of our students.

Our twenty hands-on learning centers are the place where students rehearse for the big performance task. The centers cover a broad knowledge base with such titles as Science Exploratorium, Art History, Change Makers, and Think Tank. The students are expected (with as much or as little adult guidance as is individually necessary) to complete their rehearsal contracts within a specified amount of time, choosing those activities at each center that demonstrate an advancement in their learning.

Scheduling

Design Principles

Scheduling will:

- accommodate the broad range of instructional methods and the diverse needs, learning styles, and abilities of students through simultaneously scheduled activities.

- build "pure time" into the schedule to reflect the value of task commitment and to nurture the motivation within children to learn.

- offer the students the opportunity to determine their own schedules when appropriate.

- be flexible enough to accommodate the "teachable moment."

- change each week to reflect specific educational goals and the immediate academic, emotional, social, and physical needs of students.

Structure and Format

We schedule simultaneous activities for most of the day. When a student is not engaged in an instructional group, silent reading, writer's workshop, or the like, he is working in the learning centers. While one teacher is interacting with students in centers, the other is instructing totally uninterrupted.

We have a weekly planning sheet on which we record every need that must be filled, from instructional to business to individual needs. Our weekly schedule sheet is a series of empty boxes that we fill from the needs list. We have found that we can meet an astounding number of individual needs when we stop looking at the schedule as little time blocks that repeat themselves each day and instead look at each week as a brand new forty hours to devote to whatever students might need.

Physical Environment

Design Principles

The physical environment will:

- include focal points and intimate spaces in the room that instantly engage children as they enter the door.

- include materials placed within students' reach and displayed to invite students to interact.

- include furniture arranged in such a way as to promote conversation in all areas except those requiring teacher-directed activities or quiet study.

- communicate that conversation is not just allowed but valued, by providing spaces for the express purpose of conversing.

- be designed to support a variety of simultaneous activities that can be individualized for student needs and interests.

- reflect the children who live there by providing adequate display space for their products.

- reinforce rules to reduce the need for teacher intervention.

Structure and Format

We have a very simple method for designing our physical environment. First, we list every interaction we can possibly imagine a child engaging in while learning, and then we provide appropriate spaces in the classroom. We make sure our noisy places and quiet ones aren't too close together. We provide places to be alone and to collaborate. We use space, color, light, and focal points to engage our students, and we design the classroom to be more like a home than an institution. After all, we are a family! Figure 1 is a map of our classroom and demonstrates just one way you can set up an interactive environment.

Nongraded Education **131**

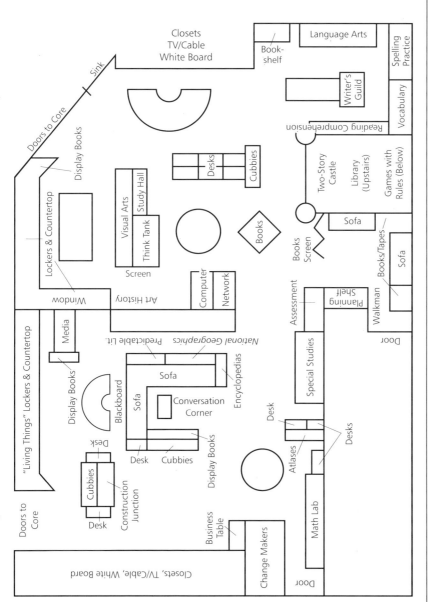

Figure 1. Classroom Map

Implementing the Change

Writing Units of Study

We have written several units of study over the past few years. For example, "A Picture's Worth a Thousand Words" was a study in communications and lifelong learning. "Bird's-Eye View" focused on global studies while "Time after Time" was a study of all the choices and changes throughout recorded history that brought us to the present.

The following excerpts are from a unit called, "Life, Liberty, and the Pursuit of Happiness." They trace one of the concepts from the unit all the way through from philosophy to action plan. I have included samples from the following pages of the unit: (1) the philosophy page (fig.3); (2) the curricular objectives matrix (table 6); (3) the performance task outline (fig. 4); (4) the instructional methods form (table 7); and (5) an action plan (table 8) that demonstrates how we put content, instruction, rehearsal, and assessment all together for implementation in the classroom. I have also included a full table of contents for unit writing so you can see where each excerpt fits into the whole system (see fig. 2).

Creating the Context

I didn't set out to teach a nongraded program in a team-taught, multiage, family-grouped classroom. I simply asked myself what the best possible setting would be for implementing an individualized, developmentally appropriate program. The answers were easy: I needed more hands, I needed more time, and I needed a more "authentic, real-world environment" in which to nurture learning. Our context gave me all these things and a few surprises as well.

I knew going in what some of the educational benefits would be, but I had no idea that we would evolve into such a powerful learning community. Our students have learned the art of relationships through multiple years with multiage friends. My partners and I have learned the art of collaboration by escaping the isolation of teaching alone. And our parents have learned to trust the teachers in whose care they place their children. That trust is so strong that they even went out and raised the money to send Betsy Ann and me to a national conference so that our program might be shared with others.

Teaching and learning for me have become more than a profession; they are a celebration of all that is possible. To think it all began with a little "whole-system" thinking and a lot of youthful idealism. Where it will end up, I couldn't begin to guess!

Figure 2. Table of Contents

    I. UNIT CONTENT
       A. Philosophy
       B. Concepts
       C. Current Issues/Questions
       D. Content Lists by Viewpoint
          1. Scientific
          2. Sociological
          3. Personal
          4. Aesthetic
          5. Linguistic
       E. Curricular Objectives Matrix

   II. UNIT PERFORMANCE ASSESSMENT
       A. Performance Task Outline
       B. Authentic Task Evaluation

   III. UNIT INSTRUCTION AND REHEARSAL
       A. Instructional Methods and Assessment
       B. Rehearsal Centers and Assessment

   IV. UNIT PLANNING AND SCHEDULING
       A. Action Plan
       B. Weekly Plans
       C. Weekly Schedule

   V. RESOURCES
       A. Authentic Task Student Guide
       B. Study Guides

Figure 3. Philosophy Page

> LIFE, LIBERTY, AND THE
> PURSUIT OF HAPPINESS
>
> Philosophy
> A child's relationship to the universe begins at birth. In the early years, this relationship consists largely of sensory experiences, familiar faces, and communicating physiological needs. As the child enters school, the universe extends to more complex intellectual and social structures that serve as a rehearsal for successful participation in our Democratic Society.
>
> "Life, Liberty, and the Pursuit of Happiness" invites children within the Learning Community to reflect upon the relationship between individuals and their expanding universe. The unit is designed to nurture the knowledge, skills, attitudes and behaviors of productive citizenship.
>
> Concept
> Our future survival is dependent on the intelligence of our decisions as to how and when to intervene in the natural evolution of the universe. (Scientific)
>
> Current Issue/Question
> On November 3, 1992, Americans will vote on a president, legislators, and a variety of issues. How will the decisions we make at the polls affect our future environmental wellness?

Table 6. Curricular Objectives Matrix

CRITICAL CONTENT	*Current Issue:* On November 3, 1992, Americans will vote on a president, legislators, and a variety of issues. How will the decisions we make at the polls affect environmental wellness? *Concept:* Our future survival is dependent on the intelligence of our decisions as to how and when to intervene in the natural evolution of the universe. *Content:* Environmental studies—global issues, environmental action groups, environmental conferences. Civics—U.S. government, elections.
FOUNDATIONS	Students will establish criteria for judging specific urban planning projects as seen from multiple viewpoints.
LOGIC	Students will construct "if/then" syllogisms about household causes of pollution.
CRITICAL THINKING	Students will formulate clarifying questions about presidential candidates' stands on specific environmental issues.
DECISION MAKING	Students will select their choice for president by stating an environmental goal, considering the options, and evaluating the options based on specific criteria.
STRATEGIC PROBLEM SOLVING	Students will devise a specific strategy for making a personal contribution to environmental wellness in their own home.
CREATE KNOWLEDGE	Students will demonstrate ideational fluency by brainstorming solutions to specific environmental crises.
COMMUNICATE KNOWLEDGE	Students will read to gain a broad knowledge base about environmental issues for effective speaking, listening, and writing. Students will present their views on the presidential candidates through written, verbal, technological, and visual communications.
REFLECT ON KNOWLEDGE	Students will clarify what they know relevant to a specific environmental issue and determine what information they need to access in order to vote in the upcoming elections.

Figure 4. Performance Task Outline

AUTHENTIC PERFORMANCE ASSESSMENT

A. Situation

Every four years the people of the United States elect a president. It is important to be informed about the issues. Then you can make an intelligent decision about who should be president. One campaign issue you will explore is the environmental well-being of our world.

1. Current Issue

   On November 3, 1992, Americans will vote on a president, legislators, and a variety of issues. How will the decisions we make at the polls affect our future environmental wellness?

2. Concepts

   Our future survival is dependent on the intelligence of our decisions as to how and when to intervene in the natural evolution of the universe.

3. Curricular Objectives

   Students will select their choice for president by stating an environmental goal, considering the options, and evaluating the options based upon specific criteria.

B. Performance Instructions

Choose a current environmental issue that concerns you. To get information, use at least four different sources (e.g., television, radio, magazines, books, newspapers, personal interviews, etc.). Make a speech that tells your classmates about this issue. Your speech may be done in writing, on an audiocassette, or on a videotape. Finally, decide which candidate's views are like yours. Make a campaign poster about that candidate. The poster should have a slogan for your issue, a quote from or about your candidate, along with cartoon artwork. Completing the guidebook will be a part of this task.

Table 7. Instructional Methods Form

LARGE GROUP TEACHER DIRECTED	• Buckminster Fuller Global Games • Compost Heap
SMALL GROUP TEACHER DIRECTED	• Research Teams • Sensory Scavenger Hunt • Braille Trail
COOPERATIVE PROBLEM SOLVING	• Presidential Debate Teams • Cafeteria Garbage • Feel a Tree • Rain Forest Purchase
INDIVIDUAL PROBLEM SOLVING	• Water Pollution Science Experiment • Water Cycles
INDEPENDENT STUDY	• Campaign Posters and Slogans • ACES Interview
MENTORS, PRESENTERS, FIELD STUDIES	• ACES Garbage Dig • Supermarket Scavenger Hunt • KSPN and Grass Roots
TECHNOLOGY	• Rain Forest Laser Disk • Kids Net/Acid Rain • Fax White House • Environmental Videos • Computer Network Pollution Solution
SIMULATIONS GAMES	• It's Your World-Urban Planning from Multiple Viewpoints • Flight to Mars
FAMILY PROJECTS	• Choosing a President
OPEN-ENDED QUESTIONS	• Question Grab Bag • What If's

Table 8. Action Plan

OBJECTIVES	INSTRUCTIONAL ACTIVITIES	INSTRUCITONAL ASSESSMENT	LEARNNG CENTERS	CENTER ASSESSMENT
Students will establish criteria for judging specific urban planning projects as seen from multiple viewpoints.	It's Your World Simulation	Anecdotal observations of role performance and related notes Written response on environmental viewpoints		
Students will analyze acid rain patterns in the United States and elsewhere.	National Geographic Kids Net Telecommunications Project	Scientist's report on team findings Experiment response sheets	Acidic plant experiment Water pollution experiments	Observation journals Graphs Response journals
Students will select their choice for president by stating an environmental goal, considering the options, evaluating the options, and then evaluating the options based upon specific criteria.	Television debates	Written guidebook Video speeches	Political cartooning	Product: Political poster on environment

References

Betts, F. 1992. How systems thinking applies to education. *Educational Leadership* 50 (November): 38–41

Burke, J. 1985. *The day the universe changed.* Washington, D.C.: PBS.

Goodlad, J., and R. Anderson. 1987. *The nongraded elementary school,* rev. ed. New York: Teachers College Press, Columbia University.

Hughes, M. 1989. *The educational master plan.* Also published as a Case Study (1991): Curriculum integration in the primary grades: A framework for excellence. *ASCD Curriculum Handbook.* Alexandria, Va.: Association for Supervision and Curriculum Development.

Wurman, R. S. 1989. *Information anxiety.* New York: Doubleday.

Recommended Reading

I recommend the following books, magazines, and articles for anyone interested in constructing a truly multiage classroom, not just a classroom with students of different ages. These resources contain material I agree *and* disagree with. However, I found all the resources to have thought-provoking information that is highly useful to the classroom teacher.

ASCD. 1991. *The curriculum handbook.* Alexandria, Va.: Association for Supervision and Curriculum Development.

Bellanca , J., A. Costa, and R. Fogarty, eds. 1992. *If minds matter.* Palatine, Ill.: IRI/Skylight Training and Publishing.

Benjamin, S. 1989. An ideascape for education: What futurists recommend. *Educational Leadership* 47 (September): 7.

Biggs, E., and R. MacLean. 1969. *Freedom to learn: An active learning approach to mathematics.* Reading, Mass.: Addison-Wesley.

Burns, M. 1976. *The book of think.* Boston: Little, Brown.

Caine, R. N., and G. Caine. 1991. *Making connections: Teaching and the human brain.* Alexandria, Va.: Association for Supervision and Curriculum Development.

Costa, A., ed. 1985. *Developing minds.* Alexandria, Va.: Association for Supervision and Curriculum Development.

Covey, S. 1989. *The 7 habits of highly effective people.* New York: Fireside Publishing.

Feldhusen, J., ed. 1985. *Towards excellence in gifted education.* Denver: Love Publishing Company.

Fogarty, R. 1991. *How to integrate the curricula.* Palatine, Ill.: IRI/Skylight Training and Publishing.

Forman, G., and S. Huschner. 1983. *The child's construction of knowledge: Piaget for teaching children.* Washington, D.C.: National Association for the Education of Young Children.

Jacobs, H., ed. 1989. *Interdisciplinary curriculum: Design and implementation.* Alexandria, Va.: Association for Supervision and Curriculum Development.

Marzano, R. 1992. *A different kind of classroom.* Alexandria, Va.: Association for Supervision and Curriculum Development.

Wiggins, G. 1989. The futility of trying to teach everything of importance. *Educational Leadership* 47 (November): 44.

This article reflects the state of Marilyn Hughes's classroom model when she left teaching in 1993. Since then, she has substantially developed the model, adding authentic assessment, portfolios, learner outcomes, a full hierarchy of thinking skills, and an updated change process. For further information, please write the author at 1425 Silverking Dr., Aspen, CO 81611.

Instructional Strategies in a Multiage Primary Classroom

Kathy Magee

> The object of teaching a child is to enable him to get along without his teacher.
>
> —Elbert Hubbard

"Hey! That big kid over there let me borrow his crayons," the youngest girl announced to her group the first day of school in my multiage class of six-, seven-, and eight-year-old students. A thought flashed through my mind when I heard this, "What am I doing here? Why did I volunteer to teach a multiage class?" I remembered that first graders wet their pants and cry the first day of school—or so I had been told.

I thought I could be successful teaching a multiage class. I had done my homework; I had read the research, visited multiage classes in Las Vegas and Tucson, and talked to many multiage teachers. Philosophically, the concept of a multiage classroom paralleled my beliefs about child development and learning.

My previous teaching experience consisted of fourth grade, third grade, a combination second-third grade, and for the past twenty years, second grade. I had always kidded my principal that if he moved me to first grade, I was going to retire because of the rumors I had heard about first grade students. However, to my relief, retiring was no longer necessary. I did make it through that first day! And to my surprise, no one cried and no one wet his or her pants.

After teaching multiage for a few years, I have concluded it is simply a new mindset. That first year there were certainly ups and downs, but I view my classroom as a community of learners—both students *and* teacher. I have taught a combination second-third grade class. Such a class is philosophically different from a multiage class. In my multiage class, the students are not segregated by grade level and grade level curriculum. When planning experiences for my students, I do not think in terms of grade level, but in terms of what each individual student can do and what he or she needs to accomplish along his or her developmental and curricular continuum. Each child must be allowed to move at a rate suitable to individual developmental needs.

> Terminology is a big factor in discussions with parents and teachers.

I have decided, after teaching a multiage class, that terminology is a big factor in discussions with parents and teachers. Clarification of terms is necessary for all who are unfamiliar with a different type of class configuration. For instance, when our school decided that some classes would be multiage, we used the term *nongraded* in our discussions with parents. Parents thought at the beginning of the dialogue that we were talking about not giving grades on report cards. We then changed the term to *multiage,* which is really a more accurate description of the class.

I refer to my students as *youngers* and *olders* rather than first and second graders—olders meaning those at a higher developmental level, regardless of age. This is to help me think in terms of individual students and their developmental levels rather than in grade level terms. I emphasize my terminology of youngers and olders to the parents of my students because I want them to view their child as moving along a developmental continuum and not stereotype them as a first or second grader.

When someone asks me what I teach, I say, "I teach six-, seven-, and eight-year-olds." Invariably, that person will ask what subject area I teach at the junior high or middle school level. They do not hear my last two words—"year-olds"—but focus only on "six, seven, and eight." People are not accustomed to hearing a teacher refer to the grade level they teach by age. This is a seventy-year tradition that is hard to break.

My multiage classroom has no social distinctions. The students function as a class. They attend specials, such as art, music, library, and physical education, as a group. The social climate of the classroom is developed at the beginning of the year, just as in a single grade, but much more quickly.

Classroom Organization

Our multiage classes are set up so that half of the students return to the same teacher the next year and a new group of six-year-olds comes in. The beginning of the new school year is wonderful because half the class already knows the teacher, the routines, and the rules. I can begin teaching right away. When I open my door a constant buzzing can be heard. The returning students are telling the new students the rules and how to behave and where the materials are located. This year I overheard a returning student telling new students, "Don't worry! Mrs. Magee is really nice. She doesn't yell at you ever. She only gets mad if you fight on the playground or throw rocks."

I arranged my class at the beginning of the year by placing older students beside younger students in a group of four desks around the room. Desks remain this way for a month. The students name their group, make a construction paper cylinder that has the group name and a picture on it, and pass the cylinder to designate a leader of the group each day. During the year, desks are changed monthly. At the first of the month, each student draws a ticket with a group name on it and moves to that area of the classroom. A student cannot stay in the same group for more than two months in a row. This mixes the students and allows them to work with and get to know other students. My students really look forward to this and keep me on my toes in case I forget to have them pick their ticket the first day of the month.

Older students provide a model for younger students. During the first month of school I do many, many activities that require the students to work with people who sit next to them, across from them, catty-corner from them, or as a group of four. For the remainder of the year, activities that require cooperation and working together occur within the group. I think the activities I do the first month are probably most important in creating an atmosphere of trust and concern for each other, and in helping students to view themselves as a class and not as first and second graders. Leadership skills, confidence, and decision making are fostered in all students through these activities.

Each student's strengths become well known and acknowledged by the class regardless of age. During our study of space, the youngest student in the class built the best mission control area from cardboard boxes. The detail he put into this was truly amazing; there were cardboard levers that moved and numerous detailed, colored dials to read. When it was time for our "Rocket to and Landing on the Moon" mission simulation, the students unanimously agreed that he should be the head of mission control, do the countdown, and tell them when it was time to walk on the moon. The mission was very successful! (This student is still an emerging reader and will be spending three years with me instead of the usual two because of his developmental level.)

> *I think the activities I do the first month are probably most important in creating an atmosphere of trust.*

Themes

The recent research into how the brain works gives educators new understanding as to the most effective and meaningful ways to teach children. Research shows that the brain is designed to deal with confusion and requires a great deal of meaningful input in order to detect patterns and make meaningful connections. The brain does not learn in sequential, logical units. An integrated curriculum that is not fragmented into subject areas is, therefore, the most efficient and effective way for children to learn.

Student-generated themes and teacher-chosen themes are the focal point for integrated instruction in my classroom. I brainstorm with the students what they would like to study. This generated list of interests and topics can be added to at any time by any student throughout the year. Students vote on the theme. After the theme is chosen, my work really begins. The research I do to find books and materials to support their choice is very time consuming. I find, though, that student interests and choice give them a feeling of being a part of what is being taught. Their interest in school, reading, and learning makes my extra efforts worthwhile. What they learn is truly amazing!

The following is an example of such learning: A parent told my principal about a shopping trip to the mall during the summer with her daughter (a younger student of mine). They saw some art prints. Jenna immediately told her mother that the painting was Monet's *Water Lilies* and went into a monologue about Monet's life and his painting techniques. She also informed her mother that he painted *Water Lilies* more than once and that each time the lilies got "fuzzier." Her mother walked over to check the artist's name and was flabbergasted to find her daughter was correct. This child was still an emerging reader at the end of her first year of full-day instruction (a first grader)!

> *"Reading to, reading with, and reading by" students is a strategy I use daily.*

I begin any theme by using the KWL strategy (Ogle 1986). We brainstorm what we **know** about the topic, what we **want** to know, and, at the end of the theme, what we have **learned**. Last year during a study of art about which I knew nothing, my six-, seven-, and eight-year-old students wanted to know many things: "What makes a great piece of art?" (I wish I knew the answer to that one—I would be rich!) "How do you become an artist?" "What tools does an artist use?" and other interesting questions.

Literacy Strategies

The New Zealand literacy model of "reading to, reading with, and reading by" students is a strategy I use daily. *Reading to* students is a shared reading that I use with my whole class. A discussion of what, how, or why the author wrote the way he or she did follows the reading with everyone participating. Sometimes the students respond to the shared reading in writing, illustrations, or drama.

All students are comfortable participating at their level in thematic study. There are certain key strategies that I use in all themes. I will discuss these strategies and explain how I applied them during our art theme. This model may be adapted to any theme.

I was at a distinct disadvantage during our art theme because most of the art books I found were written at an adult level. I brought them into class, though, so the students could look at pictures of works by famous artists, and some of my students read parts of the book that interested them. I did find an upper elementary series about famous artists that I read to my students. The students found it fascinating to figure out the age of the artists at the time of death. They were surprised that Leonardo da Vinci and Monet were so old and that Vincent van Gogh was so young. They were absolutely amazed that van Gogh cut off his ear, and that medical authorities now believe he may have had Minear Disease, a constant ringing in the ear. We discovered that Cézanne used distinctive shapes, such as the cube, in his paintings and that he had a parrot that said, "Cézanne is a great artist." We then wrote about the most interesting, appealing parts of each artist's life.

The students had a choice of writing their own stories about the artist or writing the information as a group. Some of my developmental olders wrote their own biographies of the artists. For each artist we studied (da Vinci, van Gogh, Cézanne, Calder, Picasso, O'Keeffe, Monet), we created a painting or watercolor in the style of that artist. The biographies of the artists' lives, written either by groups or individuals, were then copied by each student. Each student also wrote an autobiography as if he or she were a famous artist. The student created a drawing or painting in his or her own style. Then, the student's pictures, biographies, and autobiographies were bound together in individual books. Students shared their books with students in other classes.

Since I could not find suitable books about artists for most of my students to read during our art theme, I chose illustrators of children's books to focus on for the *reading with* part of the literacy strategy. In this part, students are guided through reading with a small group of children. At the beginning of the year, I usually group developmental youngers together and developmental olders together into about four groups by ability; however, these groups are flexible and change often. The focus of all *reading with* groups is on strategies that good readers use to figure out unknown words: saying a word and reading to the end of the sentence to determine the meaning of the sentence, then going back and rereading the sentence to figure out the word; putting in a word that makes sense and begins the way the unknown word does, etc.

Soon, some of my *reading with* groups begin to pair youngers and olders. When we come to group, we may read part of the book or story and discuss it, or we may discuss the book or story and only read the parts that justify the answers to questions, either the students' or the teacher's. The purpose of *reading with* students is the teacher-directed instruction of strategies good readers use.

During our art theme, we read almost all of the books written by Leo Lionni, Eric Carle, and Tomie de Paola. I obtained multiple copies of many of these books. We discussed the illustrators' style and what materials we thought they used to illustrate their books. We discussed their writing styles, how stories by the same author/illustrator were the same or different, and how the authors differed from each other. I read to them about their lives. We made pictures and tried to imitate their styles. We made a reproduction of *Little Blue, Little Yellow* by Leo Lionni. Finally, each child wrote his or her own story.

> *Students freely bring their individual experiences and developmental level to the activity.*

During our de Paola study, each student had a different book to read and did a "book report" focusing on the elements of story setting, character(s), problem, solution. The students made mobiles after we read *Oliver Button Is a Sissy*. Each four-by-four-inch square of construction paper contained a picture and at least one sentence retelling the story. The squares were then hooked together with yarn. I often use this mobile activity with different themes. Students freely bring their individual experiences and developmental level to the activity.

I often give my students choices when doing a book activity such as the above. After an activity has been introduced, modeled, and completed, it becomes one of the choices the students have for a book activity. They can construct a mobile, write a play to dramatize a story, write a book, or make a story map, which is a map of sequenced drawings students use to retell the story. Some choose to construct a cube made of tag board that contains drawings on each side retelling the story, and can be used in sequencing and oral language activities. These are some of the activities that I use that can be stretched to span the age levels, allowing each student to succeed at his or her own level. They can write and/or draw at individual levels or can dictate to the teacher. The students share their creations as a culminating activity.

I teach students specific skills, not in isolation, but through the use of poems. I was able to find some poems about art and color. We kept a word bank of "art" words. (I do this for each theme.) These poems and words form the basis for specific skill instruction, including spelling.

The flexible skill groups are based on student needs. Needs are determined from observation, running records, and individual conferences. It is crucial for the teacher to be familiar with the curriculum and developmental readiness of the students when planning skill groups. Phonetic rules that apply more than 70 percent of the time are stressed. These skills, taught in ten- to fifteen-minute sessions, become strategies for students to use independently in context.

> **Needs are determined from observation.**

A poem is introduced once a week and is usually duplicated for the students to put into their poetry books and illustrate at the beginning of the following week. I decide what skill each poem can be used for (e.g., contractions, compound words, rhyming words that are spelled the same at the end or spelled differently—as in bears and stairs—long vowels, short vowels, etc. After reading and discussing the poem for a couple of days to familiarize the students with it, I talk about the skill and point out words in the poem that apply to that skill. We may begin a word list of "ar" words, if that is the skill a group is working on. We then go on a hunt for "ar" words to add to our list. The students find additional words in their poetry books, classroom books, books they are reading, books they have at home, and from their parents.

The students make their lists, and they add to the class list in pencil so I can check the spelling. Then they go over their words in marker. I put these words on file cards to be used by the students for sorting and resorting as a center activity. Students that need teaching of that skill more than others work with a buddy the following week to read the words and do more sorting. The words are available to alphabetize, put into sentences, etc. The lists are posted in the room or bound together in a book that is placed in our classroom library, and then students can consult this when they are writing or reading.

I always ask the students what observations they can make about the poem. They often point out the rhyming words, periods, commas, contractions, compound words, patterning in the lines, repeated words, etc., that we have already discussed. They are very aware of the skills and can apply them.

"By-the-way teaching," a phrase a colleague of mine coined, is constantly occurring. Students are exposed to and introduced to skills, terms, vocabulary, and concepts as an aside in context when I say, "Oh! By the way, this is called . . . ." This strategy begins the first day of school and continues throughout the year. I think exposing students to as much as possible in context is critical. Mastery is not always essential at the moment, but if the child is making connections and needs the information he is exposed to, it will become something he can use or apply. If the student was not ready to learn, at least he was exposed to it, and perhaps the next time it comes up he will have the prior knowledge and be ready to build on it. Very seldom do we learn things the first time; repetition is part of the learning process.

Exposing students to as much as possible in context is critical.

For instance, during our space theme we discussed the concept of day and night. Time zones were a natural "by-the-way" topic in this discussion because we were working on telling time. I gave the students a copy of a world map divided into time zones. We discussed the International Date Line and the fact that when I went to New Zealand, I left on Friday and arrived in New Zealand on Sunday. I was aware that some of my students were not ready for this concept, but others had some understanding.

After the discussion, one of my olders, Bryan, announced, "There really are twenty-four hours in a day because I counted the time zones and there are twenty-four time zones on the world map." The next day my youngest, Michael, came up and showed me a smaller version of the time zone map he found in a book. He showed me the International Date Line and said, "Here is the line you go across where the day changes." Each student took something from that lesson at his own level!

Another strategy is sustained silent reading (SSR). This is the *reading by* part of the literacy strategy. It allows students specific time to practice reading independently and to apply the strategies learned. They choose their own books to read for ten to fifteen minutes each day.

The book box is an important part of reading by students. I picked this idea up when I was in New Zealand for two weeks at Westmere Primary School in Auckland. A book box is a box shared by two students who are at approximately the same stage of reading development. I use cereal boxes or laundry detergent boxes that the students bring in. I ask a parent to cut one edge on an angle so it looks like a magazine holder and to cover it in contact paper. Labels with the partners' names are put on the box. The box contains, if available, duplicate copies of two to four different books that the partners have read in group; two to four books a little below their level; and two to four books a little above their level. Books are changed in the book box every two to three weeks. The book boxes can be a center activity students can share with their partners or use by themselves, or they can be used during the SSR time. The purpose is to provide students with books to practice reading independently. Partners change when the need arises.

I have individual reading conferences daily with my students. These conferences focus on story structure, character development, author's language, vocabulary, etc. My olders choose their own books from a wide assortment. The books go home daily for home reading.

As Kyle said during a conference, "Let me tell you about the black mamba and this snake that has two-inch fangs. Even my dad couldn't believe it!" He was reading a book called *Exploring Poisonous Creatures* that intrigued him. It would not have been appropriate for Erin, who is reading *Superfudge* and is easily frightened by reading about snakes. Talking with students individually about what they are reading and hearing them express their opinions is something the students and I enjoy.

I also conference with my younger students every day to check on their progress, their home reading, and to see if they are employing the strategies that they have been introduced to in guided reading. We talk about what they read at home the night before, the story structure, the main character, and possible character traits. They also read a page or two for me orally.

Developmentally younger students have a choice of teacher-selected books with appropriate text for their stage of reading. I choose from the New Zealand Ready to Read books that we recently ordered, the Wright Group Storybox levels, the Mercer Mayer books, the beginning Dr. Seuss books, and other books on their level.

Talking with students individually about what they are reading is something the students and I enjoy.

In March, Travis, a younger, wanted chapter books. I gave him many of the beginning chapter books such as the Little Bear books, *Turtle Spring,* and some of the Patricia Reilly Giff books. He was very pleased. Michael, on the other hand, is still telling the story from the pictures of the books he reads. Debra wanted to read *Nate the Great.* It was a little difficult for her, but her desire was so great that I let her try it. She read the first twenty-four pages. During our conference time, I asked her if she wanted to finish it. I told her that sometimes I do not always finish a book that I begin reading. If she wanted to read another book and not finish *Nate the Great,* that was all right. She traded it for another book that was more on her level, but she did successfully complete *Nate the Great* later in the year.

The conferences take place the first half hour to forty-five minutes every morning. Students are at centers during this time or engaged in theme-related activities. I keep track of the books my students read on individual file cards. I note the date of the conference, what we discussed, their responses, the book they are reading, and its page count. If the child forgets his or her book, I note that also. I enter this information in my computer every week or two. It is available then to print out and enclose in the report cards that go home to parents so they are aware of their child's accomplishments.

I emphasize to parents at the beginning of the year at Back-to-School Night the importance of reading to and with their children. The homework every night is for each child to read fifteen minutes, or to be read to—especially at the beginning of the year for the youngers. Each week I send home a weekly reading note along with a progress report for each child. On the reading note is a space for time read each day and the parents' signatures. This is turned in every week for me to record. Having parents involved in promoting their child's reading is essential to any reading program.

Writing to, with, and by students is also an integral part of my literacy program. Students write almost daily in many forms: thank you cards and letters, letters to students in other states and countries, stories that are turned into published books and finished pieces, stories that are shared orally, reflective pieces about an experience we all had or what we have learned from a theme study, lists, reactions to reading a piece of literature, reactions to or a story about a piece of artwork, a drawing that the child has done. There is always something to write about and share with others.

During our space theme, I ordered a space shuttle with money given to us by our PTA. The shuttle was a large plastic bubble inflated by using a large fan. I obtained many cardboard boxes and after reading, research, and looking at various pictures, some of the students created the mission control while others created the inside instrumentation of the shuttle. Each student contributed to the project and constructed a section of the whole. The day of our "explorer mission," some of the students chose to be mission control officers and others were shuttle astronauts who "walked in space" to fix a broken satellite. There was no script for this; the language they used in acting out the shuttle mission demonstrated a sophisticated understanding of space. I videotaped the mission and combined it with the "moon mission" enactment done earlier in our study of rockets. The tape was sent home on a rotation basis for parents to view. My students developed oral language vocabulary worthy of any astronaut!

The questioning techniques I use span the hierarchy. Literal, inferential, creative, and critical questions are in constant use in large-group, small-group, and individual situations. I discuss different kinds of questions with students and encourage them to ask questions and to think about the kinds of questions they are asking when listening to a story or a piece of writing read by another student or myself. I constantly ask my students to explain their thinking, either orally or in writing.

Open-ended interest areas for exploration and discovery are also part of the day. Various games and activities are taught to the students so they can work independently. I have a puzzle/game center; a construction center with wooden blocks, Lincoln logs, flexi blocks, gears, and any other materials I can find; a computer center; a news center that contains a microphone, a U.S. map, a weather pocket chart, and other news materials; a math center that contains math manipulatives; a writing center; and a science center that may have an experiment or something of interest for the students to handle, read, and/or write about. These centers are often used in the morning while I am doing individualized reading.

Open-ended interest areas for exploration and discovery are also part of the day.

Spelling is integrated into my literacy program. I have been using *Spelling through Phonics* by Robert and Marlene McCracken for spelling and phonetic instruction with my students at different levels. To teach the nonphonetic words (such as the Dolch list), I use a strategy developed by Pat Cunningham. Each week I select ten or fewer words, depending on my group, from the Dolch and other lists, then write them on five-by-eight-inch file cards. I post the cards on the wall in alphabetical order with pushpins. (Pushpins make it easy to rearrange the added words when putting them in alphabetical order.) Students read the words orally during direct instruction. Then, after discussion and use of the words in sentences, I dictate any ten of the words. I tend to focus on the real toughies: because, laugh, they, what, where, when, why, about . . . . This spelling "test" is done daily. The students can look at the posted words and spell each word by copying from the word cards or by spelling without looking, which is the goal. After the ten words have been dictated, one student, acting as the teacher, asks a classmate to identify a word. The acting teacher then points to the word and spells the word orally. Then the children point to the word on their papers and spell the word correctly. The paper handed in should have each word spelled correctly. The students are working on proofreading, spelling, alphabetical order, and sight vocabulary. The words are there for them to refer to when they are writing independently.

I find this approach to teaching the "glue words," as Dr. Ray Reutzel from BYU calls them, a very workable and beneficial way to teach spelling words students need. Dictating a word like "because" ten days in a row really helps a student spell the word accurately without looking and use it successfully in writing.

Computer Use

Recently, I received a grant to buy a modem and software for a computer at school so my students can e-mail and telecommunicate with students around the world. They are fascinated by this. We have been "talking" via computer with a university student in Bristol, England. To watch the students read what he is typing onto our screen and predict the finished words or the entire answer to their question is exciting. Bryan, one of my olders, asked "our student" if he has a dirt bike. He typed back, "Are you talking about an off-the-road motorbike?" Bryan was surprised that they did not call them "dirt bikes" in England. Ben, one of my youngers, wanted to know, "Do you eat a lot of fish in England?" When I asked him why he would ask the question, Ben said, "Because England is an island, so I think they probably do a lot of fishing in the ocean." Our friend typed back, "Yes, people eat a lot of fish, but I don't like fish! Does Ben like fish?" Ben wrinkled up his nose and said "No!" which I typed in response. My students are not directly "talking" yet because of the typing involved, but they brainstorm the questions and respond orally while I type.

They do, however, go to the computer and type in the commands to telnet to the University of Michigan to get the weather forecast for our area, for a city in the United States, and for an international city that we track for a month. They print this on a daily basis and bring it into the classroom to share during our calendar time. Timothy, one of my gifted students, goes with another student whose weekly job is to bring back the most current weather conditions from the computer. They love this! Next year my returning students will already be trained, so they can teach the new students. I won't have to!

I also use the computer lab for word processing. I think it is easier for my students to type their unedited stories from rough draft into the computer. The individual students and I then edit and correct the drafts before they are printed, or we print and then we edit, and go back to the computer for a final draft. I only do this for pieces that are taken to publication. My students tend to persevere when rewriting with paper and pencil is kept to a minimum. Sometimes I may even type a piece for them on the computer for a quickly finished product.

They are beginning to see the computer as a tool for information gathering and for learning.

There are many uses for the computer other than as a glorified workbook. Although I have some good programs that my students use, I want them to be aware of the potential of computers and to think when they use them, not look at them as upgraded, expensive Nintendo machines. They are beginning to see the computer as a tool for information gathering and for learning.

Parent Questions

At our school, parents have a choice of single-age or multiage classes. We have at the present nine multiage classes, four first grade classes, and four second grade classes.

Parents often ask, "Will my older child be challenged?" This also concerned me in the beginning. I find, though, that the older child is challenged by the span of materials I use to teach the themes. When searching for materials, I check out books from our school library and the public library. If I can't find enough books on a certain topic, I go to the university curriculum and materials center. I search for books at all levels. When we were exploring our Egypt theme, many of the books I found were on a high level. The fluent readers were able to use many of them.

I was particularly worried about an older student named Jonathan. He came to me reading at a sixth grade level, according to the Slossen word list test that I gave him at the beginning of the year. I was worried that he would not progress at least a year on the Slossen, which is my goal for each of my students. But, at the parent-teacher conference held during the first nine weeks I showed his parents his improvement from a 6.0 to a 6.4. I was pleased! His parents were also pleased, but they were more concerned with his social growth. They told me that the year before, when he was in first grade, he had isolated himself and spent his whole day in class reading. He completely ignored what was going on in his class. I had no idea that he had behaved that way.

In our class he seemed interested and actively involved in what we were doing. In fact, he was especially considerate of the youngers in our class. Often, Jonathan volunteered to carry the large garbage sacks for younger classmates. The sacks contained big, class-made books that students were taking home for the evening to share with their parents. He carried the book bag to the bus for Kristy so "she [wouldn't] trip on it getting on the bus," or out to the car for Brandi, or to the bike rack for Bryan. His parents were very happy that he was interacting and showing care and concern for his classmates. Jonathan made tremendous progress in social growth and went on to third grade reading at a high school level as indicated by the Slossen word test. He was a very positive role model and a leader in our classroom.

The older children offer a positive role model and frequently encourage the younger children.

"Will my younger child learn to read?" is a concern of some parents. Younger-aged students are not intimidated by the older-aged students and do learn to read. The older children offer a positive role model and frequently encourage and tell the younger children what a good job they are doing. I have paired "reading with" children of different developmental stages so they could read to each other, sometimes the same text, sometimes different texts. At other times, children share with each other orally what they are reading. Once I overheard Jessica, an older child, telling Shauna, a younger child, "You're doing great! I read that same book last year that you are reading." Younger students have a newfound support in the multiage class. If younger children are ready to read, they will definitely learn to read.

Assessment

Finally, how do I know if these strategies are effective and my students are learning? To me, assessment and evaluation are not synonymous.

Assessment is gathering information about a child. This is done daily in some manner. It is ongoing and focuses on what the child can do and what the child needs next to enhance his learning and keep him moving forward. Evaluation occurs when I place judgment on the information I have collected.

I use many instruments, forms, and anecdotal notes to gather information about my students. I keep an individual student folder for the information I've gathered. Each nine weeks I give all my students the Slossen word test. It is stapled into the folder with the latest results on top. I am not as interested in a student's score as I am in seeing a student make progress. When I share the results with parents, I always tell them that this is just one of many lists available and that on this particular list the student scored at this level. On another test the score could be different. I stress that I am looking for improvement, not a particular score. At the beginning and the end of the year, I give children that are at an earlier stage of development the Concepts of Print test developed by Marie Clay for emerging readers. I also use her alphabet identification test.

> *I am not as interested in a student's score as I am in seeing a student make progress.*

I use running records at the beginning of the year for all my students. The running record is administered as part of a reading conference at least every two weeks for my developmental olders and every week for my developmental youngers during the first three or four months of school. By February or March I do a running record every month on most of the students unless a student is having particular difficulty. In that case, I monitor more closely.

The students enjoy reading and retelling a part of a text or the whole text into a tape recorder. About once a month they record a prepared text they selected. This is a record for the parents that I send home at the end of the year so they can hear the improvement in their child's reading. Sometimes I send the tape and a tape recorder home once a month for the child to share with parents. My students love that!

Anecdotal notes are another facet of my assessment program. I use stick-on labels on a clipboard. Each morning I select five students to focus on for the day. I write the student's name and the date at the top of a label. I jot down any observation I make about that student during the day. Sometimes I am focusing on a particular skill for the week, and I note observations on how well the students are applying that particular skill. At the end of the day, I stick the label to a blank piece of paper that is in each student's folder. For instance, on November 13, I made this observation about an older student, Suzi: "in her reading she 'mispronounced' *poked* and *woke;* work on o_e." This skill became a mini-lesson for Suzi, Jason, Rebecca, Kristy, and Brandi. On December 10, I wrote that Suzi "read *broke* and other words that ended with silent *e* with no trouble."

> **Learning logs are another type of assessment used to gather information about students.**

For Kyle I wrote "September 11, getting more involved and participated positively at centers with quieter voice"; "September 17, happy, improved attention span"; "September 24, had trouble focusing on his book during SSR time. Spoke with Kyle about appropriate reading behavior during SSR"; "October 18, attention span is now consistent and able to focus and concentrate in all areas."

These are examples of the kinds of notes I write on the labels, and the activities or actions taken for appropriate mini-lessons or behavior conferences.

Learning logs are another type of assessment used to gather information about students. I use one log for all subjects because I find it easier for my students to keep track of one log rather than one in each area. Asking students to write and explain their thinking is very enlightening and gives me insight into their thinking processes and their level of understanding in a particular area.

To assess writing, I collect rough drafts and put them in each student's folder. When a rough draft, or "sloppy copy," is going to be published, I first have my students share it with at least three other students. The student editor listens to the author read the story and asks questions to clarify unclear areas in the story. The editor helps the author add to the story to make it clearer. The editor and author then look for capitals at the beginning of sentences and periods at the end of sentences. Then each word is checked for spelling. A questionable word is circled, and different resources are consulted for the correct spelling.

The student next brings the copy to me and we conference. We discuss story elements that authors use and assess the story. We then look to make sure that all appropriate capitals and periods are included and words are spelled correctly. In New Zealand, I observed teachers using "writing ticks" (check marks) for capital letters, periods, and correct letters in a word. The ticks are checked under each correct item. Teachers also insert anything needed in a published copy. I find this works very well as an assessment tool for determining what needs to be taught in mini-lessons, and also as a record of what the student can do. The students like it because all the ticks indicate something that is correct and that they know. Comparing "sloppy copies" each nine weeks provides me with an evaluation of each student's writing development.

I also use various writing, reading, and math checklists. I find the most beneficial forms, however, are those that I modify to fit my situation and that correspond to our county and state curriculum. They also must be easy and quick to use.

Conclusion

I truly believe that all the students I have taught are better learners as a result of being in a multiage class. A knowledge of the developmental levels of students and curriculum is a critical aspect for the teacher of a multiage class. I am responsible for a broad curriculum to meet the diverse needs and abilities of my students.

A multiage classroom is a successful class configuration when you consider learning as a continuous progression, a process, a classroom of mixed ages where the focus is on the students' diverse needs. When teaching a single grade level, I taught a packaged curriculum to all students, whether or not they needed it or were able to grasp it. In multiage, the focus is on the individual student and where he or she needs to go. The curriculum becomes a road map to learning and not an end in itself.

Multiage classes benefit all students—high, low, and in between. It is a structured environment that fosters independence, thinking, and tolerance. It emphasizes working together with others who are different in age and ability. As students learn from each other, they accept individual differences and are willing to help each other. They solve problems together—academic and social—and become thinking students with opinions. Multiage classrooms more nearly replicate the real world. After all, where else in this world are we segregated by age?

References

Buchanan, E. 1989. *Spelling for whole language classrooms.* Katonah, N.Y.: Richard Owens Publishers.

Butler, A., and J. Turbill. 1987. *Toward a reading-writing classroom.* Portsmouth, N.H.: Heinemann.

Clay, M. M. 1991. *Becoming literate: The construction of inner control.* Portsmouth, N.H.: Heinemann.

———. 1993a. *An observation survey of early literacy achievement.* Portsmouth, N.H.: Heinemann.

———. 1993b. *Reading recovery: A guidebook for teachers in training.* Portsmouth, N.H.: Heinemann.

Crafton, L. K. 1991. *Whole language: Getting started . . . Moving forward.* Portsmouth, N.H.: Heinemann.

Eggleton, J. 1990. *Whole language evaluation: Reading, writing and spelling for the primary grades.* Bothell, Wash.: The Write Group.

Gentry, J. R. 1987. *Spel . . . Is a four-letter word.* Portsmouth, N.H.: Heinemann.

Johnson, T. D., and D. R. Louis. 1987. *Literacy through literature.* Portsmouth, N.H.: Heinemann.

———. 1990. *Bring it all together: A program for literacy.* Portsmouth, N.H.: Heinemann.

Learning Media. 1985. *Reading in junior classes.* Wellington, New Zealand: Ministry of Education.

———. 1988. *Books for junior classes.* Wellington, New Zealand: Ministry of Education.

———. 1992. *Dancing with the pen: The learner as a writer.* Wellington, New Zealand: Ministry of Education.

Mooney, M. 1988a. *Developing life-long readers.* Katonah, N.Y.: Richard C. Owens Publishers.

———. 1988b. *Reading to, with, and by children,* Katonah, N.Y.: Richard C. Owens Publishers.

Ogle, D. 1986. K-W-L group instruction strategy. In *Teaching techniques as thinking* (teleconference resource guide), edited by I. A. Palinesar, D. Ogle, B. Jones, and E. Carr. Alexandria, Va.: Association for Supervision and Curriculum Development.

Routman, R. 1988. *Transitions: From literature to literacy.* Portsmouth, N.H.: Heinemann.

———. 1991. *Invitations: Changing as teachers and learners K–12.* Portsmouth, N.H.: Heinemann.

Schwartz, S., and M. Pollishuke. 1990. *Creating the child-centered classroom.* Toronto: Stoddart Publishing.

Technology for Teaching and Learning

Frank Betts

> We have three information instruments in the home—the telephone, the television, and the computer—and they are all coming together to communicate on a full service network. The time is not far off when you will be answering the television and watching your telephone.
>
> —Raymond W. Smith
> CEO, Bell Atlantic

What is technology? Quite simply technology is any tool designed to fulfill a purpose. It is something to be *used* by someone—it should always be the servant, never the master. The power of technology is twofold. First, it has the potential to extend the ability of the teacher, student, or administrator to do work. Secondly, it transforms the very nature of the work itself.

In virtually every one of the dozens of schools I have visited, technology is underutilized because its transformative nature has not been recognized. Many technology planners are charging into the future with their eyes firmly fixed on the past. This leads to doing more of what we've always done. When planners and administrators work from this perspective, technology will only help us to do more of the same things faster, and often in a more costly way. The application of technology within a weak process only magnifies its flaws. The chief benefits of technology are derived from its innate capacity to permit us to do things differently—that is, to transform the nature of work, including the ways we teach and learn. To realize the benefits of technology requires the most difficult kinds of change—change in the organizational culture and individual attitudes.

Since this is not intended to be a discussion of the dynamics of organizational change, this article proceeds on the assumption that, having been warned, you will take the appropriate steps to prepare your faculty and staff. The balance of the article includes criteria for selecting technologies, suggested applications, a brief case study, and a technology wish list, which should be used with caution because of the rapidity with which technologies are changing.

Selecting an Appropriate Technology

Workability, Feasibility, and Social Acceptability

Since all technologies are, by definition, designed to fulfill a specific function, the choice of technologies for a nongraded school should be driven by the function to be performed; as in architecture, form follows function. The first criteria for selecting an appropriate technology is, therefore, workability—"Does it work?" If used, will it help get the job done?

Assuming the technology is workable, the second criteria is feasibility—"Does the prospective user have access to the technology and the skill to use it?" Many technologies are workable but are not feasible for everyone, either because they are too costly, require knowledge and skills not available to the potential user, or the demand for the technology exceeds the supply. At the moment, using a Macintosh Powerbook computer to write this article is workable, but not feasible. Although the product exists and I have the money, time, and skill needed, demand exceeds supply, so I am still waiting for the computer to be delivered; hence, it is not a feasible technology for writing this article.

Even after I have obtained a workable and feasible technological solution, it must be judged by a third criterion—"Is it socially acceptable?" For example, the use of a calculator to aid in teaching mathematics in some schools still is not socially acceptable, although it has long been established as being both workable and feasible.

These three criteria—*workability, feasibility,* and *social acceptability*—are used to determine which technologies are appropriate to a particular task. They are a necessary first step, but not sufficient for selecting the single, most appropriate application from several options. To identify the most appropriate technology for a specific situation, a second set of criteria is needed.

Efficiency, Effectiveness, and Cost Benefit

The second set of criteria is based on measuring *efficiency, effectiveness,* and *cost benefit,* or *value added.* If the first three criteria are absolute—that is, the technology passes all three tests—the criteria in the second set are relative. There is no absolute measure of efficiency, effectiveness, or cost benefit; one can only say a specific technology is efficient, effective, or cost beneficial relative to some standard. Using the typewriter is more efficient than handwriting when the two are compared on the basis of the number of words per minute produced, but typewriting has not been shown to be any more effective in terms of the quality of the writing. The choice of the typewriter over the pen or pencil rests on the perception of a relative cost benefit related to speed and readability; that is, the value added to a document in the form of quantity and legibility is judged sufficient to warrant the investment in the more costly technology even though the quality of the content is not improved.

> *Efficiency is measured quantitatively; effectiveness is a qualitative issue.*

Efficiency is measured quantitatively; effectiveness is a qualitative issue. Using another technology—the computer as a word processor—is not only more efficient (faster) than handwriting, but has also been shown to be more effective (better quality writing). The computer enjoys a relative advantage over handwriting in both efficiency and effectiveness; there is value added in speed, legibility, and quality of the contents.

Cost-benefit analysis is an attempt at constructing a global measure that includes considerations related to both efficiency and effectiveness. Which alternative is the most cost beneficial for increasing student achievement on standardized tests—peer tutoring, computer-assisted instruction using integrated learning systems (CAI/ILS), or reducing class size?

The answer can be found by calculating the ratio between the effort in time and money (an input measure of efficiency) and the change in student scores (an output measure of effectiveness). In case you're wondering about the answer, peer tutoring is more cost effective than computer-assisted learning, which is more cost effective than decreased class size.

The concept of *value added,* or return on investment (ROI), is an extension of cost-benefit analysis. In addition to the ratio between effort and outcome, we need also to look at the marginal return on the effort. Are we getting added value in proportion to the increase in effort a technology may require? It is axiomatic that increasing technological sophistication is accompanied by an increase in the effort (cost) required to make the technology fully productive. Therefore, as effort increases, there must also be a proportionate increase in the value added simply to maintain a constant cost-benefit level. As a technology approaches obsolescence, the cost of improvement increases exponentially, while benefits increase linearly, resulting in a declining cost-benefit curve. The vast majority of all schools have, therefore, become victims of industrial age thinking in the information era. Because they have treated technology, especially computers, as a capital expense rather than as a consumable raw material, they have fallen so far behind the state of the art that it's virtually impossible to catch up.

Effort Required

As technologies increase in complexity, they frequently also increase in the effort required to use them; that is, not only are they often relatively expensive, they also have steep learning curves. Nowhere is this more evident than in the example of the initial introduction of computers into the classroom. The promised benefits did not materialize in proportion to the effort required for their use. As we know, except for the most die-hard techie teacher, most of the early computers quickly found their way into the closet or the computer lab under the control of the techie teacher. In retrospect, they failed not only the cost-benefit test, but also the test of social acceptability.

The Final Decision

The choice of technology should be a decentralized decision. The final decision about which technology to use should always rest with the end user. The teacher should determine the most appropriate technology for his or her environment. After the teacher defines the desired outcome, the role of the central administration is to help the teacher obtain the best possible information to answer these six questions:

1. What technologies are workable?
2. Which of the workable technologies are feasible?
3. Of the workable, feasible options, which are socially acceptable?
4. Of the workable, feasible, socially acceptable options, which are the most efficient?
5. Of the workable, feasible, socially acceptable options, which is the most effective?
6. Of the workable, feasible, socially acceptable options, which is the most cost beneficial?

The answers to the last three questions will not necessarily be the same. Your final choice may be highly subjective, but if arrived at in this way, it will never be inappropriate.

Education Versus Application

> Question: "Why do we study and use technology in the classroom?"
> Answer: "Using technology should improve the quality of your life. If it doesn't, scrap it!"

How will we know we are using technology well enough to gain its benefits unless we study it enough to at least understand its strengths and weaknesses? The answer, of course, is that we won't. You can't enjoy the full benefits of riding a bike unless you're willing to learn to ride, practice enough to ride well, and know enough about the bike to be able to occasionally change a tire or replace a slipped chain. Bike riding is learned by doing with occasional references to the owner's manual and frequent help from your peers who have already mastered the art. This is an effective model for studying and using other technologies as well.

Children and adults don't need to know all of the theory behind a technology before using it, but its use should lead to acquisition of an ever-deepening understanding of how to use it well. The only way to do this is to use the technology in a supportive environment until it becomes a natural extension of your capacity to do work. The need to know is a powerful motivator toward learning about technology.

Getting over the Fear Factor

No one that I know is worried about breaking a pencil, so what's the big deal about breaking a computer? Sure, the initial cost of acquisition is much higher, but in normal use, the computer is much more durable, never gets consumed by being sharpened, rarely gets damaged by being thrown or used as a weapon, and will be cranking out words long after several gross of pencils has been reduced to sawdust.

> *If you cannot learn to use a technology to produce something usable in fifteen minutes or less, it has no place in the classroom.*

That's the good news. The bad news is that research indicates that it may take as much as five to ten years for teachers to fully incorporate new technologies, such as the computer, into the classroom (Sheingold and Hadley 1990). A further piece of good news is that the time span of incorporation can be substantially reduced by using one or more of the following strategies.

Strategy 1: The Fifteen-Minute Rule

I can't remember who first introduced me to this rule of thumb, but it is so eminently sensible I hope he or she will forgive me for proposing it here without having given proper credit.

The fifteen-minute rule says that if you cannot learn to use a technology to produce something usable in fifteen minutes or less, it has no place in the classroom. This rule is also handy for choosing developmentally appropriate technologies for students. The ease of use of its graphic-user interface is the single most important reason why Apple Macintosh enjoyed a competitive advantage over IBM for so many years. That advantage has now nearly been eliminated with the advent of Windows, Geoworks Ensemble, and other Mac-like graphic interfaces for IBM-compatible computers.

Strategy 2: Scaffolding

Scaffolding involves a cycle of pretesting, teaching, testing, and reteaching in easily manageable increments. When done properly, it is an instructional strategy of proven effectiveness. It is equally effective for introducing technology to adults and children. The trick to doing it properly is to introduce small increments over an extended time span with adequate support. The research unanimously cites "withdrawal of support too quickly" as the single most significant reason for the failure of scaffolding as an instructional strategy. In industry, it is not unusual to find two to three times the amount of money invested in user support as is invested in hardware. Time and effort invested upfront in making the technology accessible will be more than repaid in the long run through increased use at an accelerated rate. One effective strategy for preparing teachers is to put the next generation of technology into a teacher-only "playroom" for at least a year before it appears in the classroom.

Strategy 3: Orchestrated Immersion

The phrase "orchestrated immersion" is used by Renate and Geoffrey Caine (1991) in describing the conditions for stimulating brain-based, higher-order learning. This strategy differs from scaffolding more by degree than substance. Scaffolding is a strategy for individuals. Orchestrated immersion is a strategy for groups.

The most effective way to teach someone about technology is to immerse them in it and give them a purpose for learning. For example, several years ago, before computers were widely available in schools, teacher teams from several different elementary schools arrived at a science museum for a summer training institute. They were immediately confronted by a huge, randomly stacked pile of new computer equipment in factory-sealed boxes. Each team received a list of the bits and pieces needed to assemble a system, with the injunction that when they could demonstrate a working system, it was theirs to use and keep after the institute was over. The outcome was predictable. Through the collective wisdom and group effort, every team had a working system in less than an hour. High computer use continued throughout the institute, with individuals receiving help as needed from their peers and on-site experts (modeling and scaffolding). After the institute, computer use was higher in the participating schools than other comparably equipped elementary schools in the district.

Technology in the Classroom

Now that we have some criteria for selection and how to encourage use, let's first look at some of the technologies available for instruction, then examine one case study of technology planning.

Language Arts

The basic purpose of language arts instruction is to develop the capacity to communicate—to read, write, listen, and speak effectively. Table 1 shows the evolution of writing technologies. Similar tables can be created for the other language arts skills.

Several conclusions about the use of technology in the classroom can be deduced from this table:

- The rate of introduction is increasing.

- The more advanced the technology, the more likely it is to be a multipurpose tool, useful not only for writing but other functions as well.

- The newer the technology, the more complex and the greater the amount of energy required to use it.

A well-researched example of the current state of the art in the application of technology to language arts is the "Writing to Read" program from IBM. Primarily for children in the K–1 level, this program

Table 1. The Evolution of Writing Technologies

DATE OF INTRODUCTION	TECHNOLOGY
6000 B.C.	Stick-and-dirt
	Charcoal-and-rock
	Chalk-and-slate
3000 B.C.	Stylus-and-wax tablet
100 A.D.	Reed pen and paper
600 A.D.	Quill pen and parchment
1500 A.D.	Pencil and paper
1867 A.D.	Mechanical typewriter
1935 A.D.	Electronic typewriter
1960 A.D.	Word processor
1980 A.D.	Personal computer

Source: *Microsoft Bookshelf Encyclopedia* 1994.

combines the computer with one of several activities for broad appeal and high motivational value to children with widely varying learning styles. The instructional philosophy can be characterized generally as a whole language approach and also includes elements from direct instruction and mastery learning as the children rotate through the activities daily.

"Writing to Read" is most effective when used consistently for a short period of time each day throughout the school year. This suggests that it is best to have a separate facility that can be used by several groups throughout the day in order to increase the cost benefit of the relatively expensive technologies involved. Eduquest/IBM released in the winter of 1992–93 a follow-on program, "Writing to Write," by the same author for grade levels 2–4.

Whether or not you use a program like "Writing to Read" or create your own version with a word processor, computer technology increases productivity, fluidity of expression, quantity, and quality of writing. Ease of editing and rewriting are generally cited as the major advantages of the computer over other writing technologies, making the computer a highly desirable technology for classrooms that use the process approach to writing.

Orality, the ability to speak well, is replacing literacy as the most important language art for the future. Although the audiotape player remains the most widely used technology at present, text-to-speech computer technology, used even in basic language arts software such as KidWorks II, offers many instructional advantages because of its closely integrated multimedia capabilities. Many school applications of text-to-speech technology can be found in the adaptive technologies used by special educators. The next breakthrough in computing technology is expected soon in the area of speech-to-text and speech-to-speech conversion. IBM has produced a reasonably reliable speech-to-text system with a 30,000-word vocabulary. The Japanese have demonstrated a Japanese-English language translator. Although the translation system has a very restricted vocabulary and a high cost at present, the feasibility has been established; the "vocoder" of science fiction writing is no longer fiction.

> *Orality, the ability to speak well, is replacing literacy as the most important language art for the future.*

Science

As might be expected from its origins, computer technology for school science has already established itself as a highly desirable option. For example, computer simulations permit examination of scientific phenomena either too costly or too dangerous to do directly in a school environment.

Optical media, CD-ROM, and laser videodiscs, give students access to a vast array of data and images that can be incorporated into an interactive, multimedia instructional program. Educators can choose from prepackaged comprehensive programs such as Optical Data's "Windows on Science," Encyclopaedia Britannica's "Britannica Science System (BSS)," or "Science 2000" from Decision Development Corporation, or single-subject packages such as "The Great Space Race" from Tom Snyder Publications.

Optical media is used to store and retrieve satellite imagery, thematic maps, photographs, and text databases of sociographic data in the GEOSCOPE courseware, described as "the Interactive Global Change Encyclopedia." GEOSCOPE was developed by the Canadian Space Agency and the Canada Centre for Remote Sensing. Data is also contributed by the National Aeronautics and Space Administration (NASA), the National Oceanic and Atmospheric Administration (NOAA), and agencies of the United Nations.

Teachers who prefer to create their own instructional materials can find extensive and very inexpensive image and information bases on CD-ROM and laser videodisc. Graphic images, sound, text, even full-motion video can be combined into multimedia lessons or student presentations and portfolios using authoring tools that range from ASCD's easy-to-use Electronic Chalkboard for under $100 to programs like Adobe Premier, Macromedia Director, Asymetrix Toolbook, IBM's Linkway Live, or IconAuthor from AimTech, Inc.

The data capture and recording abilities of microcomputer-based laboratory (MBL) technologies now allows students to more closely approximate the work of scientists. Data recording using MBL probes is more accurate, more frequent, more precise, and safer with a variety of probes that now include light, heat, and motion sensors, pH meters, biofeedback detectors, and a host of measuring devices useful for science. Dr. Robert Tinker at TERC in Cambridge, Massachusetts, is a pioneer in this field. TERC contributed to the development of the very effective Personal Science Laboratory (PSL) modules available from Eduquest, and the instructional courseware and lesson plans that accompany the PSL data collection modules.

Mathematics

By now the great debate over the use of calculators in math, like the concerns over the use of spell checkers in language arts, should have been laid to rest. While it is still, and will always be, necessary to learn math facts, the calculator should now be regarded as an essential technology for the teaching of mathematics from second grade level onward. Graphing calculators should be considered a must for operations beyond basic math facts.

A word of caution—be consistent. Be sure that all calculators provided by the school district observe the algebraic order of operations. It is false economy and bad pedagogy to buy a less expensive set of classroom calculators that does not follow the algebraic order of operations, as is sometimes the case for the calculators used in the early grades.

The computer is another technology with great potential in mathematics. If I could have only one computer in a school, I would put it in the math classroom with an overhead projector and a liquid crystal display (LCD) panel to allow the computer output to be projected on a whiteboard where it can quickly be traced manually if desired.

If I could have only one computer in a school, I would put it in the math classroom.

The computer can generate and project the graphs of complex equations and the effects of algebraic transformations, factor and solve polynomials, and do other complex mathematics, saving time and effort while increasing accuracy and clarity. When more computers become available in my school, I will look for software correlated to textbooks, like the Geometric Supposer (Sunburst/Wingz) and the Geometer's Sketchpad (Key Curriculum Press), which allow geometry students to explore and examine Euclidean and transformational geometries.

A software product that should be of considerable interest to math teachers is f(g)Scholar. This program combines the symbolic processing and graphing capabilities of Mathematica and MathCad with a point-and-shoot graphic user interface and the ability to export equations and graphs to word-processed documents, all for less than $100.

Social Science

Broadcast television and videotape provide a wealth of materials for use in the classroom. CNN Newsroom supports current events broadcast daily with print materials describing scheduled broadcasts and suggestions for use in the classroom. Student-produced TV news shows offer the opportunity for performance assessment while providing interesting and useful content to other students. For example, students might be challenged to develop thirty minutes of "play-by-play" coverage of some event in history, such as the signing of the Magna Carta or the Declaration of Independence, for broadcast to the school.

Audiotape is indispensable for oral history and interviews. A polaroid-type instant camera or a digital camera allows students to add graphic images to their presentations quickly. Schools that equip at least one computer with a fax modem can use a regular fax machine to capture images from print by faxing them to the computer, where they are stored as an image file that can be printed or attached to an electronic document. With the addition of optical character recognition (OCR) software, text faxed to the computer can be converted to word-processor format and edited or cut and pasted.

> Some of the most exciting multimedia software is being produced for the social sciences.

Computer software that use a game format, such as the "Where is Carmen San Diego?" series, combined with texts, maps, or other graphic material, have proved to be an effective and popular medium. Simulations, such as the highly regarded "Decisions, Decisions" series from Tom Snyder, are also very popular and useful.

Some of the most exciting multimedia software is being produced for the social sciences, especially history and geography. The Columbus project is an outstanding example of how the next generation of multimedia materials can be used to organize and represent information. IBM's new multimedia-capable computers have brought the cost of this technology within reach of most schools, as have the comparable Macintosh 600 series computers.

Telecommunications is used very successfully to develop information and concepts in geography and science by the National Geographic Society through their Kids Network program. This is an outstanding example of building electronic learning communities by linking classrooms around the world via computer, modem, and telephone lines. Students in the middle grades gather information about their communities and environmental issues to analyze and exchange with their peers in other cites and countries.

GeoSafari is a very interesting low-tech solution for fact acquisition. Students race against the clock using electronic prompts to answer fact-based questions. This system is available for less than $100 and is suitable for readers in grades 2–4.

A wealth of information for the social sciences is available on both CD-ROM and laser videodiscs. Offerings in the larger format include National Geographic's "GTV" and "Planetary Manager," which challenge students to solve problems of deforestation, water pollution, and solid waste management. In the smaller CD format, hundreds of new titles are released each month, as are an array of multimedia atlases and encyclopedias. ProQuest offers a searchable, full text database of articles from 283 magazines on a set of CD-ROM discs, a resource for every school library.

Economics students benefit greatly from the availability of a computer for simulations and the ability to do "what if" scenarios. More advanced students can build their own economic models using spreadsheet software, while others can use simulations such as "SimCity" and "SimWorld" to examine the relationships between economic and environmental factors.

Visual and Performing Arts

Computer technology has resulted in the creation of new art forms to take advantage of its power to manipulate images and sound. Electronic music created on computer, then played or recorded through a MIDI (an acronym for Musical Instrument Digital Interface) connection is only possible through digital technology.

According to the authors of the article, "Technology and the Visual and Performing Arts," in the *ASCD Curriculum Handbook* (1993), art education has been a major beneficiary of the new technologies:

> . . . during the last ten years, the quantity and quality of art instructional resources designed for schools have substantially increased and improved. Such materials include:
> - large format, class-size color reproductions;
> - slides;
> - films and filmstrips;
> - videotapes and television program series;
> - sequential and developmental student textbook series containing reproductions of art and accompanied by a broad variety of illustrative materials and teacher's manuals;

- computer software, mainly in graphics (drawing, painting, design, and color);
- multimedia format materials (slides or filmstrips coordinated with audiotapes and published teacher's guides); and
- laser videodisc products.

Laser videodiscs provide carefully focused materials as well as very large visual databases in the form of collections of works of art and architecture from many historical periods and locations, supplemented by other imagery. Combining laser videodisc and computer hardware with the available software programs is creating electronic multimedia formats for group and individual interactive use, which is bringing extensive information and versatile opportunities for learning into classrooms. Most of these resources are designed for use in schools and include detailed teacher's manuals.

Current technology that permits high quality publication and production of these resources represents a notable achievement in support of visual arts education. In addition, the attention being given to multicultural studies is a boon to art programs because of the rapidly growing numbers of instructional packages presenting information and generous visual materials about diverse groups of people. Students can experience original works of art in schools, art galleries and museums, and in the community at large. (Hancock, Moore, and Schwartz 1993, 2)

According to recent sales figures, the art visual database on the National Gallery of Art is the laser videodisc most likely to be found in schools. The Alberta, Canada, Ministry of Education created their own videodisc, "Sightlines," with over 10,000 images to support arts education.

For music education, there are CD-ROMs like "Beethoven," which examine a single work in great depth, and software like "Play It by Ear," which helps students develop a greater appreciation of music. Composition software combined with a synthesizer and MIDI interface allows students to create and "play" original music on the computer.

Planning for Technology in the Classroom

Although I have only scratched the surface of the possibilities for using technology in the classroom, some trends should already be evident as you consider your options.

- Analog to digital technologies.

- Single sources of information to multiple sources.

- Passive reception to interactive engagement.

- Stationary to portable systems.

- Special purpose to multiple use systems.

- Magnetic storage to optical storage.

- Fixed field database retrieval to free text expert systems.

- 2-D digital simulations to 3-D virtual realities.

Clearly the rate of technological change is continuing to increase. In this environment, it is unrealistic to think that a school can stay on the cutting edge of technology. It is more realistic to expect schools to develop technology plans that take change into account and develop strategies to stay within one or two generations of the leading edge. Allow the first generation buyers to work out the bugs, then enter the field with second generation technology when prices drop with the introduction of newer hardware.

Internet: Profound or Profane?

Access to the Internet opens the door to a virtually inexhaustible supply of information. The good news is that information is readily available in both breadth and depth about almost any imaginable topic at little or no cost. It's the ultimate knowledge resource for gathering information and constructing new knowledge. It's a self-propagating, self-renewing fountain of facts and opinions. With a little creativity, effort, and assistance from intelligent web crawlers and knowbots (knowledge robots), an entire curriculum can be crafted in a matter of weeks. It can contain text, graphics, sound, video files, interactive simulations, and opportunities for real-time discussions with world-renowned scientists, philosophers, literary figures, and historians. It has the potential, largely unrealized, to revolutionize education.

The bad news is that within the mass of data and information accessible on the Internet, the profound and the profane are equally available. This leads to a paradoxical situation—there is too much good information on the Internet not to use it and, at the same time, there is too much bad information to not limit its use.

In fact, the Internet is distinguished from the world of print only by its ease of access, low cost, and interactivity, all of which make it extremely attractive for educational purposes. We solve the print problem by limiting access in school to books and other print materials judged acceptable under state adoption guidelines or by local policy makers. The same can be done for information on the Internet (at least while children are in school) by having and using filters, access restriction by address, and transactions of logging to alert administrators to questionable usage. At the same time, the chaotic condition of the Internet creates a remarkable opportunity for teaching and learning about media literacy, ethical issues related to information technology, and the use of higher-order thinking skills.

The bottom line is that access to the information on the Internet and acquisition of the knowledge and skills necessary to use it effectively have become essential elements of schools and preparation for work. The biggest barrier to access is the lack of telephone lines in classrooms. Less than 5 percent of classrooms were equipped with direct dial-out phone lines as of late 1995. Of the many schools I've visited, very few with local area networks (LANs) included the modem pools, routers, or bridges that allow them to communicate beyond the school walls. Regardless of whatever else is done with technology in schools, connection to the world outside is the defining element that divides the haves from the have-nots in the information era.

Characteristics of the High-Tech Classroom

What should we expect in a high-technology classroom? Here are some suggested benefits:

- Increased access to accurate information
- Multiple channels of communication
- Greater flexibility in the use of time
- More student centered
- Rich multiple sources of information
- Use of a wider variety of outcome measures
- High challenge, low risk

What Every School Needs

Any list of equipment is necessarily subjective. My suggestions for technology in the classroom are listed in table 2. Many of these items are already in your schools, the rest can go on your wish list after they meet the six tests of appropriateness for your classroom.

The Hardware

For ease of calculation, I have chosen a class size of thirty-two students. This is near the upper limit of the range within which the research on class size suggests there is little or no correlation between class size and student achievement. In order to increase student achievement significantly, one needs to reduce class size to seventeen or fewer students. Since few schools have the financial resources to do this, a lesser cost investment in technology for a larger class size seems to be the more realistic trade-off.

As of the spring of 1995, this configuration would cost about $5,000 per child, exclusive of installation. Since this is beyond the immediate means of most districts, a three- to five-year technology implementation plan is usually required. A typical technology planning process might look something like table 3.

Given the rate of technological development, this entire sequence can be repeated every twelve to twenty-four months. If you don't want

Table 2. Technology for the Classroom and School

RECOMMENDED HARDWARE	
FOR THE CLASSROOM	FOR THE SCHOOL
<ul><li>One computer for every four children; IBM-compatible 80486, 66 megahertz or better, or Macintosh 600 or better (8/32 children)</li><li>One CD-ROM drive for every four computers (2/32)</li><li>One multisize laser videodisc player for each classroom with barcode wand for remote control (1/32)</li><li>One overhead projector (1/32)</li><li>One active matrix liquid crystal color display panel (1/32)</li><li>One large-screen video/TV monitor (1/32)</li><li>One 300–600 dot per inch laser printer (1/32)</li><li>One MBL system for every four computers (2/32)</li><li>One dot matrix or bubble jet printer for use with the MBL (2/32)</li><li>One videotape player for each classroom (1/32)</li><li>One color xerographic copier with sheet feeder and collator for every eight classrooms (1/256)</li><li>One color scanner with sheet feeder for every two classrooms (1/64)</li><li>One digital camera for every two classrooms (1/64)</li><li>One video camera for every two classrooms (1/64)</li><li>One video editing suite for every eight classrooms (1/256)</li><li>Four portable audiotape recorders for every classroom (4/32)</li><li>One classroom set of calculators (32/32)</li></ul>	<ul><li>A fiberoptic backbone network linking all classroom workstations for distribution of digital information throughout the school</li><li>One network fileserver for every 128 computers</li><li>One computer workstation for every staff member (configuration varies by function)</li><li>A modem pool with one 28.8K bps fax/modems and direct access telephone lines; one line for every four classrooms, accessible from the classroom via the network</li><li>One computer lab (one workstation per child) for every eight classrooms (round up for partial increments over 256)</li><li>One T-1 leased line connection to an Internet Service Provider (ISP)</li><li>One voicemail system: one mailbox per child, code accessible, plus public access mailboxes for each staff member and each classroom</li><li>Sixteen multimedia workstations in the school media center (library) for every 256 children or library capacity</li></ul>

Table 3. Typical Technology Planning Process

TIME PERIOD	IMPLEMENTATION PLAN
Months 1–6	Organize, plan, assess needs, and audit existing technologies. The goals for using technology and the student outcomes are established together with priorities and a time schedule.
Months 7–12	Examine options and acquire first-priority technologies. Develop teaching strategies and assessment techniques using the new technologies.
Month 13–18	Begin classroom implementation of first-priority applications. Examine options and acquire next-priority technologies. Continue development of teaching strategies using the new technologies. Adjust school structure as needed to maximize the benefits of the new strategies and technologies.
Month 19–24	Refine and evaluate the outcomes.

to develop your own planning process, you might wish to refer to commercial planning guides such as Eduquest's "K–12 Technology Planning Guide," which includes videotapes and sample agendas and letters on diskette, or "Teaching, Learning, and Technology (TLT)," a Macintosh-based multimedia package from Apple Computer.

Case Study: Westside Elementary School

In order to help you understand how a scenario to create a technology-rich school environment might be played out, I have included a brief case study. The data is real, as is the school; however, the scenario is vastly simplified, since my purpose is to illustrate possible strategies rather than to give detailed information about solutions.

The Westside Elementary School was built in the 1980s. (The name of the school has been changed, but it is representative of dozens of schools I have visited from coast to coast.) A large main structure houses the administrative offices, multipurpose room (gym/lunchroom/auditorium), library, two kindergarten rooms, a "writing to read" lab, and a computer lab using Jostens ILS software and proprietary network management system. Three classroom clusters of six classrooms grouped around a common core area are located in an adjacent structure; two additional classrooms are housed in portable structures. Three or four computers networked to the Jostens ILS are located in each of the three permanent core spaces serving the classroom clusters. No computers are located within the classrooms themselves.

Each classroom cluster has at least one A/V cart with a large monitor and a VCR. The equipment itself is old, and although serviceable for basic use, it will not support newer applications such as digital video or display of computer-generated graphics. The "writing to read" lab is well organized and staffed and is fully functional; however, the current block scheduling scheme does not allow continuous use by children over the full school year, as is preferable. The Jostens lab fileserver is at full capacity; no additional workstations can be added at this time. The operating system has not been upgraded, which makes it very difficult to add generic software, thereby limiting the usefulness of the network for general classroom instruction.

The library resources are primarily print based, with considerable room for expansion, including shelf space for additional books. An on-line cataloging and library management system is being developed. No electronic resources are available in the library at this time.

Based on this rudimentary assessment, several strategies for enhancing the use of technology are possible:

- Reschedule use of the "writing to read" lab to gain the benefit of spaced practice in lieu of the current massed practice approach. This will improve the cost benefit at no out-of-pocket expense.

- Implement a five-year strategy to increase the size of the library collection until there are at least eighty books per student, including classroom sets. Of the total, 5–10 percent should be optical media and/or software titles.

- Obtain classroom calculator sets for all students grade 2 and above.

- Upgrade the A/V carts in each classroom cluster to include a multimedia computer workstation with laser videodisc player, CD-ROM drive, monitor with a video-in jack, and a VCR. Add four to six more mobile systems housed in the library for use in the library and as "rovers" on a reservation basis.

- Increase the capacity of the network from 32 to 256 workstations; increase the file server size and rework the operating system to allow use of generic software applications on the network.

- Charge each cluster of six teachers to develop one new technology application each semester, and then train other teachers in its use. Allow each cluster to choose the grade level and content area for the application. Set a maximum cost in advance.

- Add ten to twenty new workstations each year until there are four networked workstations within each classroom.

- Add or replace one of the network workstations in each classroom cluster core area with a laser printer shared by the cluster.

- Add at least one modem server and fax capability to the network to allow telecommunications and fax access to the outside world from the classroom or core area terminals and fax capture of images and text files.

- Establish a research area or "exploratorium" in the library with eight to twelve multimedia terminals for the on-line catalog and optical media-based encyclopedias, full text databases, maps, and other multimedia reference materials.

- Join an on-line library consortium, if one is available locally. CARL, Marmot, or OCLC, for example, allow students to locate library resources and obtain them through interlibrary loan from any member library.

Obviously, to do all of this would require an investment of a magnitude that cannot be realized overnight. But with a long-range plan it could be achieved at a cost of about $1.00 per pupil per school day over a five-year period.

The key to success in using technology does not lie in the technology itself. Rather, it is dependent on the users' ability to develop productive habits of mind. A willingness to take risks and a capacity to deal with uncertainty are required, as is an understanding that "user friendliness" is an illusion created by users, not an inherent quality of the technology. Above all, success depends on perseverance and an unshakable belief that there must be a better way.

References

ASCD. n.d. *What every professional educator should know about optical media.* Alexandria, Va.: Association for Supervision and Curriculum Development.

Becker, H. J. 1991. How computers are used in United States schools: Basic data from the 1989 I.E.A. Computers in Education Survey. *Journal of Educational Computing Research* 7 (4):385–406.

Betts, F., and, V. Hancock. 1992. HELP!: Hypermedia Enhanced Lesson Planning. *ASCD curriculum handbook.* Alexandria, Va.: Association for Supervision and Curriculum Development.

Bylinsky, G. 1991. The marvels of "virtual reality." *Fortune* (June 3): 138–50.

Caine, R. N., and G. Caine. 1991. *Making connections: Teaching and the human brain.* Alexandria, Va.: Association for Supervision and Curriculum Development.

Currence, C. 1986. Making effective educational use of advanced technology. *Time for results: The Governors' 1991 Report on education.* Washington, D.C.: National Governors' Association Center for Policy Research.

Dede, C. 1989. The evolution of information technology: Implications for curriculum. *Educational Leadership* 7 (September):23–26

Dickinson, D. 1991. *Positive trends in learning: Meeting the needs of a rapidly changing world.* Atlanta: International Business Machines Corporation.

D'Ignazio, F. 1988. Bringing the 1990s to the classroom of today. *Phi Delta Kappan* 70 (September):26–27.

Getty Center for Education in the Arts. 1991. *Future tense: Arts education technology conference summary.* Los Angeles: The Getty Center for Education in the Arts.

Gibbons, S., P. Greenfield, and R. Kubey. 1991. Technology's impact on children. *Future tense* (an invitational conference). Los Angeles: The Getty Center for Education in the Arts.

Hancock, V. E. 1991. Curriculum reform through technology integration. *ASCD Curriculum/Technology Quarterly* (Spring):1–3.

———. 1992. LOCATE: Matching media with instruction. *ASCD Curriculum/Technology Quarterly* (Summer):1–4.

Hancock, V. E., B. Moore, and B. Schwartz. 1993. Technology and the visual and performing arts. *ASCD Curriculum Handbook.* Alexandria, Va.: Association for Supervision and Curriculum Development.

Merrion, M. 1992. Theater instruction via interactive television. *Phi Delta Kappan* 74 (December):338–40.

Moore, B. 1992. Music, technology, and an evolving curriculum. *NASSP Bulletin* 76 (May):42–46.

Nachmanovich, S. 1990. *Free play: Improvisation in life and art.* Los Angeles: Jeremy P. Tarcher.

Pogrow, S. 1990. A Socratic approach to using computers with at-risk students. *Educational Leadership* 47 (February):61–66.

Schwartz, B. 1991. The power and potential of laser videodisc technology for art education in the 90s. *Art Education* 44 (May):8–17.

Sheingold, K., and M. Hadley. 1990. *Accomplished teachers: Integrating computers into classroom practice.* New York: Center for Technology in Education, Bank Street College of Education.

Van Horn, R. 1991. Educational power tools: New instructional delivery systems. *Phi Delta Kappan* 72 (March):527–33.

Warger, C., ed. 1990. *Technology in today's schools.* Alexandria, Va.: Association for Supervision and Curriculum Development.

SECTION IV

Insights

*It requires
a very unusual
mind to make
an analysis
of the obvious.*

—Alfred North Whitehead

SECTION IV
Insights

Just as this anthology opens with a section on images of multiage classrooms, it closes, in bookend fashion, with a similar, visually appealing section. "Insights" contains two authors' firsthand exprences with implementing the multiage philosophy in their classrooms.

Kay Williams' essay, "Critical Insights from the Classroom," discusses how she used a multiage approach in her first grade class. Although her students are not in different grade levels, she allows them to work at their own pace. Williams notes that through experimenting with different models to find what would truly help her students learn, she became a student as well. As she put it, "I have changed from a teacher to a facilitator and colearner." Williams also discusses a multiage program, Partners in Learning, that she and another teacher developed. She briefly outlines a three-day activity from it in the second half of the article.

In a comparison piece, Jacquie Anderson invites the reader to accompany her on a personal journey into the classroom. Anderson, although a young teacher, has great insight. Immersed in the change process, she reveals her thoughts on the biggest obstacle to change—herself. Her thoughtful reflection takes the reader into the painful experience of role change, moving from sage to collaborator in classroom interactions. In addition, Anderson includes discussions of practical concerns, such as schedules, as well as the more philosophical issues of students as individuals and the role of parents.

This final section complements the other three sections of the book and provides a visceral experience for the knowing reader.

Critical Insights from the Classroom

Kay J. Williams

"Guess who this story is based on?" a first grade student asked as she displayed her newest book from her writing portfolio. I mentally recorded that she understood character development, both as a writer and a reader. With her comment, "I think I'll add borders to the illustrations," I knew she applied author/illustrator knowledge to the publication of her book.

"How do you spell *there?*" another student asked. A classmate grabbed her by the hand, pulled out a fairy tale book, and said, "Remember, *Once upon a time there* . . . " I realized then that the students have learned how to learn and that the classroom climate fosters collaboration, not competition.

"When I first went down to your room to work with first graders, I thought, 'it's too childish.' But as I worked, I learned new things such as cooperating with others and helping youngsters. And I realized that even if their faces weren't cute, their gestures and way of talking made me get interested in young children," an exiting sixth grade Partner in Learning wrote to me in a thank-you letter—and I rejoiced that students of all ages and all backgrounds can learn from each other within the same classroom.

My classroom has changed from a *factory* model—one that has a teacher producing information and students trying to retain the facts—to a meaning-based, collaborative working environment. I have changed from a teacher to a facilitator and colearner, not as an innovator but as a *motivator,* emphasizing intrinsic rewards and desires to learn. In the process, I have learned a lot and retain an enormous desire to learn more.

This article will describe to you what prompted the change in my methods and philosophy, how I implemented the change, and what you will find in my elementary classroom today. The students in my classroom are no longer tracked in reading groups determined by a basal. The first grade students work both independently and collaboratively throughout the content curriculum in a child-centered classroom focusing on student interest.

I share my experiences to give ideas and courage to promote or support change, not to say that this is *the* method. Each classroom, each teacher, each district, is as different as each individual on this earth. Collaboration must take place to implement change and to develop philosophy. Change must be accepted and supported.

What Promoted Change?

Prior to earning a master's degree, I taught my first grade classroom in the only way I knew. Students were slotted into a basal reading group, usually three groups to a classroom. Since it was a first grade classroom, it was understood that I had to somehow test students to determine each child's ability level. If only I had realized then that I was determining the student's ability level for the rest of his or her life! Once the groups were established, I tried to disguise the level by calling them by different names, i.e., the Bees, Bears, and Butterflies, or the Red Group, Blue Group, and Yellow Group. I was only fooling myself. The students knew.

I said to parents, "Your child is in the lowest group, but if she does her work and catches up with the next group, she can move up." In reality, that task was nearly impossible. It rarely happened.

While attending classes to receive my master's in curriculum and instruction, I began to read books and articles reflecting the whole language philosophy. I studied developmentally appropriate practices and began to realize that while I *felt* each child develops quite differently in the primary years, I had been forcing students into slots determined by me so as to fit into my three reading groups and to meet the expectations of subsequent teachers. I was not allowing them to develop at their own pace, to discover the fun in learning, and to use the natural language and curiosity innate in every child to reach their full potential. Slowly, I began to change my teaching methods to become a facilitator, kid-watcher, and inquirer.

True to my own developmental learning stage at that point, the first change I incorporated was the use of writing as a tool to enhance the students' relationship to language, *but only on Fridays*. Now, I realize that I had placed writing as a reward at the end of the week for continuing the other format. It was fun for both the students and myself, and the underlying message that school is not supposed to be fun, unless it is a reward, was still within me.

> *Slowly, I began to change my teaching methods to become a facilitator, kid-watcher, and inquirer.*

I assigned topics and sat in the center of grouped desks, placing myself within easy access to spell words for the children. Again, I had not yet realized I was demonstrating to students that they were incapable of choosing an appropriate topic—something of interest to them—and that I felt it was unacceptable for them to use the natural writing ability they possessed.

Later, as I began to understand developmental/invented spelling, I began to encourage the students to proceed appropriately. I also began modeling how to find words already in print to aid spelling and to encourage them, I placed print everywhere in the classroom.

Big books became an integral part of my classroom. They allowed easy viewing by the entire class as I read the text, modeling expression and demonstrating the use of context clues, punctuation, interpretation of illustrations, etc. Often we would illustrate our own big book of the same title and text. These books were sent home daily with one student at a time to share with their family, instilling within the student a sense of pride in accomplishment and allowing practiced reading of familiar text, incorporating natural language patterns and memorization of words frequently used. Later I used trade books as the model for writing our own books.

Gradually I developed my own philosophy of teaching. I believe this is the essence to successful, meaningful learning experiences within a classroom. Development, practice, and maintenance of individual philosophy is the core meaning-based classroom learning. Through personal study, I read about whole language philosophy. I agreed with the educators who emphasized the importance of real purposes as learning experiences, as opposed to worksheets with no real meaning. As I read *Whole Language: Inquiring Voices* by Dorothy Watson, Carolyn Burke, and Jerome Harste, I saw the value of collaboration and grasped the idea that by collaborating, we learn from each other rather than by trying to convince others that ours is the best solution. I was learning by inquiring and realized that students learn best by inquiring. I discovered that real comprehension is the meaning I bring to the text from my personal prior experience, thus students should be given the opportunity to develop individual comprehension of a text.

> *Unsuccessful learning experiences are not failures, but should be evaluated and seen as risks that permit growth.*

Now I have a reason for procedure within the classroom and for the physical arrangement of the room. I can respond with research-based theory put into practice when questioned. Often I can provide an anecdote of a student's successful experience for many of the practices I maintain.

Risking as a teacher is as important for modeling and for my personal growth as it is for students within the classroom. My change has been gradual. It has taken place over several years. Once I learned I was able to put into practice ideas that I wanted to try, I did them as I became comfortable. Some practices or projects did not work for a variety of reasons. The makeup of personalities within the classroom plays a large role in the success of activities and methods. The attitude and acceptance of colleagues can influence success or failure. But more importantly, my own attitude was, and is, the key to success. Unsuccessful learning experiences are not failures, but should be evaluated and seen as risks that permit growth.

How My Classroom Changed

The physical climate of my classroom changed dramatically a few years ago when I changed rooms within my building and seized the opportunity to request round tables rather than individual student desks. This simple change allows frequent physical movement for primary students not developmentally ready to stay seated for long periods of time. Young children learn through total body integration—an active rather than a passive process. Staying seated at an individual desk tends to prohibit this active process. Tables allow me to change seating arrangements daily with "portable" nametags. However, I am not the only one who decides on seating arrangements. Student choice is also used throughout the day and week as determined by various projects and activities.

Students are encouraged to talk to table neighbors during work time. This allows them to engage in oral language while learning about each other and discussing issues that interest them. As a kid-watcher, I receive some of my most valuable information and anecdotal material while listening and contributing to these conversations.

Often tables are pushed together to create large working environments and groups. If appropriate, tables are easily shoved to the wall and the floor is used. Tables have been one of the most freeing changes in my classroom.

The walls are covered with print and pictures, both student-generated and trade-book generated. Posters of trade books, book characters, and letters from author-friends are displayed in any available space. Class-written lists and stories, as well as individual papers and projects, are displayed. It is a stimulating and fun environment. The print on the wall also becomes a resource for students to locate words for spelling or for help with words recognized in unfamiliar context but needing to be related to a familiar context before decoding can occur.

Tables have been one of the most freeing changes in my classroom.

Another integral part of the classroom is my large personal collection of trade books, many of which are autographed. The collection relays a message to students that books are very important to me. And the fact that I am willing and eager to share the books with them—with most being available on a daily, personal checkout system to take home to share with their family—makes the students feel valued.

As trade books became more and more important to me, I began to use them to integrate my curriculum and create a literature-based study. This was a significant step in my realization that students do not need to be grouped by ability or by age. I used my district's scope and sequence to make sure I was covering the skills deemed important and saw to it that these skills were woven within the various subject areas.

Literature allows hands-on learning and integration of curriculum. It also subtly demonstrates to the students the reading/writing/listening/thinking/learning connection. Nonfiction books can be used, when appropriate, to introduce objectives in the various curriculum areas: social studies, science, health, math, art, music, physical education. I have also begun to connect content curriculum areas and skills within fiction books.

Students do not need to be grouped by ability or by age.

Now when I call reading groups, rather than asking for the "Bees" or the "Red Group," I call for the *Chrysanthemum* Reading Group (Henkes 1991). I have acquired several class collections of trade books. Some collections have ten copies, some only four. The number of copies I have available is the only factor that determines how many students can be in a reading group. Students are allowed to choose from four or five selections. As these selections are depleted, new selections are added. One week appears to be the length of time appropriate for a first grade interest level in a trade picture book. If the interest is still apparent, we continue with the book. We use *Pumpkin Pumpkin, If You Give a Mouse a Cookie, Jump Frog Jump!, Hattie and the Fox,* and *The Doorbell Rang,* as well as others. We have previously enjoyed these choices through shared reading, so the students are familiar with the content. These titles are appropriate for first grade age and interest level, but there are many other books available for whatever the age and interest level.

Within the group we read chorally or independently. The choice may be determined by me or by the group. At this age level, the first day of reading should include a choral reading so the emergent readers feel as secure as the independent readers. It is a time for familiarizing the readers with content and expression.

Comprehension questions are phrased to help the readers develop meaning from personal prior experiences. Examples of such questions include: What was your favorite part of the book? Why? Read aloud to me the page that meant the most to you. Why did you choose that page? If you wished to change a part of the story, what would you change? Why? If you had the opportunity to meet the author, what would you ask? These questions often must be asked in two parts to allow the students to reflect on the personal prior experience. For further examples of appropriate comprehension questions, see *Invitations* by Regie Routman.

Students also take the book home every evening to practice and share with a family member. A list of appropriate comprehension questions is sent home to parents, but parents are encouraged to develop discussion and meaning from the text as determined by the readers.

Some students are able to read and decode every word within the trade book. Others need to have the book read with them, chorally, until they familiarize themselves with the text. As emergent readers, some students will "read" the words they have memorized as they look at the pictures. When they begin to grasp the significance of the written text on the page, they will begin to follow the text with their finger and say the words they have memorized. Eventually, the reader will begin decoding the words. Observing these reading patterns and strategies as a kid-watcher gives me anecdotal material to share with parents on report cards and in conferences, discussing the child's reading strengths, weaknesses, and formed strategies. It also provides me with information to help a student who is trying to decode new words. As the observer, I become aware of the student's primary learning style and can offer appropriate strategies to help them learn how to learn. I also believe it is an important task as a teacher to aid students in developing strategies in their secondary learning modes, which will strengthen those areas as well.

> *I become aware of the student's primary learning style and help them learn how to learn.*

Flexible skill groups for reading and writing can be formed and used within the classroom setting. As an observer and facilitator, the teacher will be cognizant of the students who are developmentally ready for understanding and application of these skills. Rather than the typical basal skill lesson taught to a predetermined ability group, practiced with a basal reading selection designed to use the skill as often as possible, and then checked for understanding with several workbook pages or worksheets, flexible skill groups allow the students to learn a skill when it becomes important to them. They, in turn, are able to apply the skill to their own writing and reading, demonstrating understanding. Only the students deemed ready by the observer are included in these flexible skill groups.

The importance of placing all levels of readers together within groups is that it benefits all readers. Emergent readers listen as fluent readers read aloud. They absorb and internalize expression in reading, interpretation of text, and fluent reading patterns. But, more importantly, high self-esteem is being developed with the realization that the teacher is confident that they can accomplish the task of reading the chosen text. One student smiled and said to me on the third day of reading a book, "I can read this whole page by myself." Another exuberantly exclaimed, "Last night I read one page, and my mom read the other one!"

> *The importance of placing all levels of readers together within groups is that it benefits all readers.*

Fluent readers are also developing self-esteem, as well as learning to collaborate and share knowledge. Students who are more developed academically need to learn to socialize, practice problem solving, and share ideas. It benefits them to recognize techniques used to arrive at a conclusion or to solve a problem. If given the opportunity to work, teach, talk, problem solve, and share with a variety of unique students, rather than being isolated in a group with similar characteristics, the strategies they verbalize become more readily attainable for later use.

When students were divided by basal reading groups within my classroom, it was apparent that the "higher" group moved more quickly through the reading lessons. It was not necessary for a lengthy focus on decoding skills, since these skills had already been internalized. Time was spent on reading, on discussion of what was read, and on how the content related to the student's prior experiences and real life. The "lower" groups often spent much more time doing worksheets and workbook pages, repetitively emphasizing the same skills because it appeared they had not mastered those skills. Now I believe they were bored due to lack of involvement. Less actual reading was taking place, as well as very little discussion. When discussion did happen, it happened at a low level. Group members had life experiences in common, and they had oral language ability in common. Ability groups tend to reflect and internalize sameness, not variety.

As I became a kid-watcher, I began to notice that students who appeared to have limited prior academic experience often had more survival, or real-life, experiences. As an example, these students were the ones quick to understand and recognize the ingredients of a recipe and more agile in actually mixing or baking. The fluent readers were often those who had limited abilities and experiences in motor skills and in collaborating. Placed together in cooking groups, each learned from the other. We became a community of learners and workers. As I began to understand this, I started to apply the knowledge to all areas of the curriculum.

I am constantly learning and trying new things. I firmly believe that a reading group does not have to read from the same text. Students can share a chosen book by reading important and meaningful passages from the text to the rest of the group and by discussing the meaning they grasped from the book. I plan to use this within my classroom this year. It takes time and modeling. I have not been ready with an entire first grade classroom until this year.

> *I am constantly learning and trying new things.*

Four years ago I was able to adopt this philosophy and formed an all-school Literature Club. It allowed members, kindergarten to sixth grade, to share a book with the rest of the group. With a large response from the students and help from other adult sponsors, three separate groups—not designated by age or ability—met after school or at lunch every other week. It has been highly successful, and, though I no longer sponsor the club, it is still meeting. For more in-depth study about literature circles, I highly recommend *When Writers Read* by Jane Hansen, *Creating Classrooms for Authors* by Harste, Short, and Burke, and *Invitations* by Regie Routman.

Since my philosophy now dictated that I was no longer bound by basal direction, I was in need of rich and meaningful curriculum. My love of literature naturally directed my path. I share with you some of the studies I have used to incorporate content curriculum and skills within a literature-based study. All of these ideas have been used within my first grade classroom, but can be adapted and used with any grade level. They are also a good starting point for developing your own studies and philosophy.

Several years ago I began an author and/or illustrator-of-the-month study. Within this study we have been able to focus on one writer and identify the author's style of writing. Eventually, the students incorporate this style into their own writing and, through trial and error, will find what works for them and what doesn't. Comparisons often take place as students reflect on similarities and differences in style between authors. Students become active critics and book reviewers. They begin to realize that critical expression does not indicate an unworthy preference but an *individual* preference by the reviewer, and includes an honest attempt at offering suggestions.

Within this author study, we complete a project to send to the author, based on a relationship with one of the author's books. As we studied Eric Carle and learned to love *The Very Quiet Cricket*, we wrote a book for him entitled *The Very Quiet Classroom*. This became an appropriate time and purposeful way to emphasize exclamatory words and exclamation marks.

By the end of the month we are ready to write a letter to our author. I model how to write a friendly letter for the students, a first grade introductory skill. The students dictate to me as I write on large chart paper. The students then write, at their own developmental level, an individual message and illustrate a picture reflecting the student's favorite book by that author.

This extension of my curriculum, now an integral part, has been extremely successful. Most authors respond to the class as a whole with a letter. Some include information fliers and posters. No matter what level, ability, or age, intrinsic satisfaction is achieved.

Thematic studies have also been incorporated within my curriculum. The theme should be based on student interest, but should be guided and directed by the teacher/facilitator. Many of the themes have been generated by holidays, such as Native American storytelling studies at Thanksgiving. Others occur naturally when content curriculum begins to flow from one to the other. This was demonstrated during our Jim Aylesworth author-of-the-month study as we read *Hanna's Hog* (illustrated by Glen Rounds), incorporated a fairy tale study of *The Three Little Pigs,* which now includes a version by Glen Rounds, and a literature-based social studies farm/city unit that included pigs and hogs.

> Real books, real writers, real purposes, real experiences offer successful affective and cognitive learning.

Fairy tale studies have been highly successful because they are familiar to the children and they reflect our literary heritage. Numerous fairy tales have been retold and illustrated. Reading several versions for comparison has proved beneficial. Students can learn new skills by graphing an individual favorite of three versions, making character analyses of characters within the same fairy tale or of the same character in different versions of the fairy tale, retelling the fairy tale and emphasizing sequencing, and charting the differences and similarities of various versions.

Little Red Riding Hood is ideal to use when emphasizing commas in a series. How many things did Little Red Riding Hood take to Grandma? What would you take? *The Little Red Hen* helps when instruction or reinforcement of quotation marks is needed. These ideas are not new. Just remember to use them as you feel comfortable and as needed and accepted by your students.

Using different types of books to study and to help develop writing skills is also successful. Cumulative tales offer a study in literature that can then be reflected in writing. A small list of very effective cumulative tales includes *The House that Jack Built, The Rose in My Garden, The Napping House,* and *Bringing the Rain to Kapiti Plain.* Pattern and predictable books such as *Hattie and the Fox, A House Is a House for Me, Fortunately,* and *Brown Bear Brown Bear What Do You See?* offer successful reading experiences for emergent readers and give ideas and a starting point for writers no matter what level.

Real books, real writers, real purposes, real experiences offer successful affective and cognitive learning. Students have related to all of these areas with pride, satisfaction, and growth.

Beyond the First Grade Classroom

As I read professional journals and books, I also developed an interest in multiage grouping. Three years ago, a sixth grade teacher and I began to develop a program that we now call Partners in Learning. Because we believe strongly in focusing the curriculum on student-generated interests, each year we try many different projects and activities. We model our belief that sixth graders and first graders can learn together and that the learning environment is not, or should not be, different from the "grownup" world of business and commerce. Within business, collaboration needs to take place to produce a product or an idea. While competition does exist in the world, more and more businesses are saying that employees lack skills for working together. It is essential that we place an emphasis on collaboration. Ability grouping and age grouping tend to stress competition.

> *The learning environment is not, or should not be, different from the "grownup" world of business and commerce.*

The first year, as we began to pair partners, we planned to keep partnerships only through one set of experiences. This, we felt, would give the students the opportunity to meet and get to know the other students. When we began another set of experiences and announced new partners, mutiny took place. Groans were heard, but we held fast, thinking we knew best and remembering that there had been some complaints with the first grouping. By the third set of experiences, we were asked, "Can we work with our real partners?" and we knew it was the students' decision, not ours.

Experiences and projects are planned around language arts, but social studies, science, and math often happen. How can they not? We use literature as the base and writing as the tool. Within the experiences, we integrate both first grade and sixth grade skills, as appropriate, from the scope and sequence.

To demonstrate how we accomplish our goal, integrate skills as well as curriculum, and give real purpose, thus, real meaning to projects, I will briefly share a three-day activity with you. This experience can be adapted for any age-level grouping or kept within one age. What is important is the understanding and use of hands-on experiences and combinations of unique individuals and untracked groups.

While the students at both grade levels were studying Jim Aylesworth as an author-of-the-month, I wished to emphasize parts of speech—nouns (naming words), verbs (doing words), and adjectives (describing words). The sixth grade was ready for emphasis in alliteration. The author's two books to be published that spring of 1992 were *The Folks in the Valley* and *Old Black Fly,* both ABC books. A real purpose for a study was now established—to create a product in the form of a backward ABC book called *Zealous Youth Xeroxed, An Aldrin ZYX Book,* to send to Jim Aylesworth with our letters.

On the first day, the first grade practiced nouns by using *The Jacket I Wear in the Snow* by Shirley Neitzel. We practiced in a variety of ways, and finally each student created a sentence and illustrated the noun on a flap over the word, creating a rebus. These sentences were celebrated by reading and displaying them on the wall with a sign saying "Words Can Name Things."

On the second day the focus with the first grade was verbs. Within our lesson we used two trade books, *Kites Sail High* by Ruth Heller and *Worms Wiggle* by David Pelham and Michael Foreman. I modeled the lesson, then we worked in small collaborative groups, and finally we created individual sentences on sentence strips with a pop-up format for the verb. Again, these were celebrated by reading and displaying them on the wall with another sign saying "Words Can Show Action."

The third day was the combined activity with first and sixth grade partners. The trade book *Many Luscious Lollipops,* by Ruth Heller, began the explanation of adjectives. As the ZYX book was explained, a sentence format was also given. The students were asked to create an individual sentence with an adjective, noun, and a verb. The nouns were to be the student's last name. The adjective and the verb were to begin with the same letter as the student's last name, thus the alliteration. To model the activity, the students and I, in collaboration, determined my sentence to be "Wonderful Williams watches." In the actual individual writing, the sixth grade partner was to help the first grade partner. Use of a thesaurus or dictionary was encouraged. Students wrote individual sentences on sentence strips, and again a celebration of the activity took place by reading and displaying them with a sign saying, "Words Can Also Describe."

To finish the book, students were photographed in groups as identified by their last name. The photos were mounted on paper and collated in reverse ABC order, students' sentences were copied on appropriate pages, and our ZYX book was published in a quantity of three. The cover was an enlarged color photostat of an entire group picture. Limited Edition #1 was sent to Jim Aylesworth with our combined package of letters, and the two classrooms each had a copy with which to share and celebrate within the classroom.

> *The process was, and is, more important than the product.*

The completed product was very impressive, but the process was, and is, more important than the product. I have never witnessed sixth grade students more proud of a finished book. They knew it was a collaboration that they shared with their partners. The reality was that they were the "higher" track. My first grade students had more limited academic knowledge and experience.

Conclusion

This article has reflected experiences within one classroom and attempts to reach beyond that classroom. All of the ideas I have shared can be adapted for any grade level. Development of a personal philosophy is key to stepping beyond these ideas. Once philosophy is established, ideas and creativity flow. There seems not to be enough time to use all of which we can dream.

Students still need to be taught and guided. By displaying confidence and the expectation that each student can succeed, a teacher taps and expands every student's potential. By observing each student's developmental stage and identifying learning modes, a teacher becomes a facilitator and can affirm and gently guide each student to enable him or her to discover numerous inherent capabilities. By collaborating with colleagues and students, a teacher becomes a learner and an inquirer and takes a place as an integral member of the community of learners.

Breaking down the barriers within my first grade classroom has taken time, patience, and effort. There are constraints within the school and district and among parents due to misunderstanding, differing philosophy, and personal educational experiences. Alone, roadblocks are difficult to break. Collaboration must be a part of the process to change. Administrative support must be available. Leaders of change must start slowly through modeling and by instigating staff development.

Cognitive growth is demonstrated when my first grade students amaze their parents in a bookstore by naming authors, illustrators, and titles of books, by mentioning the endpapers of a book, and by asking to whom the book was dedicated.

Affective influence is apparent when sixth grade students and first grade students greet each other in the hall or on the playground with a "high-five" and a smile, or when a sixth grade boy who had stopped in the school office on an errand stayed there with his first grade partner while the ill student waited for his mother. Affective influence is also apparent when sixth grade students literally bound into the first grade classroom eager to share a new picture book or information about a local author book signing.

I rejoice in the knowledge that, if given the opportunity, students of all abilities and all ages can be a community of confident, successful, and joyful learners.

References

Professional Books

Hansen, J. 1987. *When writers read.* Portsmouth, N.H.: Heinemann.

Harste, J., K. Short, and C. Burke. 1988. *Creating classrooms for authors.* Portsmouth, N.H.: Heinemann.

Routman, R. 1991. *Invitations, changing as teachers and learners K–12.* Portsmouth, N.H.: Heinemann.

Watson, D., C. Burke, and J. Harste. 1989. *Whole language: Inquiring voices.* New York: Scholastic.

Children's Picture Books

Aardema, V. 1987. *Bringing the rain to Kapiti Plain.* New York: Dial Press.

Aylesworth, J. 1988. *Hanna's hog.* New York: Atheneum.

———. 1992. *Old black fly.* New York: Henry Holt.

———. 1992. *The folks in the valley, A Pennsylvania Dutch ABC.* New York: HarperCollins.

Carle, E. 1990. *The very quiet cricket.* New York: Philomel.

Charlip, R. 1980. *Fortunately.* New York: Four Winds Press.

Falconer, E. 1990. *The house that Jack built.* Nashville: Ideals Children's Books.

Fox, M. 1987. *Hattie and the fox.* New York: Bradbury Press.

Galdone, P. 1974. *Little Red Riding Hood.* New York: McGraw-Hill.

———. 1961. *The house that Jack built.* New York: McGraw-Hill.

———. 1973. *The Little Red Hen.* New York: Clarion Books.

Goodall, J. 1988. *Little Red Riding Hood.* New York: M. K. McElderry Books.

Heilbroner, J. 1962. *This is the house where Jack lives.* New York: Harper & Row.

Heller, R. 1988. *Kites sail high.* New York: Grosset & Dunlap.

———. 1989. *Many luscious lollipops.* New York: Grosset & Dunlap.

Henkes, K. 1991. *Chrysanthemum.* New York: Greenwillow.

Hillert, M. 1981. *Not I, not I.* Cleveland: Modern Curriculum Press.

Hoberman, M. 1978. *A house is a house for me.* New York: Viking Press.

Holdsworth, W. 1969. *The Little Red Hen.* New York: Farrar, Straus & Giroux.

Hutchins, P. 1986. *The doorbell rang.* New York: Greenwillow.

Hyman, T. 1983. *Little Red Riding Hood.* New York: Holiday House.

Kalan, R. 1981. *Jump, frog, jump!* New York: Greenwillow.

Lobel, A. 1984. *The rose in my garden.* New York: Greenwillow.

Marshall, J. 1987. *Red Riding Hood.* New York: Dial Books for Young Readers.

Martin, B. 1992. *Brown bear, brown bear, what do you see?* New York: Henry Holt.

Neitzel, S. 1989. *The jacket I wear in the snow.* New York: Greenwillow.

Numeroff, L. 1985. *If you give a mouse a cookie.* New York: Harper & Row.

Pelham, D. 1988. *Worms wiggle.* New York: Simon and Schuster.

Rounds, G. 1992. *Three little pigs and the big bad wolf.* New York: Holiday House.

Titherington, J. 1986. *Pumpkin pumpkin.* New York: Greenwillow.

Wood, A. 1984. *The napping house.* San Diego: Harcourt Brace Jovanovich.

Journey of Change
The Nongraded School

Jacquie Anderson

> There was once a young man who began to study the guitar. He practiced daily, learning about melody, harmony, and composition. Earnestly he continued his work for five years. Finally, the day came for him to perform. Dressed in his finest, his family wished him well as he went off to the music hall. When it came his turn to mount the stage, the director turned to him and said, "We don't play guitar here, we play piano."

The parallels of this story to teaching are obvious. Having heard it, I considered how many times I had asked my students, verbally and nonverbally, to put away their guitars and get to work on the piano. It is from this point that I began in earnest my search for a model of teaching that welcomed all children's talents and interests, using them as a foundation for learning. I already had a developmentally appropriate program in my kindergarten, but began to emphasize more student initiation. I came to believe that a nongraded program would provide an environment in which both of these elements could be nurtured and extended almost limitlessly.

I had become aware of the numerous advantages of a multiaged class through inservices in my district. When making my decision to request a combined class for the next year, I thought that two ages would be enough of a challenge to begin with. I chose five- and six-year-olds because I felt that the freshness of the younger children could be complemented by the older children's grasp of routines and expectations. As well, the richness of a kindergarten program had much to offer children of both ages. I looked forward to the challenge and anxiously awaited my opportunity to reap the benefits of a nongraded class.

It was a delight to have those benefits realized before my eyes and ears come September. While other teachers were laying the groundwork of routines and expectations, I was delving into content. I had kept many of the children from my kindergarten the previous year, and as a result I picked up with the children right where we left off in June. The younger children followed the modeling of the older students, and the older students enjoyed the responsibility of teaching the younger ones the routines and expectations of the classroom. More importantly, however, there was a comfortable atmosphere in the room. I knew them and they knew me. The relationship of trust and support was already established. This was made clear to me when, in early September, one of my older students told me, "I can do this. It's just like in kindergarten." The significance of this statement lies in the fact that she was participating in writing, an activity she had been very reluctant about the year before. The class atmosphere had encouraged her to build on her experience by providing a setting that supported her in its familiarity.

> *The older students enjoyed the responsibility of teaching the younger ones the routines and expectations of the classroom.*

However, of all the advantages found in my combined class, none was as significant for me as the challenge it posed to my professional philosophy. The most surprising obstacle I came up against time and again was myself. I found that my vision for learning was much more limited than I thought. Despite what I said and believed, I did have a hidden agenda for my students that was hard to let go. How could I accommodate diversity in the classroom and still meet curricular objectives? Designing themes that addressed the academic needs of the children while following their interests was more daunting than I had expected. I also struggled with ensuring that the richness of kindergarten was not lost for those who needed it, and that the expectations of activities were open ended enough to challenge all the students.

Maintaining accurate and up-to-date assessments of children's progress is always a challenge. In a nongraded class it is slightly more difficult because the language is different. In order to accurately reflect the goals and principles of a nongraded classroom, evaluations cannot be based on a grade standard but need to be individualized using authentic data. Explaining this to parents, as well as alleviating their concerns about the daily program, was another challenge.

> *The first obstacle I had to face was myself.*

Meeting these challenges prodded, pushed, and nurtured my professional philosophy. In addition to enjoying the children's enthusiasm for learning and their pride in their accomplishments, refining my philosophy was significantly rewarding.

These challenges are ones we all face when beginning a nongraded classroom. The rest of this article will elaborate on my journey as I sought to resolve them.

A New Vision

The first obstacle I had to face was myself. It was with surprise and disappointment that I realized that while I spoke boldly about the merits of a nongraded, open-ended program, my actions sometimes spoke differently. My thinking was much more linear than I had admitted. By linear I mean that my vision followed a specific timeline and did not allow for individual abilities to be easily accommodated. The activities I offered did not always challenge those who needed to be challenged and occasionally involved too much risk for other children.

It became clear to me that I had perpetuated in my planning the long-held belief that children learn a standard set of skills at a roughly standard rate, and that certain activities are "too young" or "too old" for different age groups. As a teacher of a combined class based on a nongraded philosophy, I could not rightfully support those principles in my classroom. Consequently, I was obliged to reflect on my understanding about learning and begin to develop a program that was true to a nongraded philosophy.

Thus I adopted a spiral vision of learning. Children do proceed in their learning by moving from one step to the next, but they also revisit their prior experiences in doing so. In this way they build upon what they already know, adding depth to their understanding each time they return to what they learned before.

In refining my philosophy about learning, I adopted three principles that became the basis upon which I did much of my decision making. Firstly, children make continuous progress. Through a program that is developed with a spiral vision of learning, they will have opportunities to build on what they know and use their prior experiences, growing from strength to strength. Secondly, children come to school with a diverse set of experiences and abilities whatever their age. A nongraded classroom needs to accept those differences and use them to their advantage. A program that is inclusive provides a niche for every child.

In the following Venn diagram, the point where the first two principles overlap forms the uniting third principle (see fig. 1). An open-ended, student-initiated program allows children to utilize their present knowledge and prior experiences in developing new abilities through meaningful content. Such a program provides a platform from which diversity and continuous progress can be effectively addressed. While it could apply to either a straight or a multiaged class, I believe this model forms the crux of a nongraded classroom.

A program that is inclusive provides a niche for every child.

In light of these principles, I reevaluated my program. I threw out my previous plans and started again, with every new idea having to meet my recently refined philosophy. One of the tenets of my professional philosophy all along has been that children like to learn. They enjoy seeing themselves make progress and demonstrate tremendous perseverance when they are in the midst of working on something in which they have a vested interest. I knew this to be true, but I had to believe in it enough to let go of some of my agenda and provide constructive direction for their agenda. Thus began my search for a dayplan that reflected what I believed in and facilitated implementation of those beliefs.

On the Road

In developing a program that encourages student initiative, my role has become one of collaborator. I need to be able to come alongside my

Figure 1. Nongraded Classroom

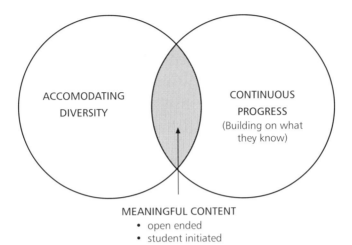

students, see what they are thinking about, and work with them toward new learning. It is not enough for me to simply watch them and congratulate myself on the fun they are having; I need to take that enthusiasm and direct it toward specific learning objectives. Sometimes those objectives are mine and sometimes they are set by the child. The significant point is using the child's interests to teach something. Meaningful content has long been known to be important in teaching, but all too often the teacher decides what is meaningful instead of watching and listening to students to discover what *they* think is meaningful.

Being flexible often means having to put aside my own interests in order to make the program more effective for students. This applies to activities and strategies as well as theme ideas. The challenge comes in marrying curricular guidelines with student interests. It is important for me to continuously evaluate the activities and strategies I am using to ensure that they are satisfactorily facilitating learning as well as reflecting my students' interests.

A significant step for me was using concept themes. Like many other teachers, I use themes in my classroom. Also like many other teachers, I had some "dud" themes—themes that went nowhere before they began. The idea of concept themes interested me because they provide room for so many "mini-themes" to develop. Everyone can find a niche within them. For instance, I had previously done a transportation theme. Some of my boys had enjoyed it, but most of the children had little or no interest in it. However, when I changed the theme to "journeys," it became a rich topic with a multitude of related ideas: mapping, transportation, destinations (other countries), vehicles, and imagery, to name a few. The possibilities seemed endless: sorting and classifying vehicles and landscapes, mapping story journeys (and real ones from field trips and walks to the park), writing stories, and discussing countries and cultures all became favorite activities that were both stimulating and academically appropriate. It was also exciting to discuss our own personal journeys. It was interesting to hear the childrens' perspectives on their own growth throughout the year. All these rich learning situations could not have been provided by a straightforward theme on transportation. Concept themes help students see how much of life is interrelated and provide opportunities for transfer of classroom learning to life learning.

Concept themes help students see how much of life is interrelated.

Another advantage of concept themes is that they last a long time. There were so many possibilities for extension that my themes often lasted two months. The depth of learning is magnified in this time. All that I had planned to accomplish through the theme will have been addressed, but the richness of the topic is provided by the extensions that the children make. It is thrilling to see them make connections and expand my limited vision for them.

This kind of planning demonstrates what I call an "unlimited curriculum." So often I have heard teachers and parents voice concerns that in a combined classroom the curriculum is modified to a happy medium, leaving some children with too little challenge and others with too much. I believe that a nongraded classroom allows for an unlimited curriculum where the content is not contained by the teacher but is left open to be expanded and extended by the students. Activities within an unlimited curriculum need to allow for a wide range of response and encourage thoughtfulness and significant learning. Activities that use higher-order thinking skills and facilitate transfer of learning inherently accommodate and encourage the diversity of learners.

When developing my previews of upcoming themes, I made a point of marking them "draft." This gave me the freedom to modify my plans to better correspond with the students' needs and interests as the theme progressed. In order to ensure a dynamic learning environment, it is important for me to be able to continuously evaluate and refine the theme activities. This also explains why I very rarely keep materials or samples from previous years. Each class of children will develop a theme in its own unique way. I found that my students usually modified my suggestions and made them their own.

> One of the most powerful elements of my classroom is play.

It is this ownership that the children feel that makes my classroom such a delight for me. Their enthusiasm and thoughtfulness are proudly displayed on the walls and are evident in group sharing times and cooperative as well as individual projects. Their delight in their learning is infectious and serves to further motivate them to embrace new challenges and take risks. Parents also comment on their child's growing self-esteem and sense of responsibility. All of these qualities are significantly influenced by the physical, emotional, and social dimensions of the learning environment.

One of the most powerful elements of my classroom is play. Much has been written about the importance of play, but all too often it is left only to the preschool and kindergarten years. As a kindergarten teacher I saw that play effectively fostered learning in my students, so when I began my nongraded teaching, I went with what I knew worked. To me, play was an activity in which all the children could participate, and its open-endedness allowed for extension and modification depending on the interests of the children. Nongradedness occurs naturally on the playground and in children's homes. Play is the medium by which children come together to teach each other and be encouraged by one another. Bringing that atmosphere into the classroom has been a tremendous asset for me. I do not need to design activities to bring the students together—they come of their own accord, drawn by the irresistible delight found in blocks, paint, and sand. My challenge became incorporating both content and process into those naturally occurring learning situations. "Teachable moments" abound when children are engaged in meaningful, enjoyable activity with appropriate materials.

I have been encouraged by the discovery that students extend the play depending on their ability. They grow more sophisticated in their use of materials and include a variety of representations within their projects. I find that I rarely need to provide them with suggestions for using their project centers. If we are talking about measurement and the measuring tapes and cups are easily accessible, the children will usually use them on their own initiative.

One day some of my students made a Unifix train that stretched along one wall and into the hallway. When I and some other admirers wondered aloud at how many cubes there were, the boys began busily counting, only to get lost again and again. It did not take long before they decided to count each ten and mark them with sticks, and then count by tens. By solving a problem that arose from a play situation, they encountered the usefulness of grouping and thus began their initial experience with place value. This project became popular with many of the children and helped me plan some rich, whole class math lessons. It also became a challenge at the math center. This is an example of how play, when extended by appropriate questions and materials, motivates students toward learning. The problem was not age-specific but arose from meaningful content.

> I find that I rarely need to provide them with suggestions for using their project centers.

In order to extend other play experiences, I place related materials nearby. Measuring cups at the sand and water, measuring tapes and rulers at the blocks, art materials for props near the sand and blocks, sponges and shaped printing blocks or leaves at the painting, and, of course, paper and pencils at each center for recording experiments, making signs or maps, or for writing out menus or plane reservations at the dramatic play. Books are also placed strategically around the room. Books on architecture for the blocks, recipe books and newspapers at the dramatic play area; math picture books (counting, patterns, etc.) at the math center; and books on water experiments for the water table. I don't feel comfortable having lovely art books at the painting center so I put up laminated art prints instead. The writing center and book corner proudly display the musings of class authors, and at the front of the room is a large selection of theme-related books gleaned from the library.

Usually there is some kind of project needing to be done for the classroom. Students enjoy cleaning the book corner by re-sorting all the books and making titles for each category. Occasionally a new poem needs to be written for the pocket chart, so a pair of students will go about gathering what they need to write it out themselves. We frequently survey class members, so there is often someone making the rounds and gathering responses to a general question from which graphs are made. All of these activities place responsibility on the children, giving them ownership of the classroom. It is often noisy. Sometimes I am momentarily embarrassed when a visitor enters the room, but I rarely put a stop to it. It is exciting, and I am proud of them. They may not realize it, but they are actively engaged in constructing their learning. Their hard work and thoughtfulness are clearly evident to visitors. In multiaged groups they are being challenged and supported through the medium of play.

In order to fulfill my role as collaborator, I need the classroom to run smoothly with little intervention on my part. I have found that several commonsense precautions are necessary. I make sure that I regularly visit the centers that have the potential for calamity—either due to the people or the processes involved. If I am going to be conferencing with a child or recording observations, I frequently position myself discretely within earshot or easy-intervention distance to centers I feel need to be closely monitored. I also use the skill of scanning to monitor the environment. Every three minutes I look quickly over the room to see how the students are managing and whether I need to reposition myself. There is also the built-in expectation—established in September—that when I appear to be busy the children rely on each other for assistance as much as possible. In addition to helping me use my time most effectively, this expectation encourages the development of independence and resourcefulness. It also facilitates an atmosphere of collaboration among students. Some students become skilled negotiators as they mediate disputes. As the children work together to gather materials and organize their projects, they develop cooperative skills. When reflecting on their projects afterward they are quick to give credit to their partners.

> *When I appear to be busy the children rely on each other for assistance as much as possible.*

In addition to the infrastructure of expectations, the physical placement of furniture and materials is important. There needs to be a sense of flow throughout the room, facilitating independent as well as group work. The hallway is a valuable extension of the classroom. Its separateness from the classroom can provide a quiet space for individual reading or writing when the classroom is particularly busy. It is also good for large group projects for similar reasons. As I mentioned previously, art materials are centrally located and the shelves well stocked so that the other centers can make props and extend their potential. Pencils, paper, books, glue, tape, scissors—all of these are easily accessible so that I needn't be interrupted in my efforts to record observations or collaborate with students.

The major difficulty I have is finding enough room for everything. I would like to get rid of desks, especially since the children rarely use them during the day, usually preferring to work on the floor or at tables. However, I have not been able to get the students to agree. Desks seem to be a status symbol for a six-year-old and a place of privacy and security. Perhaps if other classrooms had no desks it would be easier to sell the idea. As it is, I have lost the battle but will continue trying to persuade them. I believe it would make for a much more spacious and smoothly flowing environment. The younger children have a designated table in the middle of the room so that they feel included when seatwork is given. I try to steer clear of this type of situation as much as possible because it does emphasize two distinct groups in the classroom.

In light of the important role center-time plays in the shape of the day, collaboration among students and an appreciation for each other is easily established. It is delightful to listen in on their play and hear "That's a good idea," "Thank you," "Would you help me?" "Ask ___, she's good at that," and "We'll figure it out." It is also exciting to observe that they begin to see growth in each other, particularly in the areas of reading, writing, and art. What a powerful motivator it is to be congratulated and encouraged by peers!

In addition to the children supporting each other, I need to support them. I set the tone of the classroom. Some days I take on the role of a materials manager—mixing new colors of paint for murals, searching for a particular plasticene, or getting paper for mapping the blocks—all for the purpose of encouraging children to extend their play into something they can be proud of. There is always someone wanting me to staple their painting or writing to the wall, and often the children ask for permission to share their work with the whole class or go next door and share it with our neighbors. It is clear to the students that I value their work and enjoy their individuality. As a result they are more likely to value other people's efforts.

I believe it is this spirit of appreciation, respect, and collaboration that makes a classroom nongraded. A classroom of single-aged students can be more nongraded than one with all the physical trimmings of nongradedness, if the single-age class has a social climate that fosters self-esteem and encourages individual growth and the multiaged class does not. It is this concept that I have emphasized to parents in explaining the difference between a split and a combined (or nongraded) class. The social climate is paramount.

> A classroom of single-aged students can be more nongraded than one with all the physical trimmings of nongradedness.

Thus far it may sound as though my students do little other than centers during the day. This is not entirely true, although many of our directed tasks arise from their play. The day plan I have now has evolved from trial and error and many discussions with colleagues (see fig. 2). In designing the shape of the day I wanted to reflect the principal role that play occupies but also balance it with directed activities that foster literacy and math skills. The challenge came in eliminating the division between "play" in the morning and "work" in the afternoon (sending the message that younger children do not need or are not capable of directed tasks and that play is not entirely appropriate for older children for their own sake) and making the directed activities suitable for a variety of abilities. I have ended up including play twice in the day and planning two open-ended, directed activities and one teacher-directed, closed activity every day.

The day starts with general chat and a story. A large pad of chart paper is available for children to write down any news they wish to share. This is read later in the day, after recess, so that there has been plenty of

Figure 2. Shape of the Week

	MONDAY	TUESDAY	WEDNESDAY	THURSDAY	FRIDAY
8:45	Opening: Centers:	Opening: Centers:	Opening: Centers: 9:45 Gym—Mr. Wilson	Opening: Centers:	Opening: Centers: 9:45 Gym—Mr. Wilson
10:00	Shared reading:	Shared reading:		Shared reading:	
10:15	RECESS	RECESS	RECESS	RECESS	RECESS
10:30	Writer's workshop	Math	Writer's workshop	Library	Films:
11:15*	Language centers:	Printing: 11:40 Buddy reading— Ms. Hemmes	Language centers:	Language centers:	Spelling: Printing:
12:00	LUNCH	LUNCH	LUNCH	LUNCH	12:00–12:15 Recess 12:15–1:00 Computers 1:00 Dismissal Early dismissal every Friday
1:00	Story, silent reading	Story, silent reading	Project writing or silent reading	Story, silent reading	
1:30	Art talk—Mrs. Houston	Group activity:		Group activity:	
2:00	Centers:	Centers:	Centers:	Centers:	
2:45	Wraparound	Wraparound	Wraparound	Wraparound	
3:00	Dismissal	Dismissal	Dismissal	Dismissal	

*Kindergarten is dismissed at 11:15 a.m.

time for children to get around to it. The news has become one of my favorite activities because it is inclusive and instructive in meaningful ways. At first only the able writers feel comfortable with it, but as the less confident children learn to use the resources of the classroom and realize that it is a nonthreatening, enjoyable activity, they too begin to eagerly write their ideas down. The writing is never corrected—it is entirely risk free.

I use the news writing for different things. Often it becomes a resource for mini-writing lessons. After reading the news, I point out ways in which their writing follows conventional formats. This positive feedback encourages the writer and provides a peer model for other children. We then discuss how to incorporate those skills in our writing during writer's workshop. Capital letters, spaces, periods, phonics—all of these become lesson topics as they are evidenced in the children's writing. In the days following the teaching of a particular skill, I comment on its inclusion in the news writing when I see it. Some days the mini-lesson consists simply of complimenting the writers in their use of conventions we have previously discussed.

After a story we choose centers. Usually it is free choice, although I occasionally provide some direction. This may be in the form of an activity I wish everyone to complete during the next few days—an art project or a page for a class book, for example—or it may stem from the story we read. Sometimes we represent the story using the center materials. Most often all centers are open and the children are free to use them however they wish in a constructive fashion. I like to give them at least an hour of centers. It usually takes them about twenty minutes to get focused and I have found the last half hour to be the most productive time. After a particularly busy and creative center time we have "tours." We wander carefully as a group around the room to have each project described and explained to us. It is during this time that many ideas are exchanged and problems solved for future adaptations or improvements.

As the children clean up they move into shared reading. For fifteen minutes they have the opportunity to read to and with each other. It is interesting to see the ages mix and the combinations of readers and listeners. Because I do reading conferences with the older children later in the day, I frequently choose a couple of younger children to read with during this time to monitor their progress.

After recess the class participates in a whole group activity. Writer's workshop gives the children an opportunity to develop their writing in a nonthreatening setting. They work either independently or with friends on various writing projects. Most days they choose their own topics, although a few times a month I plan the writing. Some days we make class books; other days are for journal writing. We also write letters and do computer stories with our older buddies for special occasions. Writer's workshop almost always begins with a mini-lesson on writing skills. These are very short and arise from a meaningful source—i.e., news writing, their journals, or a book we have read. A helpful book in setting up a writer's workshop program is *The Art of Teaching Writing* by Lucy McCormick Calkins (1986).

We also do whole group math lessons in open-ended as well as closed activities. As illustrated previously, math frequently becomes an important element in the children's play. As a result, direct instruction in math often arises from their own math experiences during centers. Another advantage of this is that I do not feel the need to schedule math lessons every day. Instead, the day plan is flexible. I can schedule more or less math during the week as I feel it is needed. (This is also an advantage of planning weekly. Week plans help me get a vision for the direction of the next few days. I can shuffle times and activities around as is necessary but still be able to see that all areas are adequately covered during the week.) By scheduling play, math, and writing times during the morning, I feel I give the younger children an equal opportunity to be both challenged and supported in their development.

> Writer's workshop almost always begins with a mini-lesson on writing skills.

After the younger children go home for the day, the six-year-olds participate in closed, small group language activities. On Monday, the children choose where they would like to start their week: reading conferences with me, spelling and phonics with the learning assistance teacher, listening to stories on tape, or painting. For the next three days these groups rotate until they have done each center, then they choose again.

These centers reflect the four areas of language development: reading, writing, listening, and speaking. Painting is included because of the opportunity it provides children to represent their ideas and discuss them with other children. This system ensures that I am reading with every child once a week and that they are receiving some basic phonics instruction to assist them with their writing. At the end of the week we do spelling all together, reviewing the letters and sounds worked on during the week.

The afternoon consists of a second directed activity followed by another center time. The group activity is designed according to what the children have shown interest in or what I feel is needed. Sometimes we do math, sometimes writing. Occasionally we do science experiments, but I usually prefer to save those for the morning when the whole class is together. Once a week the vice principal comes to do art lessons, and we also go to the library every other month to do research writing or art projects related to our theme.

The center time in the afternoon also has some set guidelines. I may specify that I want the children to solve a math problem in their center or represent a story plot from a favorite book. I often try to relate the task to our theme in some way. When we were discussing journeys, one of the tasks was for the children to represent the journey of a favorite story in their center. The children at the writing center rewrote the story or made a map of the journey, the blocks built roads and towns, as did the sand. The water table became the ocean that Max sailed on to meet the Wild Things, complete with boat and an island.

The point of this kind of direction is to encourage the children to represent their thinking in a variety of ways. I want the play to be slightly different than the morning session so that they are encouraged to extend the materials and processes. It also accommodates the diversity of learners in that those who struggle with pencil-and-paper tasks are given the opportunity to show what they know through something they have already had success with—play. Consequently, there is a balance between challenge and support.

Of course, there are days when open-ended math and writing activities do not seem appropriate for the concepts I want to teach. There is nothing wrong with direct, formal instruction at those times, particularly when they are balanced with indirect teaching activities. When the overriding climate in the classroom is one of encouragement and appreciation, the children know that they do not need to be anxious about formal instruction. Being wrong does not carry a lingering embarrassment if there are other times in the day when children can be enveloped by familiarity, building on and using what they already know, supported by the respect of those around them. There develops a remarkable feeling of security in the classroom which allows children to venture out, take risks, and express themselves in new ways within a variety of instructional settings.

> *A remarkable feeling of security allows children to venture out, take risks, and express themselves.*

To end the day on a calm, reflective, and positive note we usually finish up with a "wraparound." Earlier in the day I ask the children to think about a particular idea as they work. For example, "For the wraparound today, I want you to tell me about how you have cooperated with someone this afternoon," or "Keep an eye on your friends' work today because we are going to compliment each other at the wraparound." I may also ask them to think about something they feel they did well today, something they tried that was new (risk taking), or a problem they solved. We quickly wrap around the circle and engage in reflecting on the day. Not only does this encourage metacognition and self-evaluation, but it brings closure to the day as a unified group.

Where Have We Been and Where Are We Going?

For developing a nongraded program, I quickly became aware of how individualized it must be in order to accommodate diversity and promote continuous progress. There is no set standard against which the children are evaluated. Instead they come with their own individual activities from which individual goals are set. As a result, the tasks children will be engaged in will usually have a slightly varied set of expectations in order to be developmentally appropriate for each child.

It is not uncommon to hear stories from parents about the inadequate expectations set for their child in previous years by teachers. Unfortunately, this has given terms like "whole language" and "child centered" a negative connotation in many communities. When children are not challenged enough in appropriate ways, parents and teachers become justifiably concerned. The same problem could arise in a nongraded classroom where individualization is interpreted as letting students do their own thing, at their own rate, within their own comfort zone. The problem with this is that too much comfort can discourage children from extending themselves and taking risks. There needs to be a balance between challenge and support.

Early in September, I set the expectation for writer's workshop by defining what writing is and what it is not. I also tell my students that I know what their ability is, that I am proud of them, and that I expect them to always try to get even better at it. From that point on I have no qualms about asking children to add more to their product or to go back over it, making sure it is their best. There are times when I simply will not accept work from a child if it does not match that child's ability. During times of sharing, writing, reading, math, printing, or art, I reinforce this expectation by commenting on a child's use of new learning. When someone learns how to use periods correctly, he gets congratulated, as does the child who is learning to use both initial and ending sounds in words. Signs of progress for the individual are applauded, thus encouraging the child in risk taking.

> *Too much comfort can discourage children from extending themselves and taking risks.*

I have found that the easiest way to set individual expectations with children and monitor their progress is through conferencing. During writer's workshop, centers, and math activities I make a point of conferencing with a few children. This way, I can see them in process and follow their thinking closely. I ask them about their work and may give suggestions for increased success if appropriate. Conferencing also affords me the opportunity to hear the child's evaluation of her work as well as offer my own. Contrary to what many may think, I usually find that the child's assessment closely matches mine and that the goals we set are mutually agreed upon. Frequently, the children know what areas require more attention by them and the steps they can take to refine their skills.

In addition to conferencing, I rely on recorded observations and anecdotal comments as assessment tools (see fig. 3). While some days my role consists of conferencing, other days I sit and "kid-watch," recording what I hear and see as accurately and objectively as I can. The children learn that I consider this important work and usually try not to interrupt. They also soon lose interest in what I am writing and seem unaffected by it as they go about their work. I try to be discreet and place myself in a position where I can see the whole class when I scan, but where I am still within earshot of conversations and/or can see the details in a student's actions. During the course of the activity, I change my position as needed to observe other children.

On days when it is not efficient for me to write down my observations, I walk around with a hand-held tape recorder and record conversations between children and my interactions with them. A video camera can also be set up to record activities that I don't always get to see. A video camera is another set of eyes that allows me to observe twice the number of interactions that I could with my own two eyes. At the end of the day, away from the hustle and bustle, I review the tape recording or video over a cup of tea or while preparing small things for the next day. I jot down significant information as I hear or see it. This relaxed, unhurried recording of observations allows me to catch many actions and interactions that I missed at the time.

Work files are also maintained. Every two weeks we try to include a math representation, an art sample, or a piece of writing. Often the children choose what goes into their collections, but there are times when I decide. Self-evaluations are part of the children's portfolios as well. Everything in the work files is gathered into the child's portfolio to be shared with pride during student-led conferences at the end of each term.

Student-led conferences have become a valued tool for me in communicating with parents about their child's progress. Parents sign up—four every hour—to come with their child and view the term's work. They have hall displays explained to them, are shown how the classroom operates, and listen as their child presents his best work from the term. I am present, but I make it clear in a letter sent home earlier that this is their child's opportunity to shine and that I will be available for a teacher-

Figure 3. Observation Grid

JASON	MARIA	DAVID
ALICE	JOSHUA	KEVIN
KIMBERLY	CHRIS J.	CHRIS H.
JULIE	ALYSSA	JOHN

On an 8 ½" x 14" sheet I make a grid for observations. A child's name goes on each square. When the sheet is full, I cut it up and glue the observations into a binder. The binder has a section for each child with color-coded sheets for center observations, reading conference notes, writing observations and conference notes, and math observations. I also include a monthly writing sample for each child.

parent conference by appointment only. Naturally there are parents with whom I feel it is expedient to conference, and I notify them, but rarely do I have parents request a private conference after the student-led conference. They are invariably pleased with the process. In the guest book they are invited to comment on the conference, and they express appreciation and pleasure in their child and in the program.

I have found that having the conferences before report cards go home usually works best. For the most part, concerns I express in the report card are evidenced in the conference so parents have a context in which to place my comments. Nevertheless, at parent education evenings a recurring concern is that this type of program can tend to overlook a child's deficiencies, which become more difficult to overcome if they are left unaddressed. Anecdotal report cards are frequently held up as examples of misleading information, allowing parents to believe their child is coping well in all areas of development until they find out in grade four that she can't read.

Parents appreciate knowing the truth about their children, but they also want to be able to help them.

Writing anecdotal report cards and being unable to rely on a graded system does require an ability to articulate thoughtfully and accurately a child's progress. Since a nongraded program seeks to appreciate the differences between children and nurture an individual pace for progress, it is important to emphasize in written reports what the child can do. This does not mean, however, that what the child can't do is left unsaid. Rather, it is said in a manner that supports the child and anticipates progress. For example, the comment, "Julia is unable to work cooperatively and prefers to work alone," simply tells what she can't do. The statement, "Though Julia prefers to work alone, I am encouraging her to respect the ideas of others and use the resources of classmates in her projects," gives more information about her and provides specific suggestions for progress.

Parents appreciate knowing the truth about their children, but they also want to be able to help them. Providing specific suggestions as well as accurate information is important. Instead of saying "Ryan does not like writing and is as yet unable to write complete words," I might say, "Ryan's participation in writing activities will increase as he develops confidence in his ability. I am encouraging him to sound out words thoroughly so that he can include more letters in each word." Though the report becomes more lengthy, the child's dignity has been protected and the parent is given a more accurate picture. Occasionally I include a suggestion for practice at home but make a point of clarifying it with the parents. Some parents put too much pressure on the child at home, making the child feel defeated and more reluctant than ever when challenged at school.

While it may seem tedious and too much work, writing report cards that are thorough, honest, and positive is an important element in a nongraded classroom. It forces me to be true to my belief in the value of every child and the reality of continuous progress. These report cards also keep parents informed about their child's progress, relieving fears that this type of program does not produce significant learning of skills and concepts. I have come to truly enjoy writing my reports because they become a tribute to the child's efforts, applauding their growth and anticipating future progress.

Parents Can Come Too!

When we as teachers, who see the benefits of a nongraded program every day, struggle with how to most effectively teach it, it is no surprise that parents express concern about it. I have found it helpful to keep this premise in mind when I talk to parents about my classroom program. They are their child's first and most influential teachers. It is in the child's best interest to draw them in to support a powerful learning environment and make them partners in their child's education.

Providing parent education nights communicates an important message to parents. It tells them that they are respected as being their child's coeducators and have the right to be informed about the learning environment the school offers. In my experience, parents attend these sessions for a variety of reasons. Some come because they are curious, some because they want to voice concerns, and some come already convinced and wanting to hear more. Whatever the reason, they do come, and immediately a significant forum for communication is established.

While parents appreciate being included and informed, I always appreciate the opportunity to articulate my beliefs about children, learning, and teaching. Each time I do this my philosophy becomes more deeply entrenched and refined.

After the first parent night of the year, communication becomes much freer and more relaxed. The more opportunity there is for parents to voice their concerns and their appreciation directly to the teacher, the less likely they will be to engage in criticisms and assumptions over coffee with their neighbors. Very rarely do I have a parent come to me with a concern we can't alleviate through talking. Making myself approachable and consistently inviting feedback has proved to be a worthwhile risk on my part. The support system for my program has gathered strength and given me a sense of freedom.

> *Very rarely do I have a parent come to me with a concern we can't alleviate through talking.*

For my parent nights I prefer to model in some way the kind of teaching I use with the children. I usually include a story that relates to the topic and use cooperative groups for discussion and brainstorming. If the meeting is in the classroom, I have the children leave their center projects on display so I can use them as examples. If we meet in the library, I find it is helpful to have samples of children's work up on the walls or for use on an overhead.

The first parent night of the year I do on my own within the first two weeks of school. This stems queries and misgivings expressed in the first few days and allows me to elaborate fully on my program. Other such nights are often done in collaboration with other teachers, thus presenting a united front for the school and providing collegial support in dealing with parental concerns. Each parent night focuses on particular aspects of our program, usually ones parents have expressed concerns about.

Figure 4 is an example of suggestions for a parent night agenda. These are only a few suggestions for parent education evenings and each contains ideas that could be easily developed into whole sessions on their own. Over time, with enough information and communication bolstered by the evidence of their child's progress and delight in school, parents will become very supportive. When this happens, the home environment begins to complement the school environment.

Figure 4. Parent Night Agenda

It is also helpful to have a handout that pertains to the evening. Short articles from parent's magazines are good resources because they are easy reading and are written from a parent's perspective.

I. THE COMING YEAR
   A. Introduction

   Who am I?

   Why I have chosen nongraded and why it has been introduced in the school.

   B. The Learning Environment

   The classroom layout, shape of the week (put up on the wall on poster paper for easy viewing), and class composition (age range, ESL, special needs).

   C. What Do You Want to Know?

   Four categories listed on the blackboard: play, curriculum, dealing with diversity, other. In cooperative groups collate the three most pressing concerns, record on strips of paper, and tape up under appropriate category. (I provide the categories because sometimes people don't know where to begin.) After several minutes, gather together and go through categories. Refer to week plan, classroom equipment, and samples to answer fully and help make it more concrete.

   D. Working Together

   Affirm parents' role as educators of their children. Provide suggestions for how home and school complement each other. Emphasize desire for frequent communication.

   E. Story

   A picture book with a message that relates to the theme of the evening—Frogs and Toads. *The Garden* by Arnold Lobel illustrates the need for a fertile learning environment.

II. COMING TO TERMS WITH NONGRADEDNESS

This could be done as a panel presentation with each teacher presenting and defining a term with examples.

   A. What Is Nongraded?

   Physical characteristics as well as curricular and philosophical.

   B. Active Learning

   The hows and whys of hands-on, experiential learning.

   C. Unlimited Curriculum

   Use specific examples of extension in the learning environment.

Figure 4. (Continued)

    D. Child Centeredness and Individualization

        How does it influence planning and teaching strategies? What does it mean to "learn at your own rate"?

    E. Continuous Progress, Assessment, and Evaluation

        How to maintain standards, building on what children know; criteria and tools for evaluation and assessment.

III. ENABLING LEARNERS

    A. Why Change the System?

        Discuss social and cultural changes that necessitate lifelong learning.

        Brainstorm in large groups the qualities of successful learners (i.e., thoughtful, creative, resourceful, persevering); record on overhead.

    B. An Enabling Environment

        In cooperative group discuss this question: What would you see children doing in a rich learning environment? Share and record on overhead. Have parents suggest ways in which they have seen these things happen in the classroom.

    C. The Unlimited Classroom

        What is a developmental program? Explain the skills continuum using samples from reading, writing, and math. How is diversity accommodated?

    D. Continuous Progress and Evaluations: Focus on Abilities.

        A child's progress is not dependent on other children in the class.

        Anecdotal reports allow us to see where the child will go next.

    E. Story

        Lizard Song by George Shannon illustrates the need to have ownership over our learning in order for it to be meaningful.

In addition to parent nights, I use a variety of forms of communication to inform parents. Weekly newsletters keep parents up to date on what we are doing and give some simple suggestions for extension at home (see fig. 5). They are amazingly quick and easy to write. I also take frequent photos of the children at work. These may be put into class books or used in hall displays. Eventually they are sent home. Rather than always having an art display in the hallway, we put up cooperative group brainstorms, writing samples, and math representations every few weeks. This allows parents to ask their child about their work and opens dialogue between them—something that parents often comment is a difficult task at home. Bringing parents into the classroom is another good way to encourage communication. Being a volunteer provides parents an opportunity to observe the learning environment and develop insights into its benefits. I have already briefly talked about student-led conferences and highly recommend them as a tool for helping parents

Figure 5. An Example of a Parent Newsletter

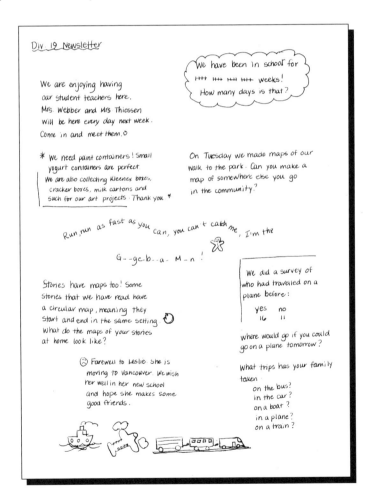

learn about their child and the workings of the classroom. For more information about organizing conferences in this way, Nancy Little's book, *Student-Led Parent Teacher Conferences* (1988), is a valuable resource.

Pressing On

This chapter has been about my journey into the realm of nongradedness. It has brought me to new understandings about children, learning, and teaching and has challenged me both emotionally and intellectually (not to mention organizationally!). It has also wrought the rewards of renewed vigor for my job and a delight in the spontaneity and freshness of teaching young children. Looking back on the illustration at the beginning of this chapter, I realize that not only do I have guitarists in my room, I also have singers, harpists, violinists, and tuba players. My journey is far from over. A conductor presses on to hear the music played with more depth and new expression. I still struggle to maintain a consistent balance, and at times I still get anxious about the children's progress, but the music of the classroom draws me back again and again. When I see the powerful learning the children are engaged in, I know I am on the right track.

I want to encourage you to begin your journey into nongradedness. My journey is just that—mine. You need to build your own program and make it a learning climate you can live with. There is no set recipe, no pattern. Our greatest resource is the children, and we can take comfort in knowing that they can and do learn despite our floundering as we seek to provide them with a learning environment that supports, challenges, and appreciates them for who they are.

Enjoy the music.

References

Ashton, W. S. 1986. *Teacher.* New York: Touchstone Books.

Baskwill, J. 1989. *Parents and teachers: Partners in learning.* Richmond Hill, Ontario: Scholastic-TAB.

Baskwill, J., and P. Whitman. 1988. *Evaluation: Whole language, whole child.* Richmond Hill, Ontario: Scholastic-TAB.

Bergen, D., ed. 1988. *Play as a medium for learning and development: A handbook of theory and knowledge.* Portsmouth, N.H.: Heinemann.

British Columbia Ministry of Education. 1990. *Primary program foundation document and resource document.* Victoria, B.C.: Publication Services, Government of British Columbia.

Calkins, L. M. 1986. *The art of teaching writing.* Portsmouth, N.H.: Heinemann.

Donaldson, M. 1978. *Children's minds.* New York: Norton.

Duckworth, E. 1987. *The having of wonderful ideas and other essays on teaching and learning.* New York: Teacher's College Press.

Forester, A., and M. Reinhard. 1989. *The learner's way.* Winnipeg, Manitoba: Peguis.

Goodlad, J., and R. Anderson. 1989. *The non-graded elementary school* (rev. ed.). New York: Teacher's College Press.

Katz, L., and A. Chard. 1989. *Engaging children's minds: The project approach.* Norwood, N.J.: Ablex.

Katz, L., et al. 1990. *The case for mixed age grouping in early education.* Washington, D.C.: National Association for the Education of Young Children.

Little, N., and J. Allen. 1988. *Student-led parent teacher conferences.* Toronto, Ontario: Lugus.

North York Board of Education. 1983. *Look! Hear! Developing programs for primary children.* Willowdale, Ontario: Board of Education.

Van Manen, M. 1986. *The tone of teaching.* Richmond Hill, Ontario: Scholastic-TAB.

Authors

Jacquie Anderson specialized in primary education at Simon Fraser University in Burnaby, British Columbia. Since completing her degree she has continued with her interest in literacy and teaching for thinking through coursework and seminars. She has written articles and conducted workshops in these areas as well as in assessment and evaluation. She is currently living in a small rural community in British Columbia with her husband and two young daughters.

Frank Betts is a senior staff member of the Association for Supervision and Curriculum Development (ASCD) and frequent presenter and workshop leader on applications of technology to education. Former superintendent of schools in Aspen, Colorado, Frank is the originator of the *ASCD Curriculum Handbook, The ASCD Curriculum/Technology Newsletter,* and *Electronic Chalkboard.* He can be contacted through the World Wide Web (http://www.ascd.org) or e-mail (fbetts@ascd.org or fbetts@aol.com).

Robin Fogarty, a leading proponent of the thoughtful classroom, trains teachers throughout the world in cognitive strategies and cooperative interaction. She has taught all levels from kindergarten to college, served as an administrator, and consulted with state departments and ministries of education. Robin has authored, coauthored, and edited numerous publications, including *The Mindful School: How to Integrate the Curricula, The Mindful School: The Portfolio Connection,* and *Integrating Curricula with Multiple Intelligences: Teams, Themes, and Threads.*

Roberto Gutiérrez received a Ph.D. in sociology from Johns Hopkins University. He received a B.S. degree in industrial engineering from the Universidad de los Andes in Bogotá (Columbia) in 1986, and an M.A. degree in sociology from Hopkins in 1991. From 1988 to 1990, he was a research associate at the Institute Ser de Investigación in Bogotá. He worked in the areas of health and local governments. His present research focuses on the psychological effects of work in the informal sector.

Marilyn Hughes has taught children from preschool through middle school in both the regular classroom and gifted resource programs. Today Marilyn is delivering keynote addresses, consulting with several school districts around the country, and conducting local and national staff development programs in several subjects pertaining to her "whole-system" model. She is the author of "Curriculum Integration in the Primary Grades," a case study published in the *ASCD Curriculum Handbook*.

Don Jeanroy has been in the field of education for more than thirty years. For the past six years he has been the principal of Concrete Elementary School in Concrete, Washington. During that time he has been instrumental in bringing about many changes in the structure, staffing, and instructional direction of the school. He has also participated in numerous workshops dealing with cooperative learning, student assessments, multiple intelligences, and other curriculum areas that directly relate to the activities taking place at Concrete Elementary School.

Mardi B. Jones is a professional writer with a degree in marine science and literature from the College of Notre Dame in Belmont, California. She has worked in the field of education for fifteen years. She is the author of two books, *Identifying Fish in the Estuary* and *Growing Miniature Roses*, and also writes general interest articles and juvenile fiction.

Kathy Magee began teaching in 1969 and has taught grades 2, 3, and 4, and a multiage primary class. She has received several awards, including the 1994 Milken Family Foundation National Educator Award, 1991–92 Nevada Teacher of the Year, the Clark County School District Teacher of the Year for 1991–92, the 1983–84 Clark County School District Teaching Excellence Dissemination Program Award, and Outstanding Leader in Elementary and Secondary Education in 1976.

David Marshak is an assistant professor in the Master's in Teaching Program at the School of Education at Seattle University. His previous professional experience includes teaching at several grade levels in public schools, extensive work in curriculum development, and consultation with schools in many states and provinces. Prior to his current position, Marshak served as the curriculum and assessment coordinator in the Addison Northeast Supervisory Union in Bristol, Vermont.

Barbara Nelson Pavan is professor of educational administration at Temple University (Philadelphia). After completing her doctoral dissertation on nongradedness at Harvard University, she served as the second principal at Franklin School in Lexington, Massachusetts, which was the first nongraded team teaching school in the United States. Pavan has been a regular presenter at the annual conferences of the American Educational Research Association (AERA) and the Association for Supervision and Curriculum Development (ASCD).

Robert Slavin is currently codirector of the Center for Research on the Education of Students Placed at Risk at Johns Hopkins University. Robert has authored or coauthored more than 140 articles and 14 books, including *Educational Psychology: Theory in Practice; School and Classroom Organization; Effective Programs for Students at Risk; Cooperative Learning: Theory, Research, and Practice;* and *Preventing Early School Failure*.

Kay J. Williams, a first grade teacher in Schaumburg, Illinois, has gained life experience as a wife, homemaker, mother, and foster mother prior to returning to college and completing her degree. Her graduate studies focused on children's literature, whole language, integrated learning practices, and creative writing. As a freelance writer for Silver Burdett Ginn, Kay assisted in the development of a theme-based social studies curriculum entitled *Primary Place* for grades 1 and 2.

Index

Ability grouping, 51, 53, 65–66
Acceleration policies, 38
Affective influence, 205
Allington, R. L., 50
Anastas, Betsy Ann, 113
Anderson, Jacquie, 189–90, 207, 235
Anderson, R., 47, 49, 50, 51, 56, 62–63, 65, 113
Anecdotal comments as assessment tools, 157–58, 224, 225, 226
Art of Teaching Writing, The, 220
ASCD Curriculum Handbook, 176
Ashton-Warner, Sylvia, 6
Aspen, Colorado, nongraded education in, 111, 113–38
　assessment, 125–27
　characteristics of valid systemic process, 115–17
　constructing valid change process, 115–17
　creating context, 132–33
　designing components of curriculum content, 123–25
　empowering change, 121–23
　implementing change, 132
　instructional methods, 127–28
　justification of, 117–18
　philosophy statement on current role of education, 119–20
　physical environment, 130–31
　scheduling, 129
　student outcomes in, 120–21
Assessment
　anecdotal comments in, 157–58, 224, 225, 226

　authentic, 8–9, 19
　conferencing in, 29–31, 223, 224–26
　in multiage classroom, 156–59, 209, 222–27
　narrative report card in, 30
　portfolio, 9
At-risk children, concerns over, 43
Audiotape, 175
Authentic assessment, 8–9, 19
Aylesworth, Jim, 201, 203, 204

Back-to-basics, 37, 41–42
Bangert, R. J., 65, 67
Basal reading group, problems with, 192–93, 198–99
Best-evidence synthesis, 52
Betts, Frank, 112, 115, 235
Big books, 193
Birch, John, Society, 42
Book box, 150
Bringing the Rain to Kapiti Plain, 201
"Britannica Science System (BBS)," 172
Brophy, J. E., 65
Brown Bear Brown Bear What Do You See?, 201
Burke, Carolyn, 194, 199
Burke, James, 117, 119
Burroughs, John, 35
By-the-way teaching, 149

Caine, Geoffrey, 169
Caine, Renate, 169
Calkins, Lucy McCormick, 220
Camus, Albert, 109
Carle, Eric, 147, 200

Carnegie report, 43
Cemetery Study Unit, 3–4, 12–13
Center-time, role of, in nongraded school, 216–17, 219
Chalfant, L. S., 53
Change
　empowerment of, 121–23
　factors promoting, 192–94
　need for whole system approach to, 115
　process of, 115
　teacher as obstacle in, 189–90, 207–32
Children, role modeling for, 22
Choral reading, 196
Civil War cemetery as setting for multiage classroom, 12–13
Classroom organization in multiage classroom, 143–44
Cleary, Beverly, 10
CNN Newsroom, 173
Coalition of Essential Schools, 37
Cognitive growth, 205
Collaboration
　role of teacher in, 210–11, 215
　value of, 194
Columbus project, 175
Comprehension questions, phrasing of, 196–97
Comprehensive nongraded programs, 56–57, 72–73, 80
Computer
　in multiage classroom, 154–55
　potential of, in mathematics, 174
Concept themes in nongraded classrooms, 211–13
Concrete Elementary School, Continuous Progress Program at, 4, 19–32
Conferences
　in assessment, 223
　parent, 29–31
　student-led, 224–26
Cooper, M., 60
Cooperative learning, 27–29
　models for, 44–45
　training for, 27
Cost-benefit analysis, 165–66
Courage, multiage classroom study of, 13–16
Creating Classrooms for Authors, 199
Cross-age grouping, 61, 65, 66
　tutoring in, 23, 27–29
Cunningham, Pat, 153
Curriculum, integration of, 3, 9

Decision Development Corporation, 172
de Paola, Tomie, 147
Developmental/invented spelling, 193

Developmental kindergarten, 51
Developmentally appropriate practices, 52
Dewey, John, 40
Dolch list, 153

Education, current role of, 119–20
Effectiveness in selecting appropriate technology, 165
Efficiency in selecting appropriate technology, 165
Effort required in selecting appropriate technology, 166–67
Elms, Hallie, 24–25
Emergent readers, 198
Encyclopaedia Britannica, 172
Engel, B. M., 60
Eubanks, E. E., 50
Evangelou, D., 67

Facilitator, role of teacher as, 191
Factory model, 191
Family grouping, 113, 114
Feasibility, in selecting appropriate technology, 164
Fifteen-minute rule, 168–69
Flexible skills groups for reading and writing, 197–98
Floyd, C., 55
Fluent readers, 198
Fogarty, R., 3, 5, 9, 235
Folks in the Valley, The, 203
Foreman, Michael, 203
Fortunately, 201
Franklin Elementary School, Lexington, Massachusetts, nongradedness at, 39–47

Gallagher, Jaci, 25, 28–29
Geometer's Sketchpad, 174
Geometric Supposer, 174
GeoSafari, 175
GEOSCOPE courseware, 173
Giaconia, R. M., 65, 67
Giff, Patricia Reilly, 151
Glasrud, G. R., 59
Glass, G., 52
Glue words, 154
Good, T. L., 65
Goodlad, J. I., 43, 44, 45, 49, 50, 51, 56, 62–63, 65, 113
"Great Space Race, The," 172
Group, family, of children, 19–32
"GTV," 176
Guarino, A. R., 46
Gutiérrez, R., 38, 49, 52, 236

Hanna's Hog, 201
Hansen, Jane, 199
Harste, J., 194, 199
Hartman, A., 67
Hattie and the Fox, 201
Hauenstein, Mimi, 113
Hawkings, Barbara, 25–26
Heathers, G., 53
Hedges, L. V., 65, 67
Heller, Ruth, 203
Hemingway, Ernest, 15
High-tech classroom, characteristics of, 179–80
Historical trackings, xii
Hoffman, M. S., 46
Holmes Group, 43
Horak, V. M., 65, 67
House Is a House for Me, A, 201
House that Jack Built, The, 201
Hubbard, Elbert, 141
Hughes, Marilyn, 111, 113, 236

IBM, 170–72
I/D/E/A, 54
Independent reading, 196
Individualized instruction, incorporation of, into nongraded programs, 57–58, 74–75, 80
Individually guided education (IGE) program, 54, 59, 64, 76–77, 80
Ingram, V., 53
Instructional strategies in multiage primary classroom, 111–12, 141–60
Integrating curricula, 3, 9
Intermediate setting, multiage classroom in, 3, 9–16
Internet, 178–79
Invitations, 199

Jacket I Wear in the Snow, The, 203
Jeanroy, Don, 12, 19–22, 236
Jeffreys, J. S., 58
Jones, Mardi, 12, 19, 236
Joplin-like nongraded programs, 55–56, 64, 70–71, 80
Junior kindergarten, 51

Karweit, N. L., 51
Katz, L., 67
Kettering Foundation, 54
Kids Incorporated, 3–4, 9–13
Kids Network program, 175
Kinc. See Kids Incorporated
Kites Sail High, 203
Klausmeier, H. J., 54, 59

Kulik, C., 65, 67
Kulik, J., 65, 67
KWL strategy, 145

Lane, Marilyn, 24–25
Language arts
 technology in, 170–72
 writing in enhancing student relationships in, 193
Learner-centered schooling, 37
Learning
 spiral vision of, 209–10
 technology for, 112, 163–85
Learning logs, 158
Levine, D. U., 50
Lionni, Leo, 147
Literacy programs
 integration of spelling into, 153–54
 strategies in multiage classroom, 145–54
Literature, and integration of curriculum, 196
Literature Club, 199
Little Bear books, 151
Little Blue, Little Yellow, 147
Little Red Riding Hood, 201
"Little Red Schoolhouse, The," 3, 5–16
Loomis, Meridith, 25, 28–29

Madden, N. A., 50
Magee, Kathy, 111–12, 236
Mann, Thomas, xi, xii
Many Luscious Lollipops, 203
Maresh, R. T., 53
Marshak, David, 38, 87, 236–37
Material manager, role of teacher as, 216–17
MathCad, 174
Mathematica, 174
Mathematics, technology in, 173–74
Mayer, Mercer, 151
McCracken, Marlene, 153
McCracken, Robert, 153
McGaw, B., 52
McGill-Franzen, A., 50
McLoughlin, W. P., 49, 62, 63, 64, 66
Microcomputer-based laboratory (MBL), 173
MIDI, 177
Miller, R. L., 65
Money, Deborah, 25–26
Motivator, role of teacher as, 191
Multiage programs
 acceleration/deceleration of student progress, 61–63
 advantages of, 207–8
 agenda for, 229–30
 application of, at Concrete Elementary, 4, 19–32

in Aspen, Colorado, 111, 113–38
assessment in, 156–59, 209, 222–27
benefits of
    for parents, 103–5
    for students, 91–97
    for teachers, 97–103
book corner in, 214–15
categories of, 54–55
center time in, 216–17, 219, 221
computer use in, 154–55
concept themes in, 211–13
defining qualities of, 88–91
definition of, 22–23
disadvantages of, 38, 105–7
for first-grade, 189, 191–205
individualized instruction in, 57–58, 74–75, 80
instructional strategies in, 111–12, 141–60
    classroom organization, 143–44
    literacy strategies, 145–54
    terminology in, 142
    themes in, 144–45
in intermediate setting, 9–16
news writing in, 217, 219
parent education nights in, 227–30
parent questions in, 155–56
physical placement of furniture and materials in, 216
play in, 213–14
principles of, 45–46
rationales for, 50–52
research in, 49–80, 55
    base for, 38
    comprehensive nongraded programs, 56–57, 72–73, 80
    individually guided education (IGE) programs, 59, 76–77, 80
    interactions with study features, 60–61
    Joplin-like nongraded programs, 55–56, 70–71, 80
    nongraded programs incorporating individualized instruction, 57–58, 74–75, 80
    relevance of, 67–68
    studies lacking an explicit description of the nongraded program, 59–60, 78–79, 80
review methods, 52–54
    methodological inclusion, 53–54
    substantive inclusion criteria, 52–53
in setting, 3, 5–9
teachers' perspectives on, 87–107
waning of, 40–42
waxing of, 42–47
working definition of, 113–14
shared reading in, 219–20
teachable moments in, 213
teacher
    as collaborator in, 210–11, 215
    as material manager in, 216–17
    as obstacle in, 208, 209
    philosophy of, 209–10
unlimited curriculum in, 212
whole group activity in, 220
wrap around in, 222
writing center in, 214
Multiple intelligences, 27
Multi-Unit Individually Guided Education (IGE) program, 43
Musical Instrument Digital Interface, 176

Napping House, The, 201
Narrative report card, 30
Nate the Great, 151
National Gallery of Art, 177
National Geographic, 176
Nation at Risk, A, 42, 43
Neitzel, Shirley, 203
New Look at Progressive Education, A, 40
Newsletters, communicating with parents in weekly, 230–32
News writing, as resource for mini-writing lessons, 217, 219
New Zealand literacy model, 145
New Zealand Ready to Read books, 151
Nonfiction books in first-grade classroom, 196
Nongraded programs. See Multiage programs
Norman, Jean Mary, 1

Old Black Fly, 203
Oliver Button Is a Sissy, 147
One-room schoolhouse as a metaphor for multiage grouping, xi–xii
Open classrooms, 37, 40
Open education, 41
    American receptivity to, 40
Open-ended interest areas, 153
Optical Data, 172
Orchestrated immersion, 169–70
Organic learning in the primary cluster, 5–9

Parent conferences, 29–31
Parent education nights, 227–28
Parent questions in multiage classroom, 155–56
Parents
    benefits of multiage classrooms for, 103–5
    communicating with, 230–32

Patterns in Learning, 202–4
Pavan, B. N., 37, 40, 42, 45, 47, 49, 63, 64, 237
Pelham, David, 203
Performing arts, technology in, 176–77
Piaget, Jean, 40
"Planetary Manager," 176
Play in classroom, 213–14
Plowden report, 40
Portfolio assessment, 9
Prefirst programs, 51
Primary setting
    multiage classroom in, 3, 5–9
    whole language approach to reading in, 6–7

Questioning techniques, 152–53

Readers
    emergent, 198
    fluent, 198
Reading
    choral, 196
    independent, 196
    whole language approach to, in primary classroom, 6–7
Recorded observations as assessment tools, 224, 225
Report card
    anecdotal, 226
    narrative, 30
Retained students, standardized test scores of, 44
Retention, negative long-term effects of, 50–51
Return on investment (ROI), 166
Reutzel, Ray, 154
Role modeling for children, 22
Rose in My Garden, The, 201
Rossmiller, R. A., 54
Rothrock, D., 65
Rounds, Glen, 201
Routman, Regie, 197, 199
Running records, 157

Saily, M., 54
Scaffolding, 169
Schools for the 21st Century program, 19
Science, technology in, 172–73
Science table, 10–11
"Science 2000," 172
Self-esteem, development of, in fluent readers, 198
Senior cluster, philosophy study for, 13–16
Sentence booklet, 5

Shared reading, 219–20
Shepard, L. A., 44, 50
Short, K., 199
Site-based management (SBM), 45
Sizer, Ted, 37
Slavin, R. E., 38, 49, 50, 52, 53, 56, 237
Smith, M. L., 44, 50, 52
Smith, Raymond W., 163
Snyder, Tom, Publications, 172
Social acceptability, 164–65
Social science, technology in, 173–76
Spelling
    developmental/invented, 193
    integration of, into literacy program, 153–54
Spiral vision of learning, 209–10
Split grades, nongraded plan as solution to problem of, 52
Squire, J., 40
Student assessment, 29–31
Student-led conferences in assessment, 224–26
Students, benefits of multiage classrooms for, 91–97
Sustained silent reading (SSR), 150

Teachable moments, 213
Teacher
    benefits of multiage classrooms for, 97–103
    as collaborator, 210–11, 215
    as facilitator, 191
    as material manager, 216–17
    as motivator, 191
    as obstacle to change, 189–90, 207–32
    perspectives on multiage classrooms, 87–107
    responsibility of, in team teaching, 26
Teaching, technology for, 112, 163–85
Team teaching, 23–26
    benefits of, 24, 25–26
    preparation for, 25
Technology
    benefits of, 163–64
    for the classroom, 181
    definition of, 163
    education versus application, 167–70
    in language arts, 170–72
    in mathematics, 173–74
    planning for, in the classroom, 177–78, 182
    power of, 163
    for the school, 181
    in science, 172–73
    selecting appropriate, 164–67

in social science, 173–76
for teaching and learning, 112, 163–85
visual and performing arts in, 176–77
TERC, 173
Thematic studies, 200–201
Three Little Pigs, The, 201
Tinker, Robert, 173
Total body integration, 195
Track Sheet, 10
Trade books, use of, in first-grade classroom, 195–96
Training plus cooperative learning, 27
Transitional first grade, 51
Turtle Spring, 151

Unlimited curriculum, 212

Value added, 166
Venn diagram, 210
Vertical arrangements, 22
Very Quiet Cricket, The, 200
Visual arts, technology in, 176–77

Wasik, B. A., 51
Watson, Dorothy, 194
Way, R. S., 59
Westside Elementary School, technology at, 182–85
When Writers Read, 199
"Where is Carmen San Diego?," 175
Whitehead, Alfred North, 188
Whole group math lessons, 220
Whole language approach to reading, 192, 194
 in the primary classroom, 6–7
Whole-system approach, 115
Williams, Kay, 189, 191, 237
"Windows on Science," 172
Word processing, use of computer lab for, 154–55
Word study time, 5–9
Word webs, 15
Workability in selecting appropriate technology, 164
Worms Wiggle, 203
Writer's workshop, 220, 223
Writing
 assessing, 158–59
 use of, in enhancing student relationship to language, 193
Writing ticks, 159
"Writing to Read," 170–72
Wurman, R. S., 117

Learn from Our Books *and* from Our Authors!

Bring Our Author/Trainers to Your District

At IRI/SkyLight, we have assembled a unique team of outstanding author/trainers with international reputations for quality work. Each has designed high-impact programs that translate powerful new research into successful learning strategies for every student. We design each program to fit your school's or district's special needs.

Training Programs

IRI/SkyLight's training programs extend the renewal process by helping educators move from content-centered to mind-centered classrooms. In our highly interactive workshops, participants learn foundational, research-based information and teaching strategies in an instructional area that they can immediately transfer to the classroom setting. With IRI/SkyLight's specially prepared materials, participants learn how to teach their students to learn for a lifetime.

Network for Systemic Change

Through a partnership with Phi Delta Kappa, IRI/SkyLight offers a Network for site-based systemic change: *The Network of Mindful Schools.* The Network is designed to promote systemic school change as possible and practical when starting with a renewed vision that centers on *what* and *how* each student learns. To help accomplish this goal, Network consultants work with member schools to develop an annual tactical plan and then implement that plan at the classroom level.

Training of Trainers

The Training of Trainers programs train your best teachers, those who provide the highest quality instruction, to coach other teachers. This not only increases the number of teachers you can afford to train in each program, but also increases the amount of coaching and follow-up that each teacher can receive from a resident expert. Our Training of Trainers programs will help you make a systemic improvement in your staff development program.

To receive a FREE COPY of the IRI/SkyLight catalog or more information about trainings offered through IRI/SkyLight, contact **CLIENT SERVICES** at

TRAINING AND PUBLISHING, INC.
2626 S. Clearbrook Dr., Arlington Heights, IL 60005
800-348-4474 • 847-290-6600 • FAX 847-290-6609

There are
one-story intellects,
two-story intellects, and three-story
intellects with skylights. All fact collectors, who
have no aim beyond their facts, are one-story men. Two-story men
compare, reason, generalize, using the labors of the fact collectors as
well as their own. Three-story men idealize, imagine,
predict—their best illumination comes from
above, through the skylight.
—*Oliver Wendell*
Holmes